IMAGES OF WAR
THE ALLIED NEUTRALIZATION OF RABAUL
JAPAN'S MAJOR SOUTH PACIFIC BASE

RARE PHOTOGRAPHS FROM WARTIME ARCHIVES

Jon Diamond

Pen & Sword
MILITARY

First published in Great Britain in 2024 by
PEN & SWORD MILITARY
an imprint of Pen & Sword Books Ltd
Yorkshire – Philadelphia

Copyright © Jon Diamond, 2024

ISBN 978-1-03610-203-6

The right of Jon Diamond to be identified as the author of this work has been asserted by him in accordance with the Copyright, Designs and Patents Act 1988.

A CIP catalogue record for this book is available from the British Library.

All rights reserved. No part of this book may be reproduced or transmitted in any form or by any means, electronic or mechanical including photocopying, recording or by any information storage and retrieval system, without permission from the Publisher in writing.

Typeset by Concept, Huddersfield, West Yorkshire, HD4 5JL.
Printed and bound in England by CPI Group (UK) Ltd, Croydon, CR0 4YY.

Pen & Sword Books Ltd incorporates the imprints of After the Battle, Aviation, Atlas, Family History, Fiction, Maritime, Military, Discovery, Politics, History, Archaeology, Select, Wharncliffe Local History, Wharncliffe True Crime, Military Classics, Wharncliffe Transport, Leo Cooper, The Praetorian Press, Remember When, White Owl, Seaforth Publishing and Frontline Books.

For a complete list of Pen & Sword titles please contact
PEN & SWORD BOOKS LTD
47 Church Street, Barnsley, South Yorkshire, S70 2AS, England
E-mail: enquiries@pen-and-sword.co.uk
Website: www.pen-and-sword.co.uk
or
PEN & SWORD BOOKS
1950 Lawrence Road, Havertown, PA 19083, USA
E-mail: uspen-and-sword@casematepublishers.com
Website: www.penandswordbooks.com

Contents

Acknowledgements 4

Abbreviations 5

Chapter One
Strategic Overview of the War in the SWPA and SPA (1942-44) 7

Chapter Two
Battle of the Bismarck Sea (2-5 March 1943) and the Air War over New Guinea 39

Chapter Three
Commanders and Combatants 77

Chapter Four
MacArthur's Invasions of Arawe and Cape Gloucester (December 1943 to March 1944) .. 125

Chapter Five
US 1st Cavalry Division's Invasions of Los Negros and Manus in the Admiralty Islands (February to March 1944) 155

Chapter Six
The Aerial Neutralization Campaign against Rabaul 177

Epilogue 209

Bibliography 211

Acknowledgements

This archival photograph volume in the 'Images of War' series is dedicated to the multinational Allied Armed Forces' service members who fought, were wounded, captured and perished during the hellacious land, sea and air combat in the SWPA and SPA to defeat the Japanese in 1942–44, to isolate the Japanese bastion at Rabaul and dramatically assist in bringing the Pacific War to a conclusion. We ponder upon viewing these photographs about the heroic sacrifice made to maintain freedom over military aggression, hegemony and brutality, lest we forget. The author is indebted to the able assistance of the archivists at the Still Photo Section of the National Archives and Records Administration (NARA) in College Park, Maryland, and at the USMC Archives in Quantico, Virginia. Their diligence is much appreciated as they maintain and safeguard these superb historic images for the present tome as well as for future viewers.

Abbreviations

AA – Anti-aircraft
ADC – Assistant Division Commander
AF – Air Force
AIF – Australian Imperial Force
AirSols – Aircraft, Solomons
ANGAU – Australian New Guinea Administrative Unit
AP – Armour piercing
AT – Anti-tank
CAP – Combat Air Patrol
CBI – China-Burma-India theatre
CG – Commanding General
C-in-C – Commander-in-Chief
CINCPAC – Commander-in-Chief, Pacific Fleet
CINCPOA – Commander-in-Chief, Pacific Ocean Area
CNO – Chief Naval Operations
CO – Commanding Officer
ComAirSols – Commander, Air, Solomons
COMINCH – Commander-in-Chief, US Fleet
ComSoPac – Commander, South Pacific
COS – Chief of Staff
CPA – Central Pacific Area
DFC – Distinguished Flying Cross
DP – Dual Purpose
DSC – Distinguished Service Cross
ETO – European Theatre of Operations
FA – Field Artillery
GMC – Gun Motor Carriage
GOC – General Officer Commanding
HE – High explosive
IJA – Imperial Japanese Army
IJAAF – Imperial Japanese Army Air Force
IJN – Imperial Japanese Navy
IJNAF – Imperial Japanese Navy Air Force
IMAC – I Marine Amphibious Corps
IMB – Independent Mixed Brigade
IMR – Independent Mixed Regiment
IR – Infantry Regiment
JCS – Joint Chiefs of Staff
LCM – Landing Craft Mechanized
LCP(R) – Landing Craft, Personnel (Ramp)
LCT – Landing Craft, Tank
LCVP – Landing Craft, Vehicle, Personnel
LOC – Lines of Communication
LST – Landing Ship, Tank
LVT – Landing Vehicle Tracked
MAW – Marine Air Wing
MG – Major General
MG – Machine gun
MLR – Main Line of Resistance
MTO – Mediterranean Theatre of Operations
NAA – North American Aviation
NEI – Netherlands East Indies
NGVR – New Guinea Volunteer Rifles

PBY – Patrol Bomber, Consolidated Aircraft
PIR – Parachute Infantry Regiment
PT – Patrol Torpedo
RAAF – Royal Australian Air Force
RN – Royal Navy
RCT – Regimental Combat Team
RNZAF – Royal New Zealand Air Force
SBD – Scout Bomber Douglas
SEAC – Southeast Asia Command
SMLE – Short Magazine Lee-Enfield
SNLF – Special Naval Landing Force
SPA – South Pacific Area
SWPA – Southwest Pacific Area
TB – Tank Battalion
TBF – Torpedo Bomber Grumman
TD – Tank Destroyer
TF – Task Force
TG – Task Group
US – United States
USAAC – United States Army Air Corps
USAAF – United States Army Air Force
USAFFE – United States Army Forces Far East
USMA – United States Military Academy
USMC – United States Marine Corps
USN – United State Navy
V FC – Fifth Fighter Command
VMSB – Marine Scout Bombing Squadron
WP – White Phosphorus
XO – Executive Officer

Chapter One

Strategic Overview of the War in the SWPA and SPA (1942–44)

The Japanese juggernaut following the 7 December 1941 attack on the US Pacific Fleet at Pearl Harbor rapidly acquired British, American, Australian and Dutch possessions and resources in the Philippines, Malaya and Singapore, the Dutch East Indies, Burma, New Guinea, the Bismarck Archipelago, and the Solomon Islands and Gilbert Islands (see Map 1). Strategically, seizure of extant airfields or building new aerodromes expedited Japan's advance towards northern Australia and southeastwards to sever the sea lanes from America to the Antipodes.

IJN and USN carriers were sunk, with significant air crew and aircraft losses, in solely airplane versus surface ship battles, first in the Coral Sea from 4 to 8 May 1942 and then at Midway from 3 to 7 June 1942 (see Map 1). On 3 to 4 May 1942, Japanese forces occupied Tulagi on Florida Island, opposite Guadalcanal in the southern Solomon Islands (see Map 2), to base IJN seaplanes and tenders to interdict Allied LOC, while the IJN's Fourth Fleet's Carrier Striking Force sailed from Rabaul, protecting transports with 10,000 naval infantry towards the Coral Sea to amphibiously assault Port Moresby. On 8 May, USS *Lexington* was sunk and USS *Yorktown* damaged, while the light Japanese carrier *Shōhō* was sunk and the fleet carrier *Shōkaku* damaged. The Port Moresby invasion was thwarted and the Japanese sailed back to Rabaul. At Midway, three USN carriers surprised an IJN four-carrier invasion force steaming to seize the American airfield on Midway Island to threaten the Hawaiian Islands. Four Japanese carriers were sunk by SBD Dauntless dive-bombers, while most USN torpedo bomber squadrons were decimated. The USS *Yorktown* was sunk.

In July 1942, the Japanese moved from Tulagi to Guadalcanal to build an airfield, which was observed by both Allied aircraft and by a British Army/colonial administrator/coastwatcher, Captain W.F. Martin Clemens. When Admiral Ernest King, COMINCH US Fleet and CNO, was apprised, the

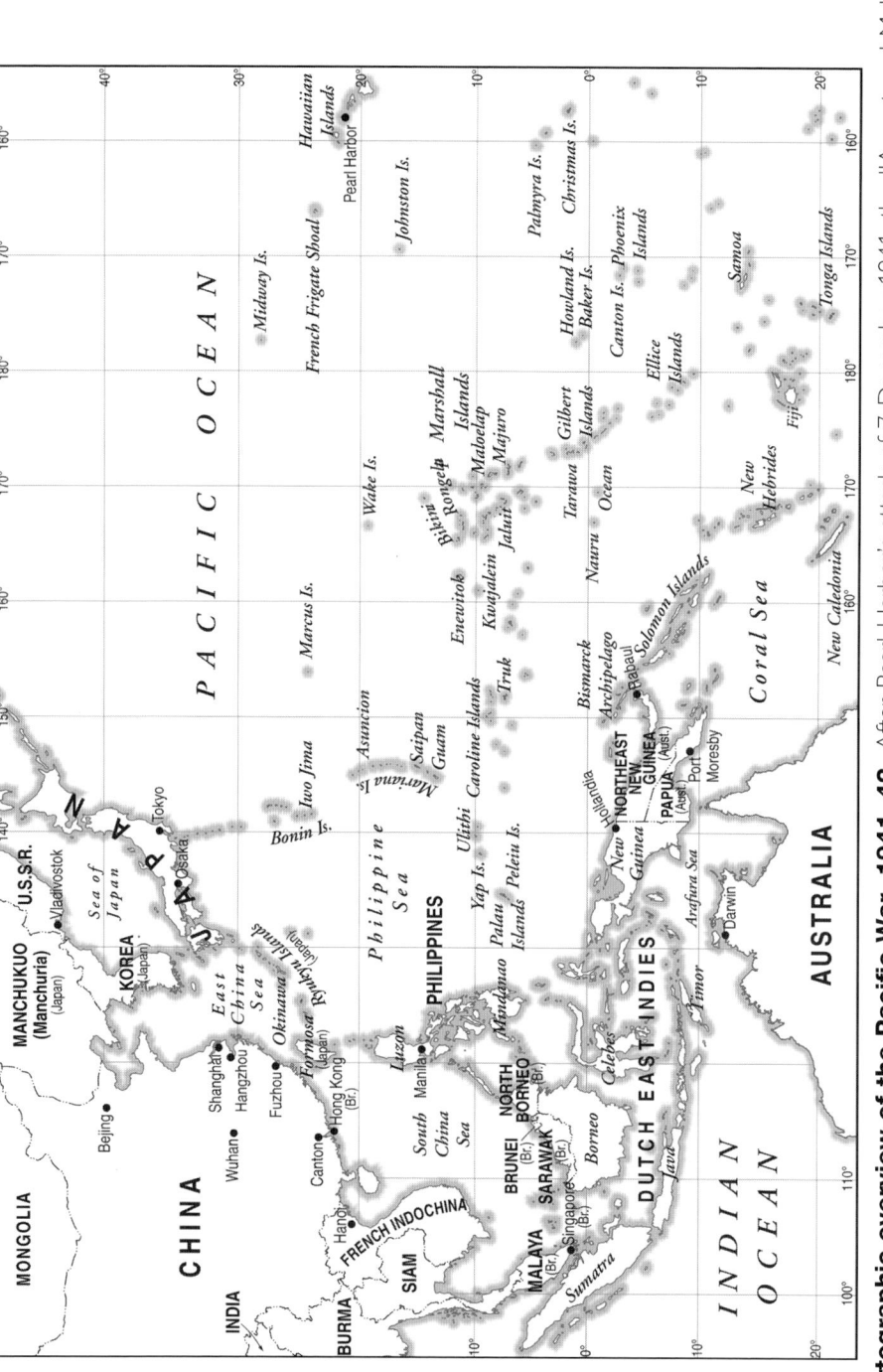

Map 1. Cartographic overview of the Pacific War, 1941–42. After Pearl Harbor's attack of 7 December 1941, the IJA captured Malaya and Singapore; occupied Borneo, Sumatra, and Java in the NEI; marched from Siam to evict the Allies from Burma, further isolating China; while defeating Filipino-American forces to capture the Philippines. Japanese forces swept south and east, capturing Rabaul on New Britain Island; setting up garrisons along New Guinea's northern coast; and occupying British-controlled Tulagi in the southern Solomons and the Gilbert Islands, all threatening Australia. (Meridian Mapping)

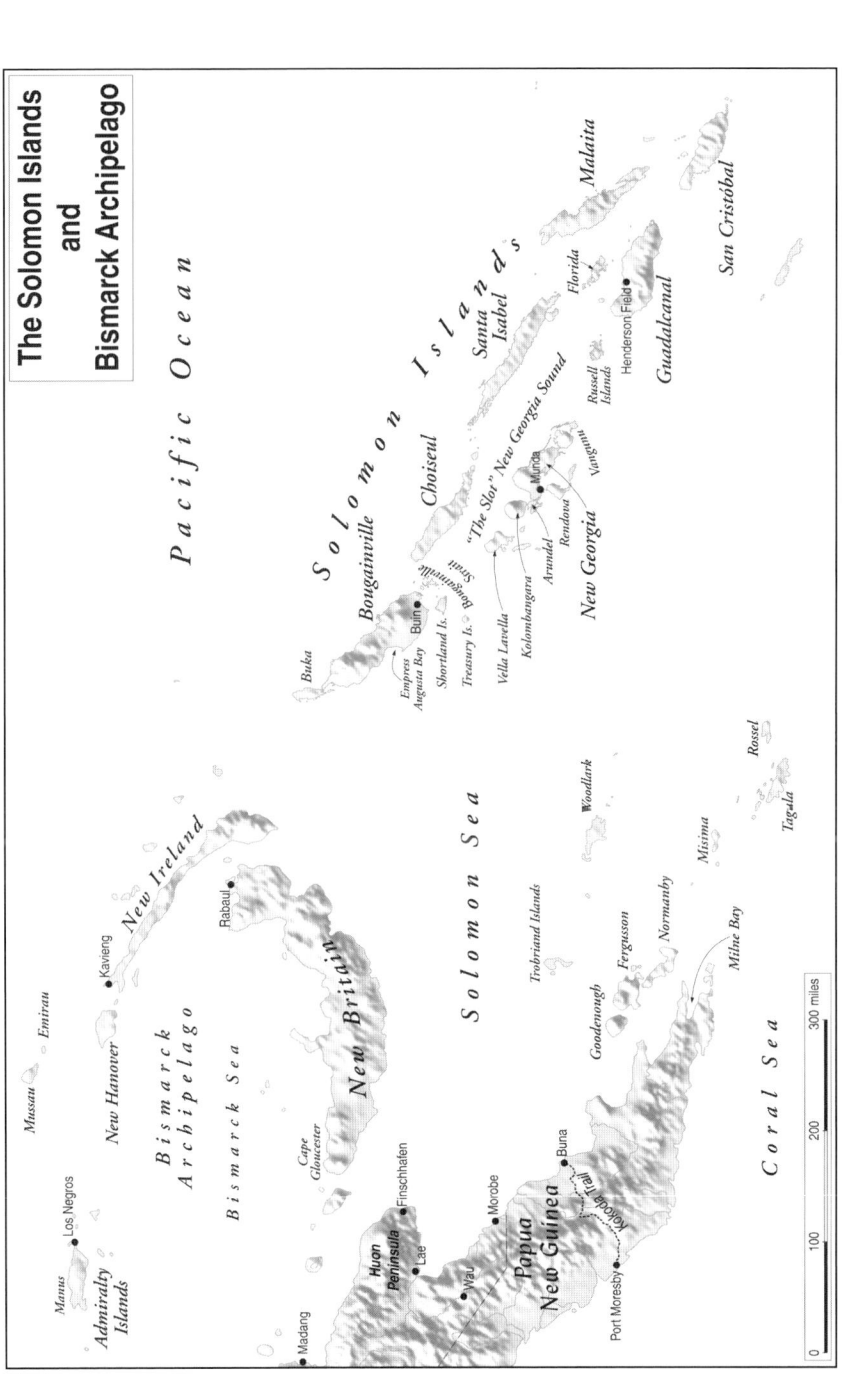

Map 2. The Solomon Islands, New Guinea and the Bismarck Archipelago in the SPA and SWPA, 1942–43. The principal areas of Allied counteroffensive to encircle Rabaul in a 'double envelopment' for its aerial neutralization rather than a direct invasion included the Solomon Islands, New Guinea and its offshore Solomon Sea islands (Goodenough, Woodlark and Kiriwina, the largest of the Trobriands), western New Britain at Cape Gloucester and Arawe, and the Bismarck Archipelago's Admiralty Islands and Emirau Island in the St Mathias Group. The Allied 1942–43 campaigns in Papua and on Guadalcanal diluted Japanese strength in both areas, posing dilemmas that Japan never overcame. A common theme of all the Allied and Japanese campaigns in these areas was establishment and control of extant airfields to aerially cover land operations by ground forces and to interdict LOC by contesting IJN resupply operations and amphibious assaults. Although the USN launched only two carrier raids against Rabaul in November 1943, newly developed American bases developed at Cape Torokina on Bougainville in December 1943; and on captured Henderson (Guadalcanal) and Munda (New Georgia) airfields, August 1942 and 1943, respectively, became stationary 'aircraft carriers' for USN and Marine SBDs, TBFs and F4U Corsairs. *(Meridian Mapping)*

USN and USMC hastily assembled the 1st Marine Division (Reinforced), under Major General Alexander A. Vandegrift, to amphibiously seize both Tulagi and the airfield on Guadalcanal. Hellacious jungle combat, aerial conflict and naval battles ensued from 7 August 1942 (Marine invasion) until 7 February 1943 (Japanese evacuation) to defend the American Guadalcanal lodgement and the newly completed Henderson Field.

On 22 to 23 January 1942, the Japanese seized Rabaul, on New Britain Island's northeastern tip in the Bismarck Archipelago (see Map 2), from an Australian 1,400-man garrison (2/22nd Battalion and NGVR militia units). Rabaul's Simpson Harbour was a sheltered, deep and vast anchorage for the largest IJN ships and fleet, 640 miles south from the main IJN base at Truk in the eastern Caroline Islands. Japanese bombers attacked Rabaul on 4 January. The small RAAF contingent was destroyed or withdrew to Lae. Rabaul had excellent airfield sites and its town was large enough to maintain an IJA corps.

Lae, at northeastern New Guinea's Huon Peninsula base, and the Admiralty Islands' Los Negros and Manus, were within 400 miles of Rabaul's multiple airfields (see Map 2). With Port Moresby on Papua New Guinea's southern coast and Guadalcanal 500 and 650 miles, respectively, away from Rabaul, the Japanese bastion became the staging area for troops, aircraft and resources to northern New Guinea bases and the Solomon Islands from Japan through the Marianas to Truk and then New Britain (see Map 1). On 1 April 1942, the Japanese Eleventh Air Fleet arrived at Rabaul with 150 Japanese aircraft operating from the Vunakanau and Lakunai airfields. By June, Rabaul had 21,000 troops and another 20,000 on surrounding islands, notably at Kavieng on New Ireland (see Map 2). By the start of 1943, Rabaul had 100,000 men based in northern New Britain's Gazelle Peninsula as 400 miles of new paved roads, hangars, warehouses, barracks, radio facilities, control towers, repair shops, docks and gun positions were created from 1942 to 1943. With oil storage and ammunition dumps within 10 miles, Rabaul became Japan's logistics centre in the SWPA, competing with the IJN Combined Fleet base at Truk.

To secure Rabaul, the Japanese extended southeastwards, seizing the Solomon Islands, and southwestwards, taking Papua New Guinea after having previously landed at Lae, Finschhafen and Salamaua on northeastern New Guinea's Huon Gulf from 8 March to 7 April 1942 to capture Australian airstrips. On 22 July, IJA troops from Rabaul landed at Gona, Sanananda and Buna, all located on Papua's northern coast. Buna Airfield, built pre-war by Australians as an emergency grass-surfaced landing ground, was extended by the Japanese in late July, and in early August was ready for use as a forward Japanese military airfield. At Kokoda (see Map 3), a 1,000-yard grass strip was occupied by the Japanese on 10 August, but abandoned two months later. Buna and Kokoda strips based Japanese aircraft providing air cover for IJA ground troops marching 130 miles south over the Owen Stanley Range along the Kokoda Trail to seize Port Moresby from the rear. These locales were converted into garrisoned outposts to prevent the Allied Air Forces from using any as an airstrip to attack Rabaul.

In early June 1942, US Army engineers surveyed Buna and Milne Bay for airfield sites, but flying over Papua on 11 July, they determined the kunai grass plains at Dobodura be developed instead of Buna Airfield. A month later, several thousand troops and two US Army engineer battalions carved out a small grass airfield for RAAF P-40 Kittyhawks near eastern Papua's Milne Bay. Previously, Allied engineers in Papua hacked airstrips out of jungle and bush wherever there was a well-drained level area, naming each field for its distance from Port Moresby (e.g., Seven Mile Field or Jackson Drome). Japanese aircraft raided these sites to delay completion as MacArthur and his SWPA planners were preparing to assault Buna.

In June 1942, General Douglas MacArthur, C-in-C SWPA, dispatched additional 'green' Australian Militia units to Port Moresby as the US 32nd and 41st Infantry Divisions arrived in Australia. Previously, the Australian Militia's 39th Battalion, already deployed at Port Moresby, was ordered north to defend Kokoda, which was attacked by the Japanese on 29 July. Eventually reinforced by Middle East veteran AIF formations, the Australians combated IJA units across the Owen Stanley Range (see Map 3). By mid-September, stiffening Australian defence and Japanese orders to cease advancing saved Port Moresby. Also, a second amphibious Japanese invasion at Milne Bay during late August to early September aimed at seizing Port Moresby was turned back by Australian forces. Americans and Australians began their offensive up the Kokoda Trail and through the Papuan jungle to drive the Japanese from Buna, Gona and Sanananda.

On 10 September 1942, MacArthur ordered Lieutenant General Robert Eichelberger's I Corps HQ in Australia to deploy Major General Edwin Harding's 32nd Infantry Division to capture the 11-mile-long group of Japanese installations at Buna. After a few months of arduous marching and combat against a bunkered Japanese foe, the unprepared American former National Guardsmen, with the aid of battle-hardened Australians, evicted the Japanese from their installations by January 1943 with a steep Allied 'butcher bill', compelling MacArthur to vow, 'No more Bunas.'

Beginning in 1943, three separate axes of Allied advances were conducted in the SWPA, SPA and CPA (see Map 4). Japan was now on the defensive in both the SPA and SWPA theatres of the Pacific War. In March,

Allied air strikes neutralized the main Japanese airfield at Lae. In May, the Australians began attacks against the Japanese forces holding Lae, while a seaborne landing was being planned. On 23 and 30 June 1943, respectively, MacArthur's forces took the Woodlark Islands and Kiriwina Island (the largest in the Trobriand group), giving the Allies airfields closer to New Britain (see Map 2). On 16 July, the Australians gained a foothold on Mount Tambu, south of Salamaua and northeast of Wau (see Map 3), and by 12 August, it was encircled, forcing a Japanese retreat a week later. On 4–5 September, an Allied amphibious landing prepared the way for the capture of Lae on 15 September. On 11 September, the Allies captured Salamaua to Lae's south, along Huon Bay. These two Allied victories pushed the Japanese inland from North-East New Guinea's Huon Peninsula. Finschhafen – at the far eastern end of the Huon Peninsula between the Vitiaz Strait and the Solomon Sea, formerly a Japanese stronghold – was seized by the Australians on 2 October. The capture of Lae and Finschhafen placed newly acquired Allied airfields across the Vitiaz Strait and the Dampier Strait from New Britain.

As early as 2 July 1942, the US JCS called for Rabaul's recapture as an enumerated operation in SWPA. However, on 28 March 1943, this directive was cancelled and replaced with Operation CARTWHEEL, a strategy to seize lightly held islands around Rabaul in order to build new airfields or improve existing ones, thereby encircling the Japanese bastion and bombing it with near continual Allied aircraft raids, turning it into an irrelevant military base to isolate and bypass rather than directly invade and occupy. The Allied vacillation correlated with the horrific naval and ground force losses during the 1942 Guadalcanal and Papua New Guinea campaigns. Operation CARTWHEEL was at the junction of two major Allied Commands: SWPA under MacArthur and SPA under Halsey (see Map 4).

The attack on Rabaul drew the resources of three independent air commands: Lieutenant General George Kenney's 5th USAAF under MacArthur; the 13th USAAF as part of SPA; and USN and USMC air assets

Map 3. Papua and North-East New Guinea campaigns, July 1942 to September 1943.
The Japanese expanded their presence at Salamaua, Lae and Finschhafen on North-East New Guinea's Huon Peninsula by establishing bases along Papua's northern coast, notably at Buna during the late spring of 1942. Lieutenant General Kenney, CO Allied Air Forces and 5th USAAF in SWPA, built new airfields in late 1942 to 1943 at Wanigela near Collingwood Bay, at Pongani near Oro Bay, and an airfield complex at Dobodura, situated within Papua's interior, east of the Girua River and south of Buna, in addition to numerous dromes constructed in the vicinity of Port Moresby. After the Allied victory in Papua in January 1943, MacArthur conducted separate amphibious and land campaigns, capturing the above Japanese key sites, airfields and IJA bases in North-East New Guinea, enabling his occupation of the Huon Peninsula for the December 1943 invasion of western New Britain at Arawe and Cape Gloucester. (*Meridian Mapping*)

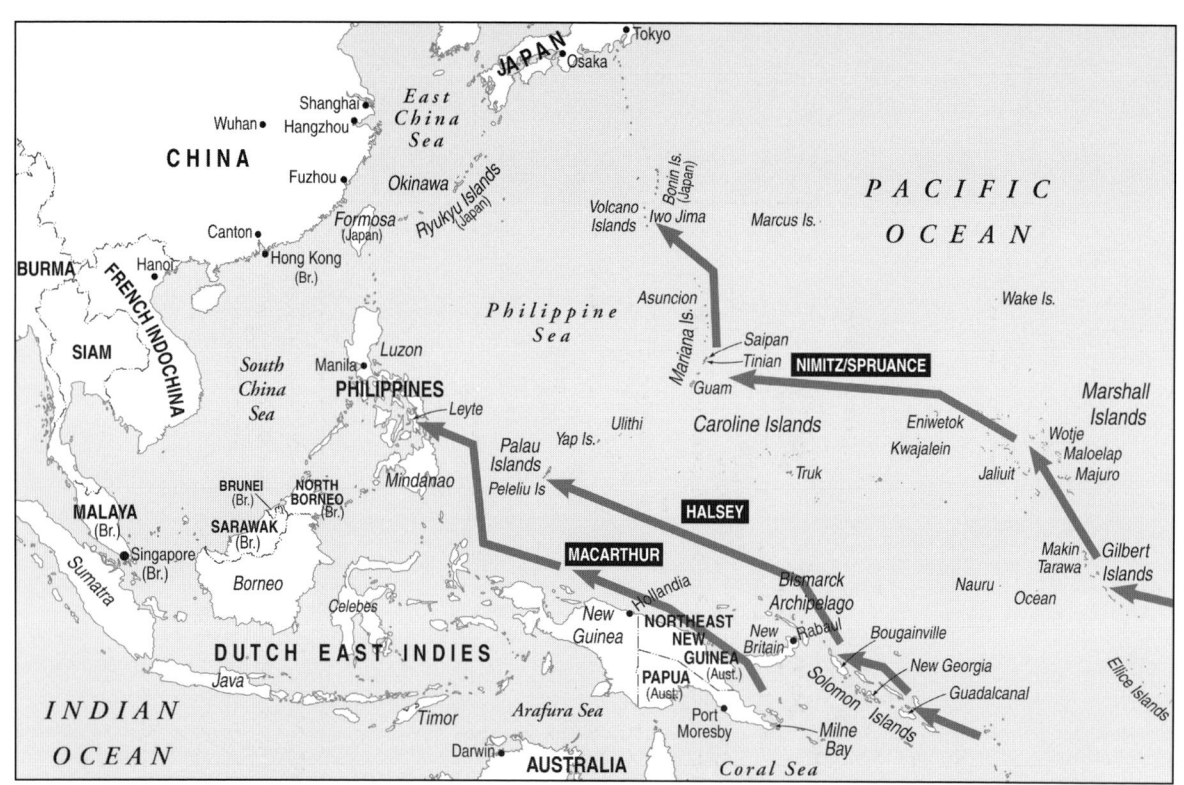

Map 4. Allied Counteroffensive Axes in the Central, South and Southwest Pacific Areas of Operation, 1943–45. Vice Admiral Raymond Spruance, Nimitz's COS, was assigned to command the Central Pacific Force (later redesignated Fifth Fleet in April 1944) in the CPA campaigns involving USN, Marine and Army forces advancing in separate hotly contested invasions of the Gilbert Islands (November 1943), the Marshall Islands (January–February 1944), the Mariana Islands (June–August 1944) and the Iwo Jima invasion of 19 February 1945. As commander of SPA, Admiral Halsey was given command of the tenuous Guadalcanal campaign in October 1942, and after the Japanese evacuation in early February 1943, he led the Allied forces in this theatre for the drive up the Central Solomons to Bougainville throughout 1943. In April 1943, Halsey assigned Rear Admiral Marc Mitscher to become ComAirSols, and lead Army, USN, Marine and New Zealand aircraft up the Solomon chain, culminating in the Rabaul raids starting in December 1943 after Halsey's two daring Simpson Harbour carrier raids the preceding month. In May 1944, Halsey was promoted to CO of the newly formed Third Fleet, leading the naval campaigns to take the Palau Islands, Leyte and Luzon, and later raid the Japanese Home Islands. General Douglas MacArthur, CO SWPA, led his US and Australian ground forces, Lieutenant General George Kenney's Allied Air Forces and 5th USAAF, and USN's Seventh Fleet vessels, under Vice Admiral Thomas Kinkaid, and Rear Admiral Daniel Barbey's VII Amphibious Force, driving along the northern coast of Northeast and Netherlands New Guinea, western New Britain at Cape Gloucester and Arawe, and the Admiralty Islands invasion, all in 1943–44 as a prelude to assault Leyte in October 1944 and Luzon in December 1944. *(Meridian Mapping)*

in the Solomon Islands. The 13th USAAF with the USN and USMC aircraft in SPA were consolidated into 'AirSols' under a unified, rotating commander, 'ComAirSols', which operated with Kenney.

In the SPA, now-Admiral Halsey's forces of Marines and Army troops quickly occupied and constructed airfields in the Russell Islands in late

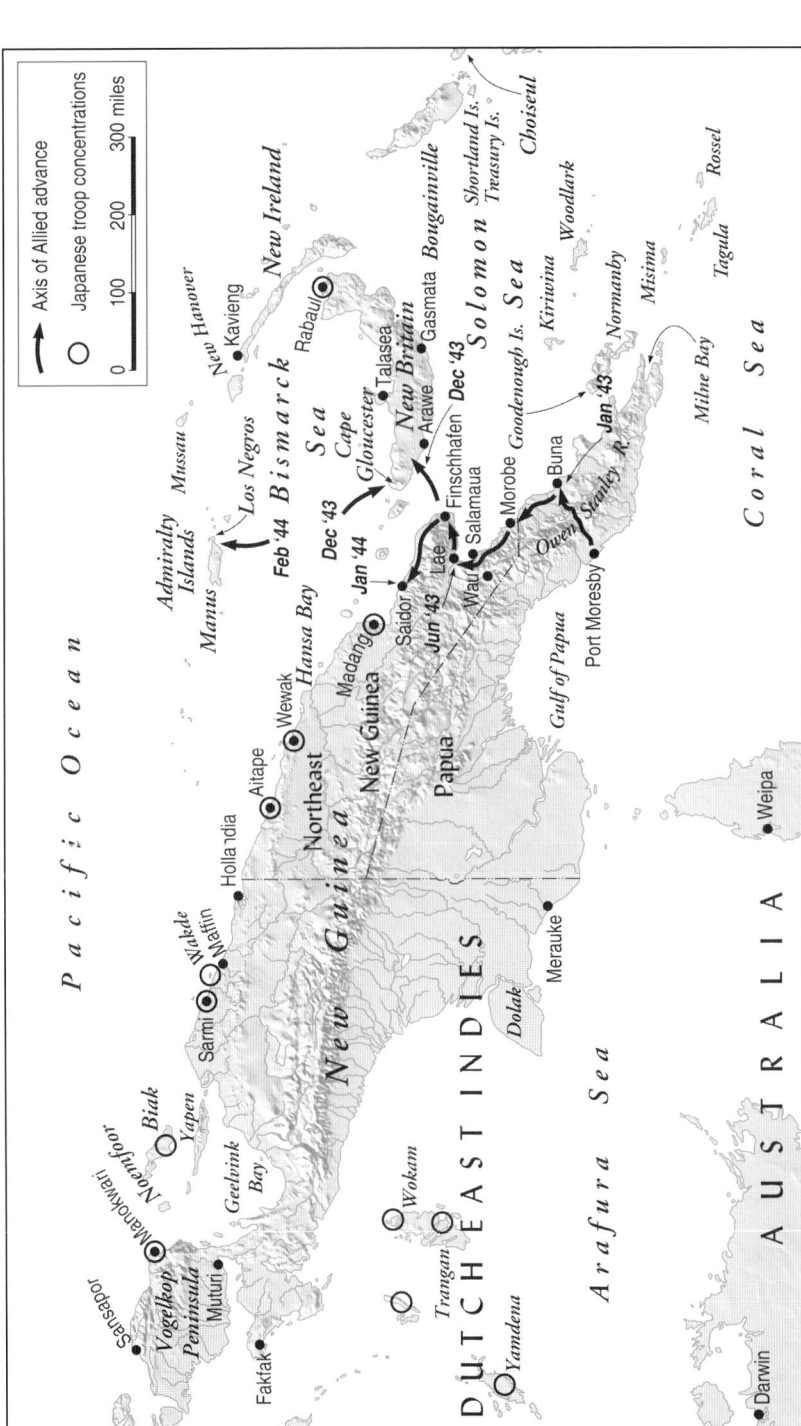

Map 5. New Guinea Campaign and the Nidus of Operation CARTWHEEL 1943. Map of New Guinea, the world's second largest island, divided into Papua, North-East New Guinea, and Netherlands New Guinea. Rabaul, situated at the northeast end of New Britain Island, along with Cape Gloucester and Arawe, and dates of SWPA amphibious assaults there. The Japanese had garrisons and airstrips at Gasmata on the southern coast and Talasea on the east coast of New Britain's Willaumez Peninsula. MacArthur's forces captured and built airfields on the islands of Woodlark, Goodenough and Kiriwina, which would be vital as staging areas and bases for aircraft raiding Rabaul. The Admiralty Islands of Los Negros and Manus, with their airfields, were captured in February–March 1944 to strengthen the 'aerial noose' around Rabaul, which was the intent of Operation CARTWHEEL, to avoid a land invasion. Along the northern coast of North-East New Guinea, MacArthur's forces 'leap-frogged' over strong IJA garrisons after neutralizing the Japanese airfields there in 1943.

(Meridian Mapping)

February 1943. The Central Solomon Islands campaign (see Map 2) continued with the New Georgia group's invasion in early July. After several weeks of combat against stubborn Japanese defenders, notably at Munda Airfield, New Georgia Island fell, with operations continuing at other islands in the group: Arundel, Kolombangara, and Vella Lavella. Diversionary assaults on Choiseul and the Treasuries were a prelude to the invasion of the heavily defended and largest Solomon Island of Bougainville, along Cape Torokina at Empress Augusta Bay, on 1 November by IMAC, commanded by Marine MG Roy Geiger, comprising the 3rd Marine Division and other Marine battalions (see Map 2).

MacArthur wanted Halsey's aircraft established on new airfields at Cape Torokina, within fighter range of Rabaul, in time to cover the 1st Marine Division's invasion of Cape Gloucester on 26 December 1943, as well as elements of US Sixth Army at Arawe on 15 December 1943 at the southern end of New Britain Island, and to participate in Rabaul's aerial neutralization (see Map 3).

Throughout the earlier part of 1944, MacArthur's SWPA ground forces, comprising Lieutenant General Walter Krueger's Sixth Army's 6th, 24th, 32nd and 41st Infantry Divisions, with attached elite cavalry, parachute, engineer and scout units, transported by the USN's growing amphibious fleet, moved inexorably westwards along the northern coast of Netherlands New Guinea with successful missions at Saidor (2 January), the Admiralty Islands (29 February), Talasea (6 March), Aitape (22 April), Hollandia (22 April), Tanahmerah Bay (22 April), Wakde Island (18 May), Biak Island at the entrance of Geelvink Bay (27 May), Middelburg Island (30 June), Sansapor on the Vogelkop Peninsula (30 June), and Noemfoor Island (2 July) (see Map 5).

(**Opposite, above**) An IJN Nakajima B5N Type 97 three-seat carrier and land-based attack torpedo/horizontal bomber (Kate) flies above a fiery and smoking Pearl Harbor on 7 December 1941 during Admiral Chūichi Nagumo's six-carrier raid. The B5N was the counterpart to the Aichi D3A Type 99 (Val) carrier dive-bomber during the IJN's 1941–42 *blitzkrieg* across the Pacific and into the Solomon Sea and Indian Ocean. The Kate carried an external torpedo and bomb load of over 1,700lb. The carrier-borne torpedo attacks devastated 'Battleship Row' as these USN capital ships were moored side by side near Ford Island in the middle of the harbour. (*Author's collection*)

(**Opposite, below**) The smoking USS *Lexington* has its ship's crew climbing down ropes into the water for rescue by an awaiting destroyer on 8 May 1942, during the Battle of the Coral Sea. A total of 2,735 of *Lexington*'s crew were evacuated, while 216 sailors perished. As the naval battle was fought solely by aircraft, an emerging stratagem was reinforced that aircraft carriers could be sunk but defended airfields sustained. Also, although the Japanese carrier *Zuikaku* was not sunk, it lost so many aircraft and trained pilots that it was unable to participate in June 1942's Battle of Midway. (*NARA*)

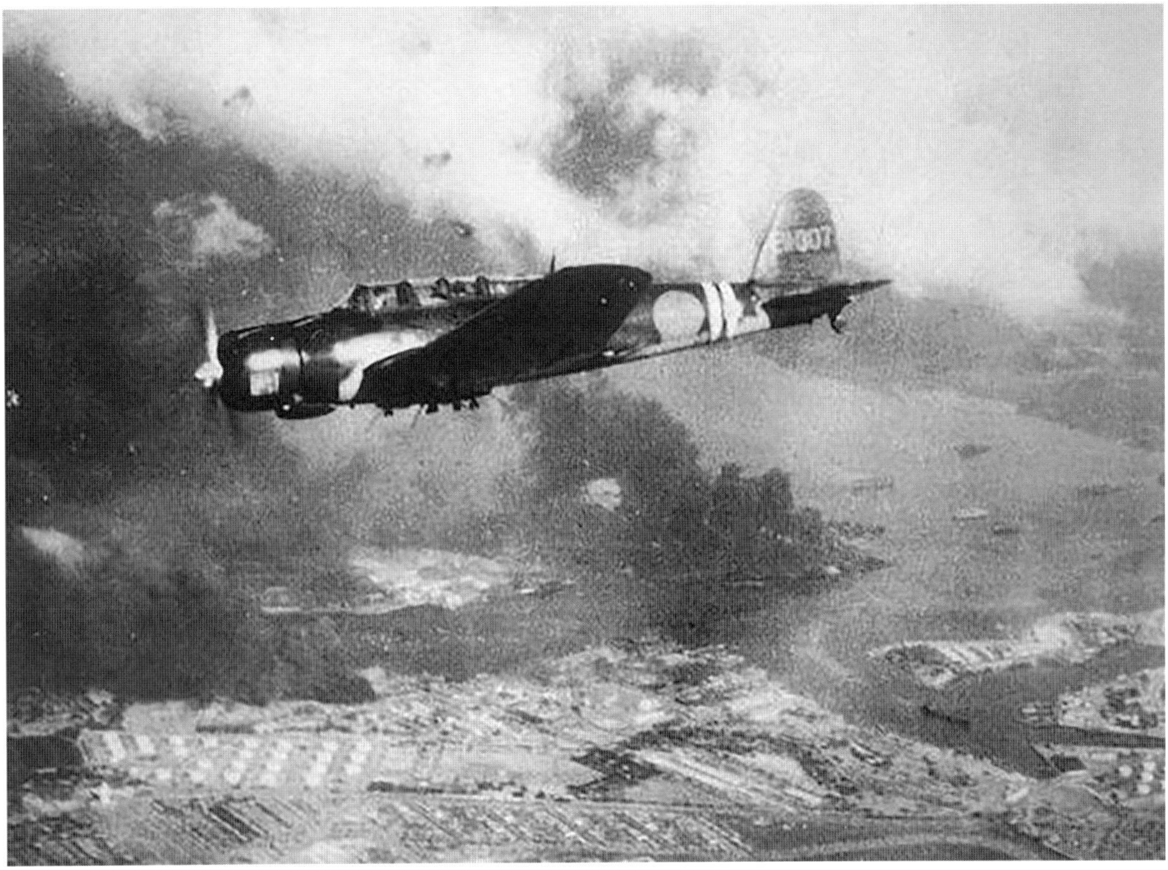

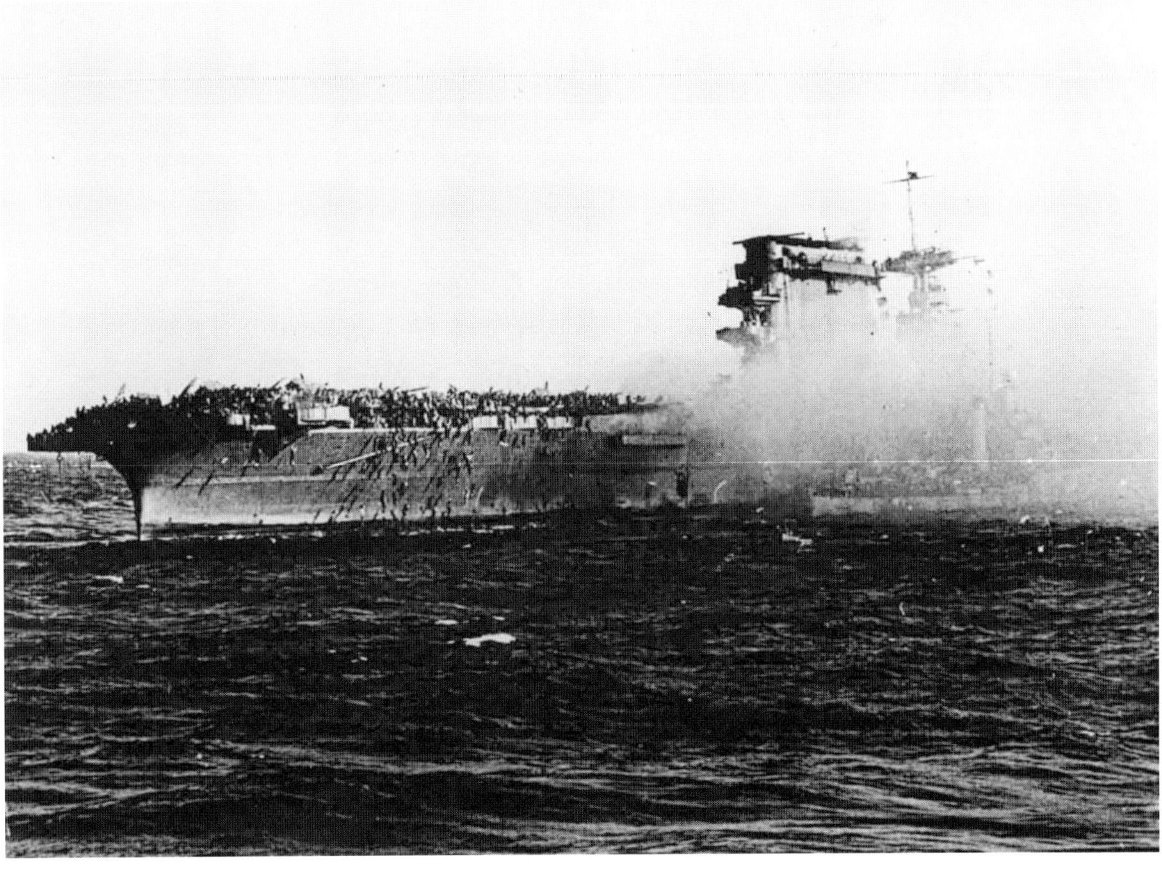

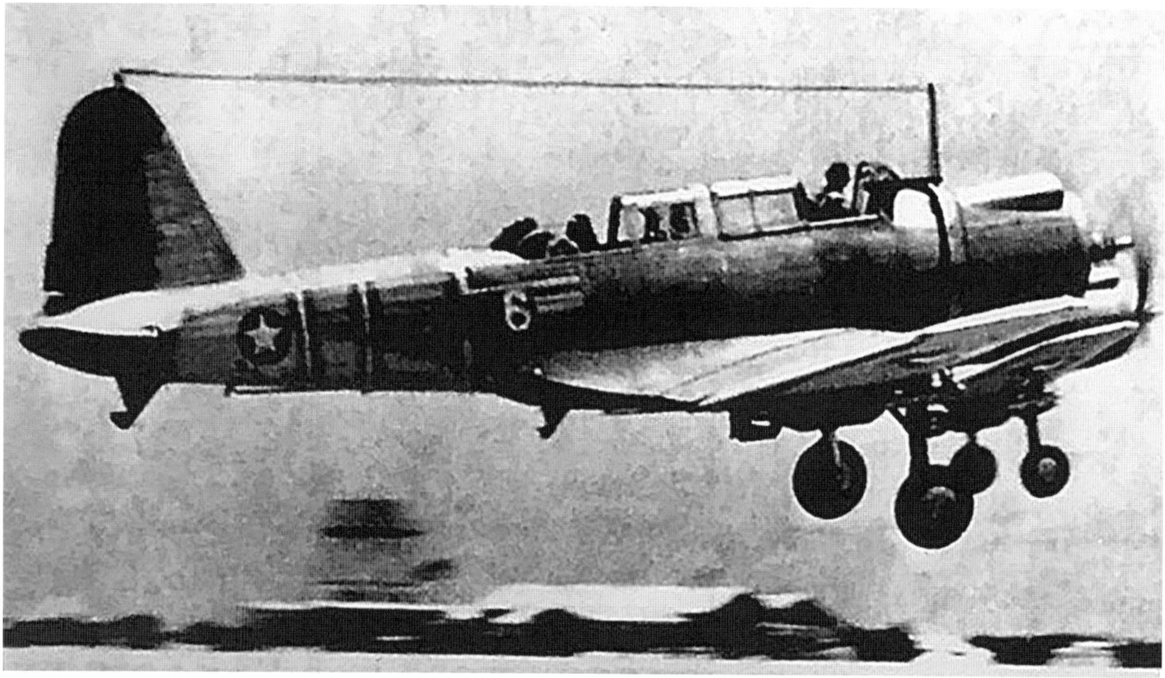

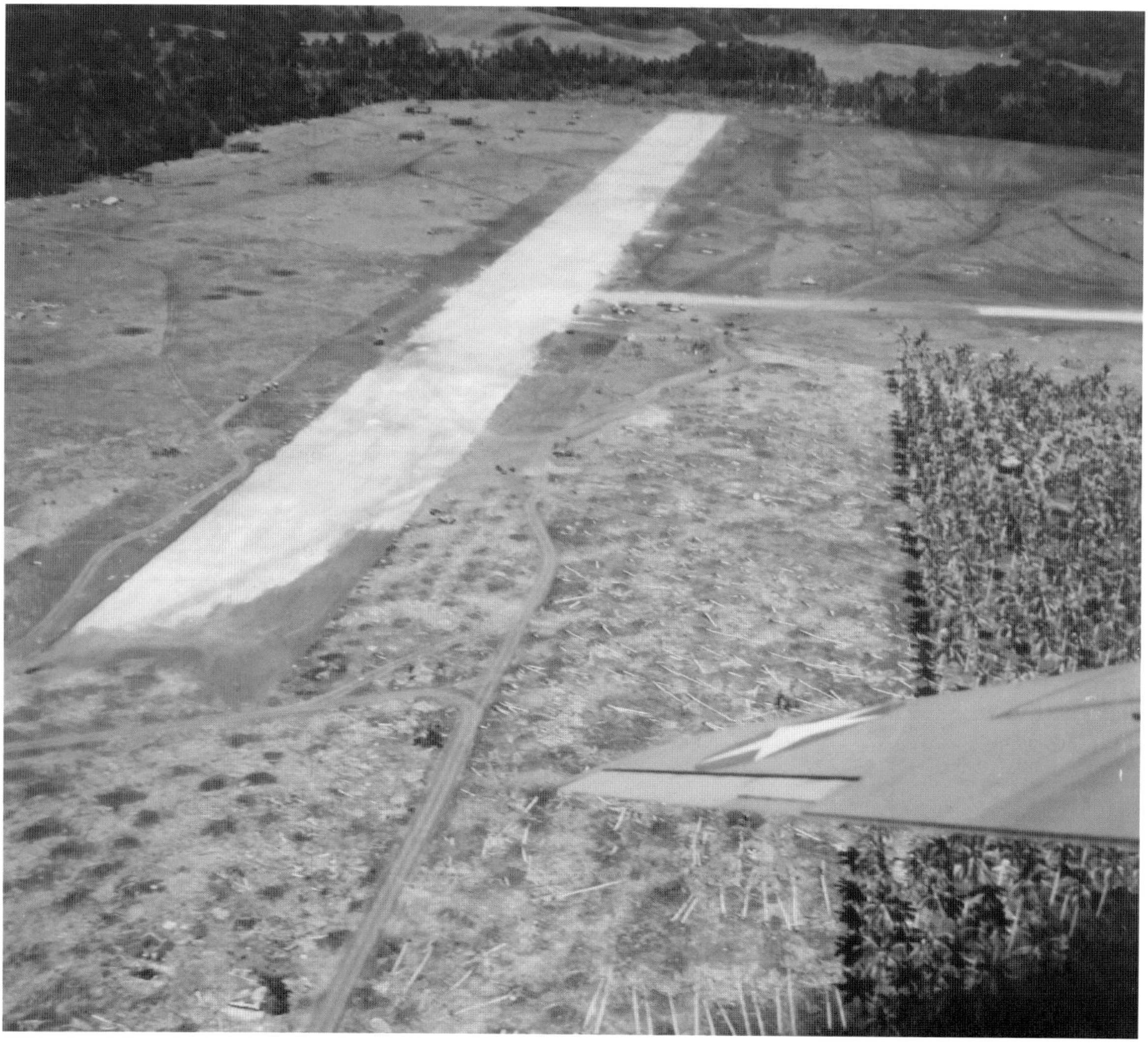

(**Opposite, above**) One of the seventeen USMC Vought SB2U Vindicator dive-bombers of VMSB-241 takes off from Midway Atoll's Eastern Island airfield on 4 June 1942 after the IJN fleet was spotted and IJN aircraft were en route to Midway. The Vindicator was the first USN monoplane. During the Pearl Harbor attack, seven Vindicators were destroyed on the ground at the Marine Air Station, Ewa Field. At Midway, Marine Captain Richard Fleming's Vindicator attacked the IJN cruiser *Mikuma* on 5 June 1942 but was shot down. Fleming received the Medal of Honor. The Japanese cruiser was sunk the following day by USN carrier planes. Marine aviators disparagingly referred to the Vindicators as 'vibrators' or 'wind indicators'. *(NARA)*

(**Opposite, below**) Guadalcanal's nearly completed airstrip at Lunga Point, except for the unfinished runway corner as seen from a low-flying USN airplane after the 1st Marine Division landed on 7 August 1942, renaming it Henderson Field after Marine Major Lofton Henderson – a dive-bomber squadron commander shot down at Midway leading an attack on IJN carriers on 4 June 1942. By 7 August, the runway was 3,800ft long by 150ft wide. *(NARA)*

(**Above**) Marines work on Henderson Field to preserve it as an 'unsinkable aircraft carrier' as a Marine Douglas SBD Dauntless dive-bomber takes off. The IJN frequently pounded Henderson Field with their cruiser and battleship guns when these warships moved down 'the Slot' from Rabaul into 'Ironbottom' Sound opposite Henderson Field. Bomb craters had to be filled and burning or demolished planes removed from the runway soon after the bombardment to keep the airfield operational. *(NARA)*

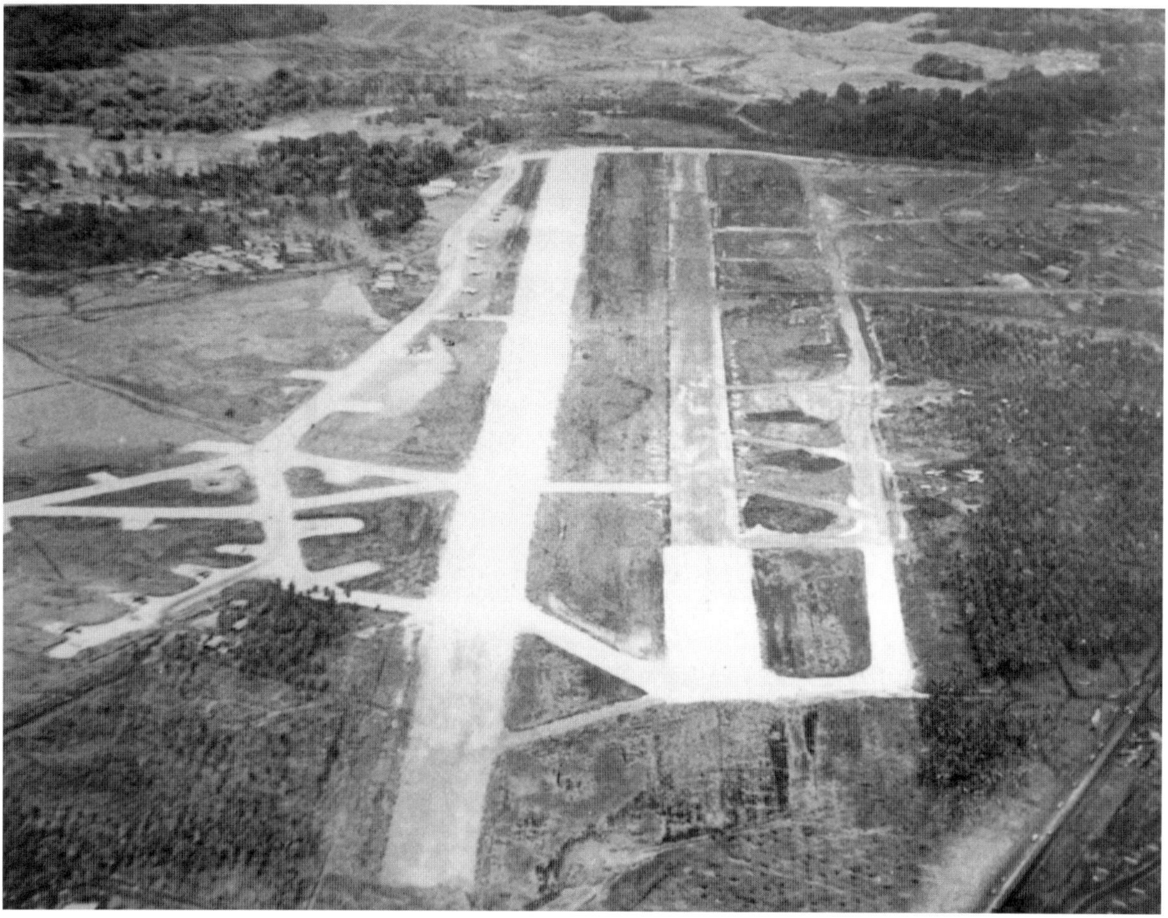

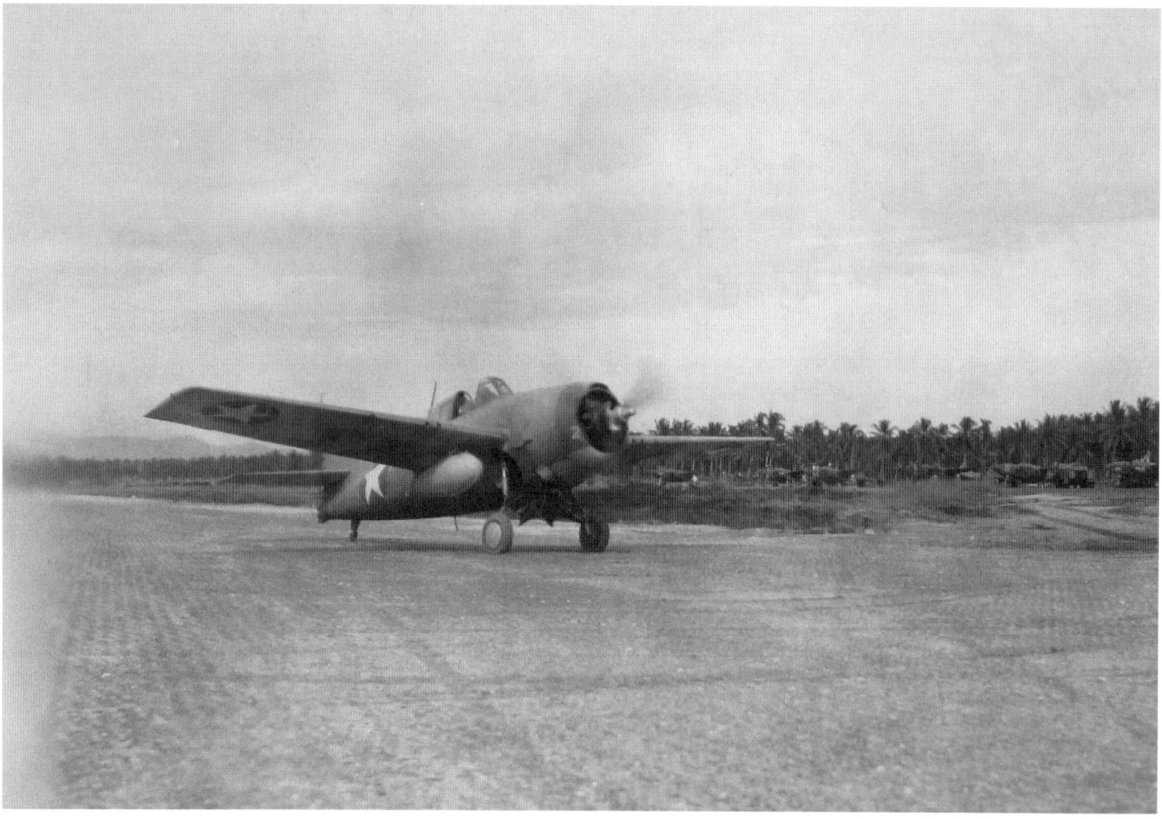

(**Opposite, above**) An aerial view of the completed Henderson Field complex after Guadalcanal was secured in February 1943 with taxiways, revetments, and American planes lined up along the runways (top left). The challenge of 'island-hopping' and coastal assaults throughout the South Pacific was to create or seize existing airfields in order to bring aerial attack closer to the enemy, usually in preparation of upcoming amphibious assaults or to isolate Japanese garrisons, such as Rabaul, by an overwhelming air interdiction of either enemy supply or evacuation. (NARA)

(**Opposite, below**) A Marine Grumman F4F Wildcat fighter with extra wing fuel tanks stationed at Henderson Field soon after the February 1943 Japanese evacuation of Guadalcanal. Extra fuel tanks gave the fighter longer airborne patrol range farther up the Solomon Island chain, providing protection for American bombers or flying CAP over Guadalcanal against Japanese air attacks with its six 0.5-inch calibre forward-firing machine guns in the leading edges of the wings, especially during Yamamoto's Operation I-GO, the southern Solomon Island air assault emanating from Rabaul in the spring of 1943. The F4F was the USN and USMC's most important fighter at the war's outbreak. American pilots devised special tactics for aerial combat against the Mitsubishi A6M Reisen Zero IJN fighter. (NARA)

(**Above**) A Lockheed USAAF P-38 Lightning fighter readies for take-off into the Central Solomons from Guadalcanal's Fighter One airstrip. A P-38 flown from Guadalcanal by USAAF Lieutenant Thomas Lamphier shot down the IJN Combined Fleet Admiral Isoroku Yamamoto's transport plane, a twin-engine IJN Mitsubishi G4M3 Betty bomber, over southern Bougainville on the morning of 18 April 1943. Yamamoto was on an inspection tour of the northern Solomon Islands for the start of Operation I-GO, the April 1943 aerial counteroffensive launched by Japan against Allied forces in the Solomon Islands and New Guinea to give Japan additional time to prepare a new set of defences after recent defeats on Guadalcanal and the Bismarck Sea. The IJN air units for this operation were under the command of Admiral Yamamoto and Vice Admiral Jinichi Kusaka at Rabaul. The P-38 became one of the most successful Allied interceptors in the Pacific, as it possessed four M2 Browning 0.50-inch calibre machine guns and one Hispano M1 20mm cannon in the plane's nose. The P-38's range was superior to any of the other American fighters in the South Pacific, allowing it to make the round trip from Guadalcanal to Bougainville. It had a unique appearance, with twin booms located behind each supercharged Allison engine and tricycle landing gear, with the aircraft's central nose containing the cockpit and armament. (NARA)

A Grumman (TBF) Avenger torpedo bomber is armed for a Solomon Islands sortie from Guadalcanal's Henderson Field with the torpedo on a carrier (foreground). After a disastrous debut at Midway in June 1942, the Avenger became the USN's major torpedo bomber for the war's remainder. It had a crew of three, carried a 2,500lb torpedo/bomb load, and could sustain Japanese fighter gun and cannon fire. The TBF Avengers participated in Halsey's carrier attack by the *Saratoga* and *Princeton* on Rabaul's Simpson Harbour on 5 November 1943, days after the Bougainville invasion at Cape Torokina in Empress Augusta Bay. (NARA)

A pair of RNZAF Lockheed Hudson bombers from Henderson Field fly on a bombing sortie in the Central Solomons. The Hudson was a six-seat coastal reconnaissance bomber with a maximum range of 1,900 miles and could deliver a bomb load of 1,350lb. (NARA)

Japanese-controlled Munda Airfield on New Georgia Island's west coast, under attack by Marine Guadalcanal-based SBD Dauntless dive-bombers in July 1943. Marine Raiders and the Army's 43rd, 37th and 25th Infantry Divisions, comprising Major General Oscar Griswold's XIV Corps, invaded at both eastern and western ends of New Georgia, fighting the Japanese from 30 June to 25 August 1943, ultimately converging to capture Munda Airfield on 5 August 1943. (NARA)

(**Above**) A Marine Vought F4U Corsair takes off from battle-scarred Munda Airfield on New Georgia after its capture on 5 August 1943. The Corsair, with inverted gull wing design, was planned as a carrier-borne fighter for the USN, but became an excellent ground-attack and close-support fighter, fulfilling Marine aviation philosophy to support the Corps' rifle platoons. The Corsair entered service in 1943 and was armed with external bombs or a rocket load of 2,000lb to complement the six 0.50-inch calibre forward-firing machine guns in the leading edges of the wings The Marine fighters based on Munda proved vital as CAP in protecting Admiral Halsey's TF 38 conducting the 5 November 1943 full-scale carrier aircraft raid on Simpson Harbour's shipping. (NARA)

(**Opposite, above**) Australian infantrymen of the 2/9th Battalion, 18th Brigade, and an M3 Stuart light tank of the 2/6th Armoured Regiment with a 37mm turret gun confront a Japanese bunker at close range in a Cape Endaiadere coconut grove in December 1942 during MacArthur's Papuan counteroffensive against Buna, Gona and Sanananda after the failed Japanese September 1942 overland and amphibious attacks to capture Port Moresby. Allied victory against the Japanese garrisons enabled the ongoing construction of airfields in northern Papua to bomb Japanese positions along the northern New Guinea coast. (NARA)

(**Opposite, below**) A 127th Infantry Regiment, 32nd Division's 37mm AT gun in a sandbag-protected position fires across the Girua River at Buna Village, just southwest of Buna Mission, in December 1942. The 37mm AT gun was effective against lightly armoured Japanese tanks, and in a close-range direct-fire capacity against Japanese pillboxes, caves and buildings. When firing canister or fragmentation rounds, it functioned like a 'giant shotgun' to disrupt enemy infantry attacks. Weighing 900lb, this gun did not require motor transport, making it suitable for jungle combat. (NARA)

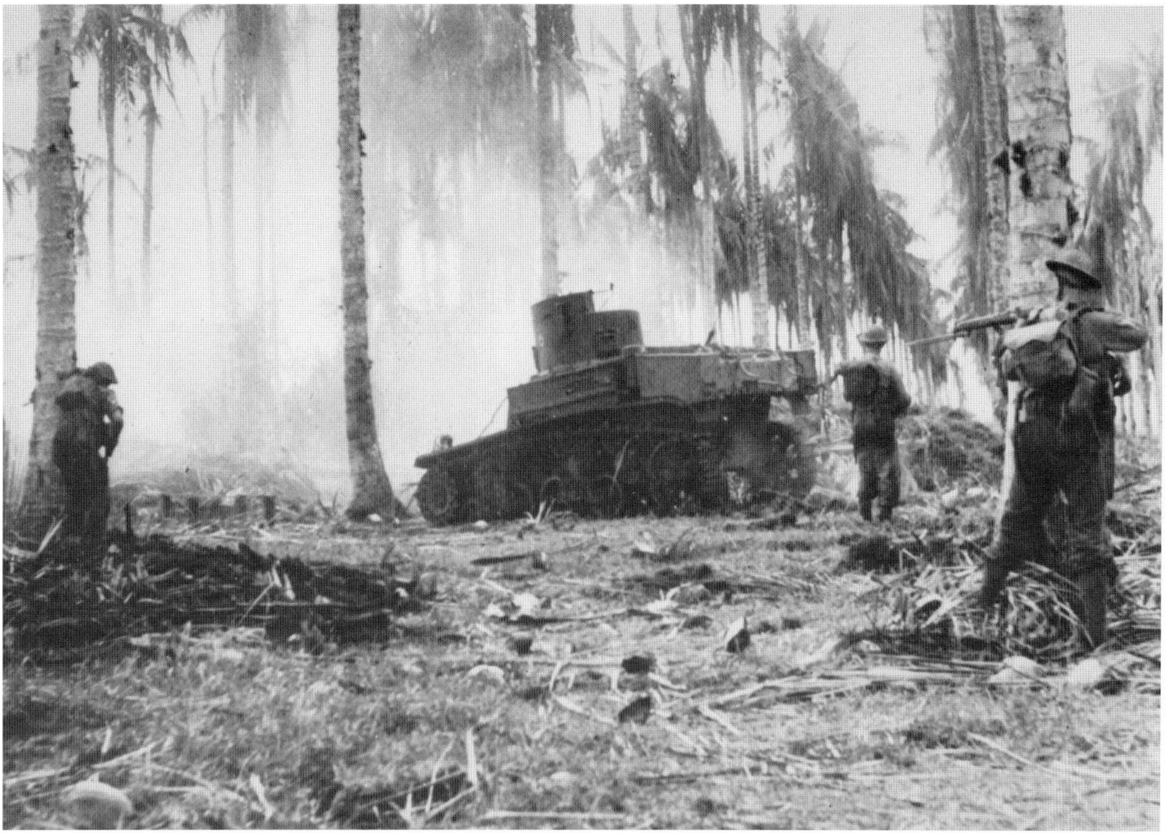

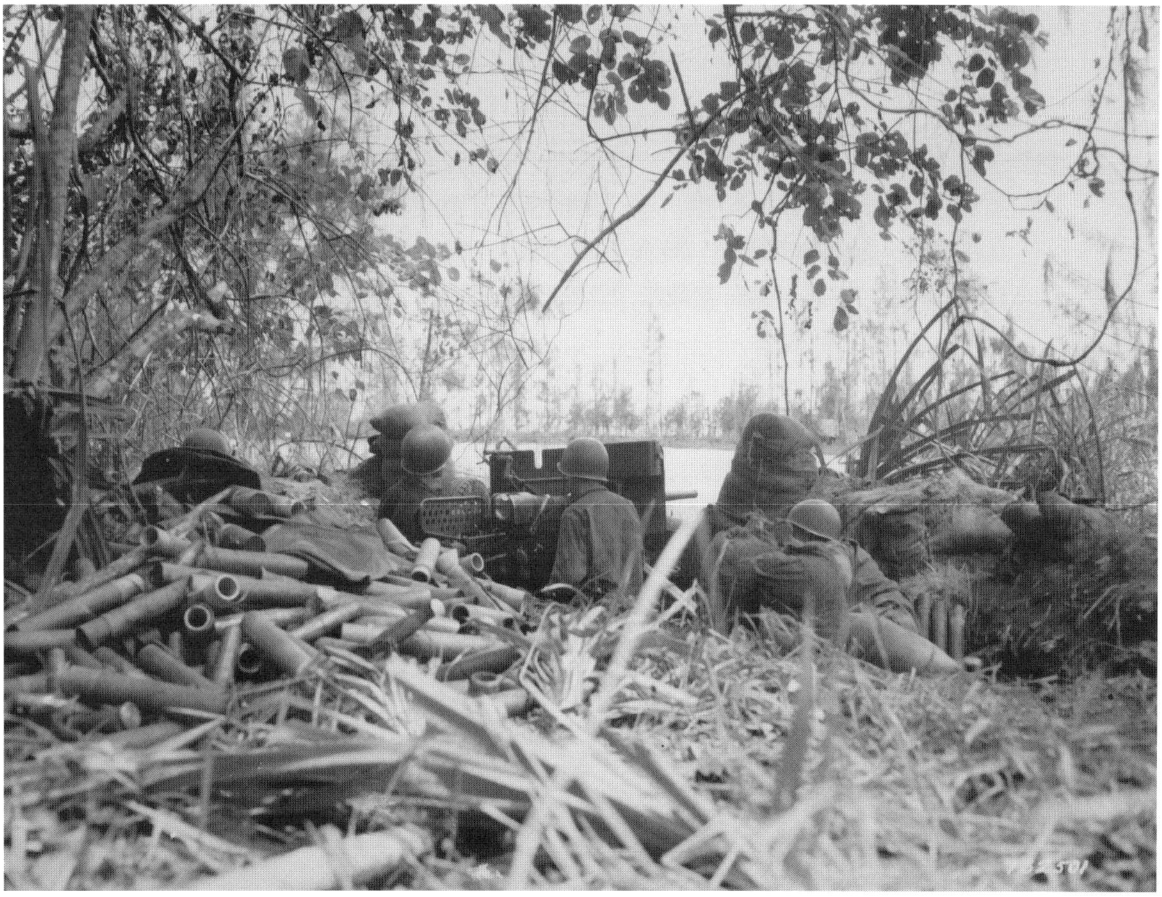

(**Above**) Volunteers of the 163rd Infantry Regiment, US 41st Division, inch forward through mud on a beach to outflank IJA roadblocks at Sanananda Point in early January 1943. The Allied struggle to capture Sanananda started on 19 November 1942, continued through 22 January 1943, and was contemporaneous with American and Australian infantry assaults against Japanese defences at Buna and Gona along Papua's northern coast. (NARA)

(**Opposite, above**) American pilots race towards their Lockheed P-38 Lightning fighters on a newly built Papuan airfield complex at Dobodura. Shortly after their arrival in the SWPA, these high-altitude fighters shot down forty-two enemy aircraft in three days. The Lockheed P-38 Lightning was also able to carry a maximal load of either external bombs or rockets, making it a fighter-bomber. When Lieutenant General George C. Kenney assumed command of air units in SWPA, he asked General Henry Arnold, USAAF CG, for P-38s to replace the older Bell P-39 Airacobras and Curtiss P-40 Warhawks, both of which were inferior to their Japanese counterparts. On 27 December 1942, the first Lightnings sortied in SWPA. (NARA)

(**Opposite, below**) The five-man crew, comprising a pilot, co-pilot, navigator/radio operator, bombardier and gunner of a North American B-25 medium Mitchell twin-engine bomber called *Grass Cutter* of the 38th Bombardment Group at Port Moresby, New Guinea, stand by their aircraft as personal gear is delivered. The several airfields or 'dromes' situated near Port Moresby provided the 5th USAAF numerous sites from which to mount offensive, low-level strafing missions to interdict IJN reinforcement and supply operations as well as against IJA airfields and installations along the northern New Guinea coast in 1942–43. (NARA)

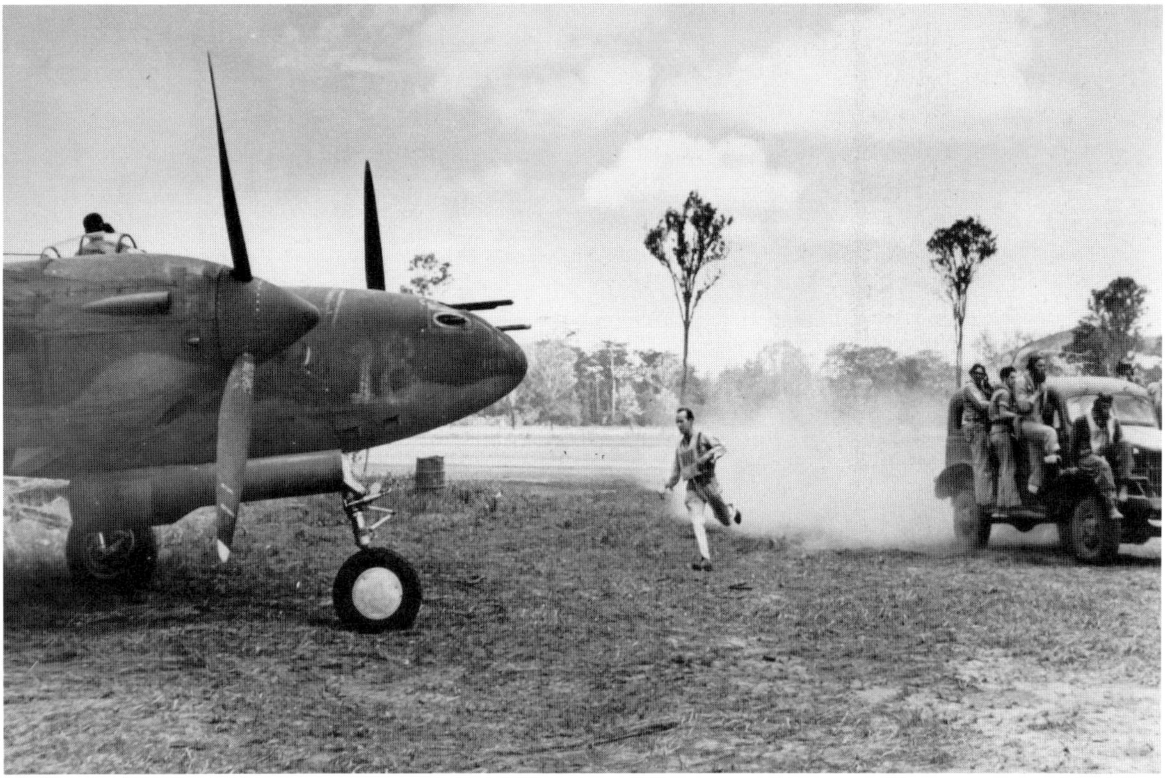

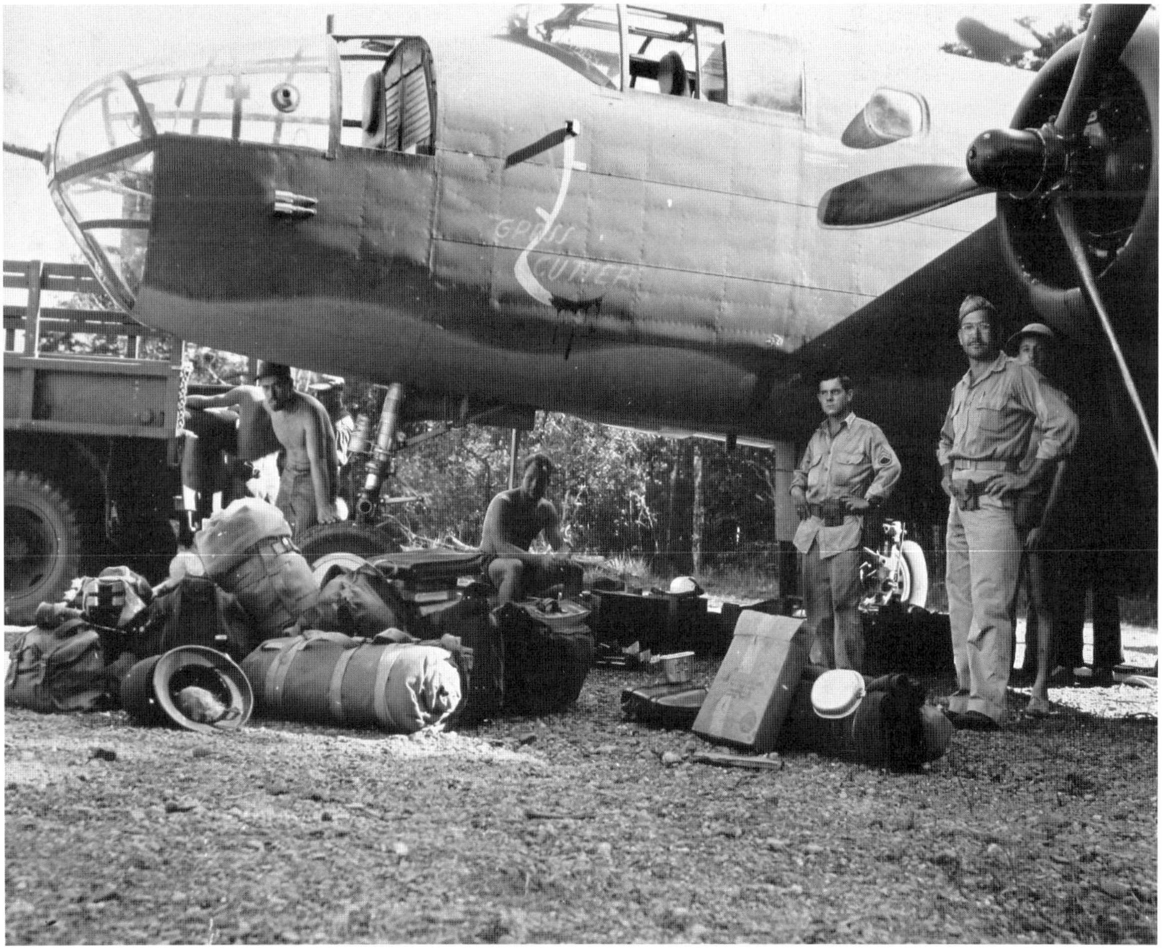

(**Above**) Two 5th USAAF Boeing B-17 Flying Fortresses situated at Port Moresby airstrip. Utilized as strategic bombers in the ETO, Lieutenant General George Kenney employed these four-engined heavy bombers in a tactical interdiction role during the New Guinea campaign of 1942–43. The B-17 had a maximal range of 4,400 miles and was capable of carrying an 8-ton bomb load in addition to up to thirteen 0.50-inch calibre machine guns. On 7 December 1942, Lieutenant General Hatazō Adachi, the new IJA 18th Army CG, attempted reinforcing New Guinea's northern coastal garrisons by dispatching the IJA 170th Infantry Regiment in six destroyers from Rabaul with a strong fighter escort. However, nine B-17s, in successive low-level waves, attacked the enemy surface force. Three of the IJN destroyers were set afire, with many dead aboard, while seven enemy fighters were shot down, without the loss of any American heavy bombers. Adachi's reinforcing ships reversed course for Rabaul. (*NARA*)

(**Opposite, above**) A downed IJN Mitsubishi A6M2 Reisen Zero single-seat carrier-borne or land-based fighter destroyed at Buna's 'Old Strip', after an Allied air raid on 28 December 1942. In dogfights over Papua, 5th USAAF P-38 Lightnings outperformed the vaunted A6M2 fighter. The newer A6M3 Zero had more power; however, its range was shorter until fitted with external fuel tanks, enabling it to fly from Rabaul to escort bombers to attack Guadalcanal and Tulagi during Operation I-GO in April 1943. (*NARA*)

(**Opposite, below**) A wounded Australian is carried while other wounded walk to an aid station during the Lae battle in September 1943. To complement both the Australian overland advance from Wau through the Markham River Valley and an amphibious landing of 8,000 9th AIF Division troops 18 miles behind Japanese defences to Lae's east, C-47 transports, escorted by 200 fighters and bombers of Kenney's 5th USAAF, ferried the US 503rd Parachute Infantry Regiment to Nadzab, 20 miles northwest of Lae on 5 September (see Map 3). The PIR completed a *coup de main* unopposed low-level jump in five minutes, securing the landing zone. On 7 September, C-47s flew AIF 7th Division units into the airhead. MacArthur's land, sea and airborne envelopment threatened Lieutenant General Adachi's IJA 51st Division at Lae, so he ordered its disastrous retreat to Finschhafen, 50 miles east of Lae, claiming 25 per cent of the 8,000 Japanese, mainly from starvation. (*NARA*)

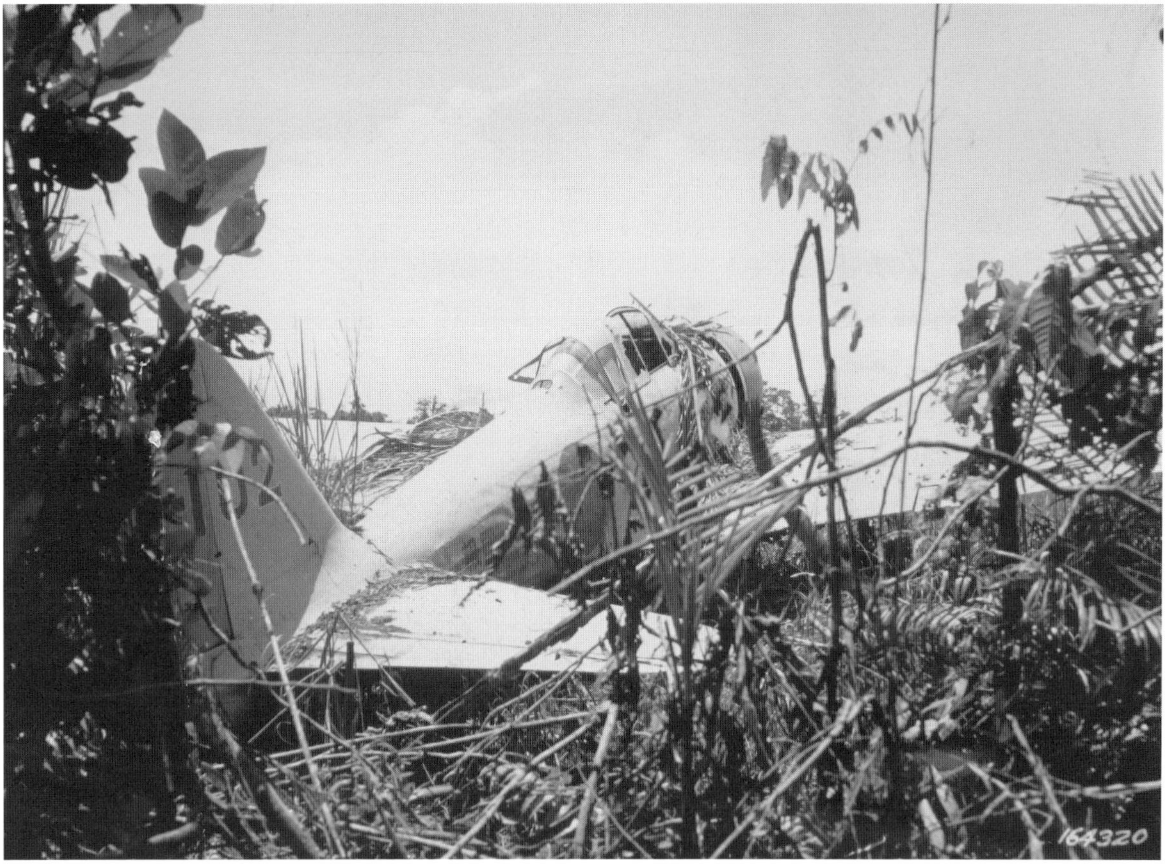
164320

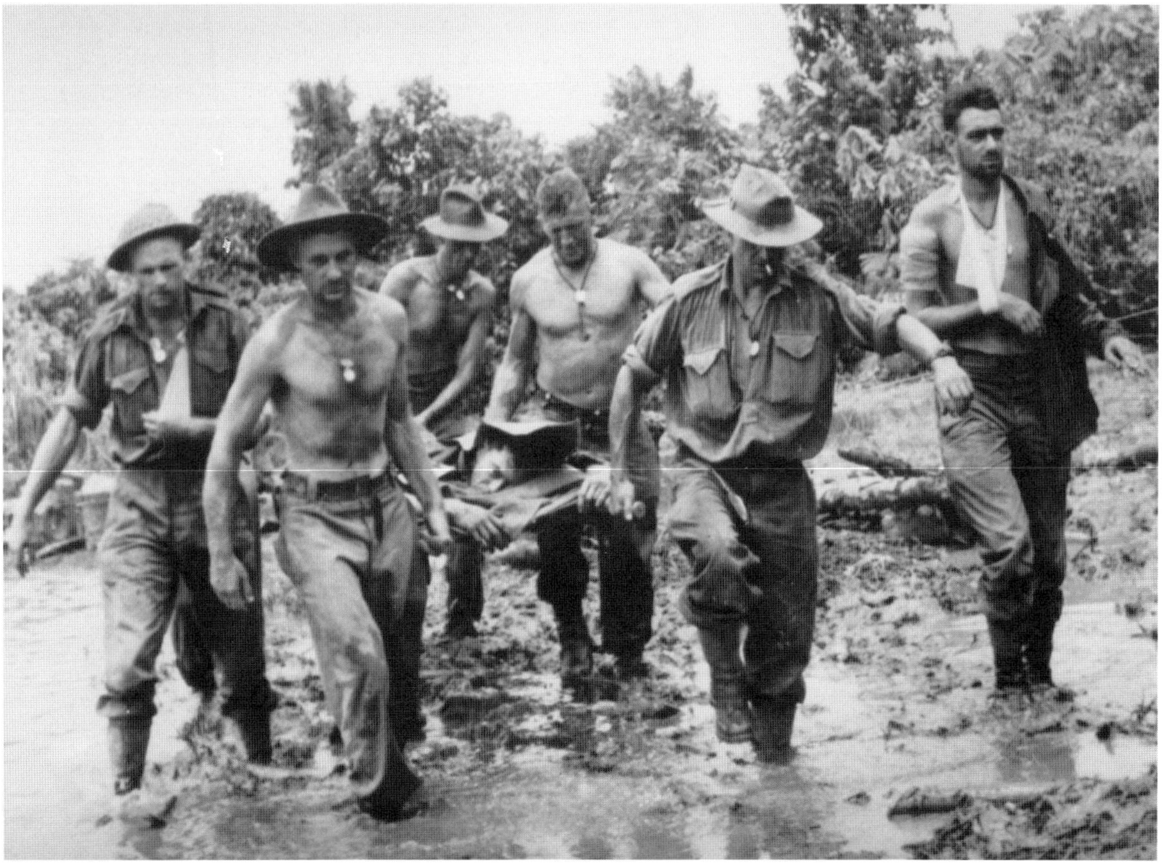

An Australian 25th Brigade infantryman with his shouldered Owen gun and an American paratrooper greet one another at Nadzab's airfield in the Markham River Valley in September 1943. The AIF's 25th Brigade, 7th Division was airlifted in on 9 September to begin its advance through the Markham River Valley, compelling the Japanese to abandon Lae to the southeast. Nadzab over time replaced Dobodura as the major forward New Guinea airbase for the 5th USAAF. (NARA)

Wrecked Japanese aircraft at Lae's airfield after its capture in September 1943. As the Japanese withdrew from Guadalcanal in early February 1943, the IJA and IJN High Commands ordered that air operations continue on New Guinea, principally using IJAAF aircraft at Lae, Salamaua, Wewak and Madang (see Map 5), which were to be strengthened with aircraft from Rabaul. After Allied bombers demolished the small airfield base at Buna in January 1943, near-constant attacks on Japanese airfields at Lae and Salamaua commenced, especially by RAAF Beaufighters and Bostons in early March 1943 during and after the Battle of the Bismarck Sea (see Chapter 2). When one of the Japanese freighters, filled with replacement aircraft and parts for Lae, was sunk during the Bismarck Sea battle, the long-term prospect of Lae remaining a sustainable IJAAF base waned. On 25 March, Japan's High Commands reaffirmed the importance of the New Guinea front, specifically maintaining Lae and Salamaua, so the IJAAF continued to stage aircraft out of Lae for the short term. As Allied bombers made low-level attacks on the Lae airfield, they were often unable to distinguish undamaged enemy aircraft on the ground from the wrecks littering the airfield (above). (NARA)

(**Above**) An RAAF twin-engine Bristol Beaufighter flies above New Guinea's mountains. The Beaufighter was planned as an interceptor with a top speed of 300mph and four forward-firing 20mm cannons and six 0.303-inch calibre machine guns. As a heavy interceptor or night-fighter, it had no bombardier or bomb bay. About 100 British-manufactured Beaufighters arrived in the SWPA for battle; this was a lighter and faster plane than the Douglas A-20 Havoc (also called 'Boston'). Like all of the 5th USAAF strafers, the Beaufighters were a scourge to Japanese shipping and land-based aircraft, as they demonstrated at the Battle of the Bismarck Sea and Lae, respectively, in early March 1943. (NARA)

(**Opposite, above**) A 162nd Infantry Regiment, 41st Division 81mm mortar crew fires a round at enemy troops at Boisi near 'Roosevelt Ridge' on 1 August 1943. Driving on Salamaua from several different axes and also to establish a port with which to relieve the aircraft that were supplying the Allied force, a landing at Nassau Bay was made in early July by 162nd IR units, who drove north along the coast. By mid-July, the 162nd IR faced strong Japanese forces at a ridge overlooking Tambu Bay, later dubbed 'Roosevelt Ridge' after Major Archibald Roosevelt, CO 3rd Battalion, 162nd IR, as his troops advanced along Lake Salus towards Tambu Bay. Japanese units around Boisi defending Tambu Bay included SNLF troops and the IJA 3rd Battalion, 66th Infantry Regiment. (NARA)

(**Opposite, below**) Captain R.M. Martin and Colonel William Jackson (on telephone) at a B Battery, 205th Field Artillery, 41st Division gun position at Lake Salus north of Nassau Bay on 17 July 1943. The battery's four 75mm howitzers were welcomed by the leading battalion of the 162nd Infantry Regiment, 41st Division, which landed at Nassau Bay earlier in July, to secure a beachhead supply point for shorter Allied LOC for the proposed attack on Salamaua. Throughout early and mid-July, two more battalions of the 162nd IR, 41st Division landed at Nassau Bay along with other Australian and American artillery batteries to shell Japanese positions. (NARA)

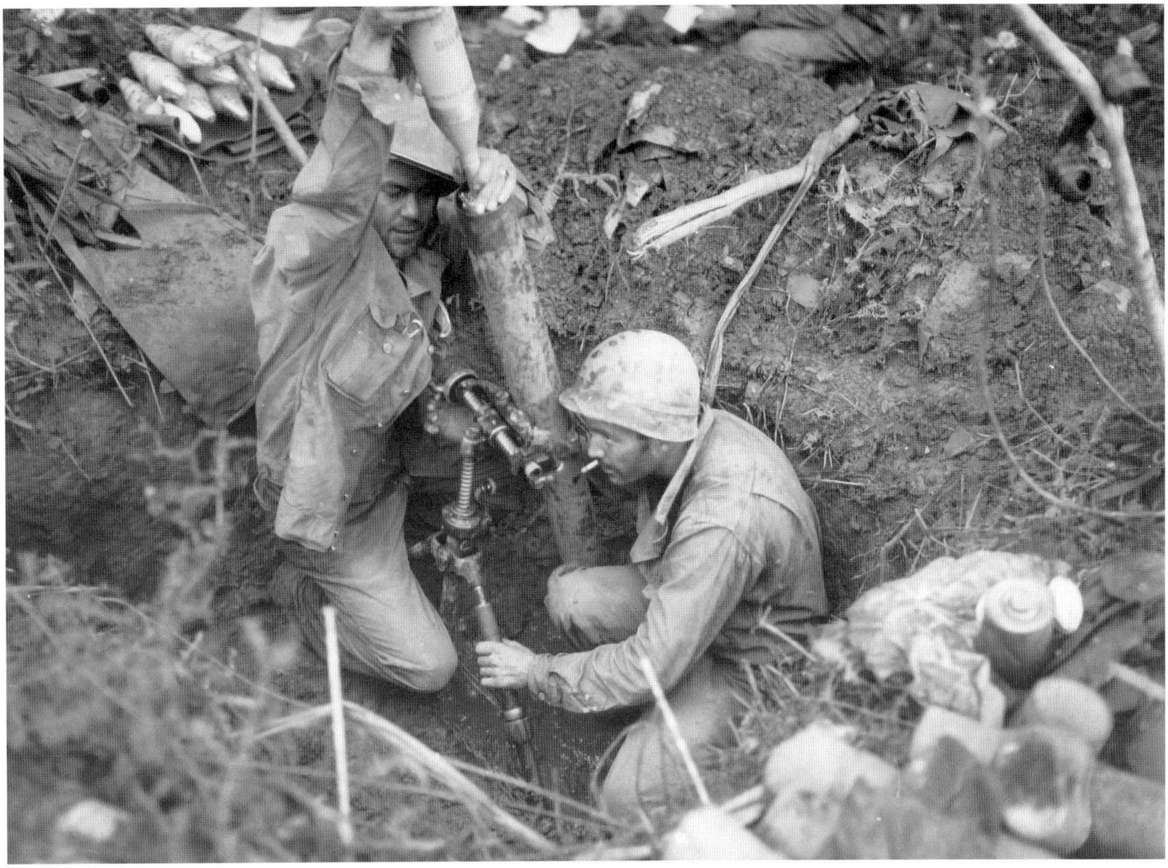

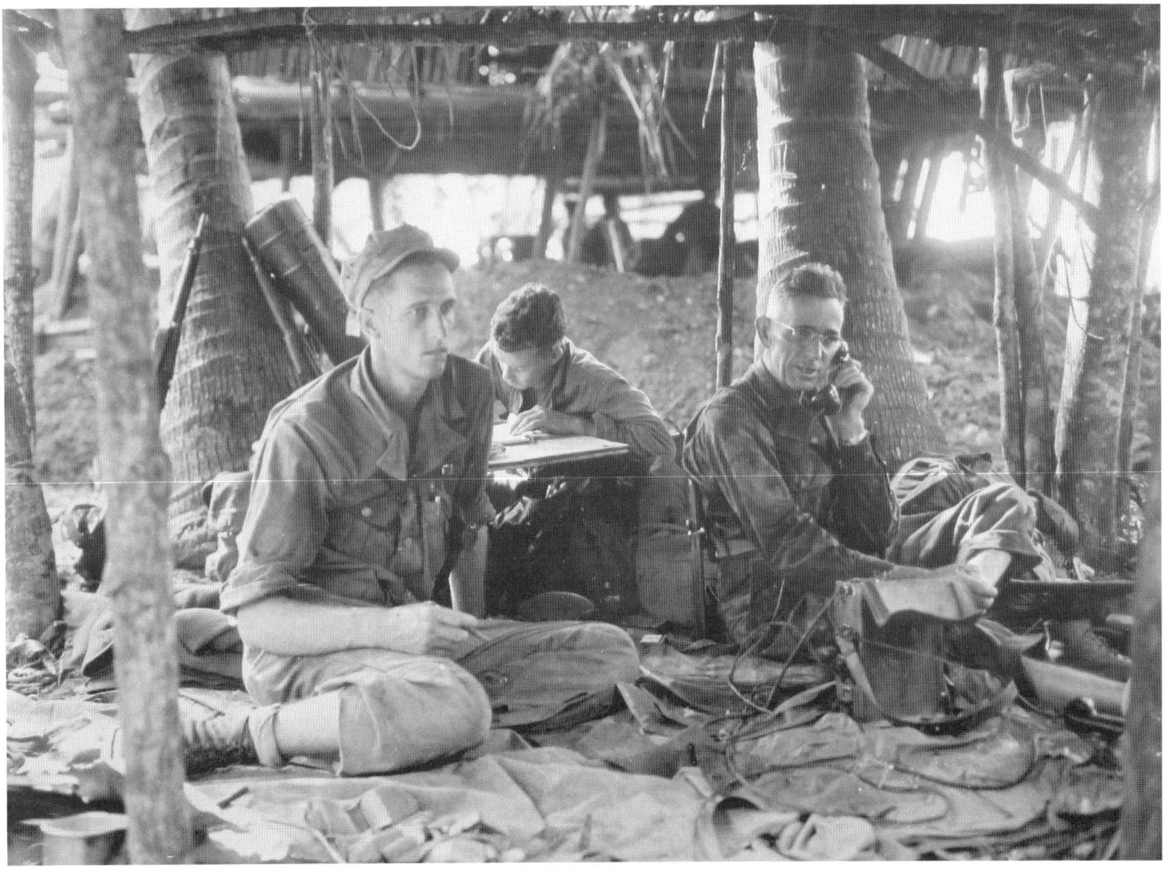

(**Above**) A 41st Division officer uses a walkie-talkie to communicate with LST at the Humboldt Bay beach (right). American units of Lieutenant General Eichelberger's I Corps' 41st Division landed at Humboldt Bay near Hollandia on 22 April 1944, simultaneous with the 24th Division assaulting Tanahmerah Bay, the latter becoming a nightmare as vehicles could not exit the beach due to non-existent roads and a swamp 30 yards from the shoreline. Due to these problems, the remainder of the 24th Division was diverted to the now-secured Humboldt Bay. The linkup with the 41st Division was soon followed by the seizure of the airfield complex at Hollandia, captured by 26 April. The 5th USAAF transports flew in supplies on 3 May to a hastily built airfield to relieve the logistic nightmare. The Allied landings leaped 500 miles west up the New Guinea coastline to capture Hollandia, a major Japanese air and supply base, and isolate the IJA 18th Army to the east at Wewak (see Map 5). In addition, SWPA planners wanted to bypass the large Japanese garrison at Hansa Bay to Wewak's east. (*NARA*)

(**Opposite, above**) A 41st Division mortar crew moves inland from the Humboldt Bay beachhead with its weapon broken down for the trek to the Hollandia airfield, starting on 22 April 1944. For MacArthur, Eichelberger's I Corps and Barbey's VII Amphibious Force, these landings proved to be the decisive operation on New Guinea that replaced the previously scheduled late April operation against Hansa Bay, midway between Madang and Wewak, the two strongest Japanese garrisons on New Guinea's north coast, with the latter being HQ for Lieutenant General Adachi's IJA 18th Army. Allied planners feared strong opposition at Hansa Bay, since the Japanese had predicted such an Allied move to capture its excellent natural harbour 150 miles west of Saidor (see Map 5), with Adachi moving two IJA divisions to that anchorage. When Allied intelligence sources revealed that Hollandia's land defences were scant, MacArthur and Krueger reactivated Eichelberger's I Corps, comprising the 24th and 41st Divisions with the 32nd held in reserve, for the amphibious operation. In the meantime, Kenney's air groups made many large-scale raids on Japanese airfields at Hollandia, destroying or causing evacuation of 300 enemy planes. (*NARA*)

(**Below**) Australians with native scouts in a jeep after the American amphibious assault on Aitape on 22 April 1944 to secure the Tadji fighter and bomber strips situated a few miles to the southeast of the beachhead and northwest of Wewak (see Map 5). After its capture, Australian engineers repaired the north runway for Allied fighters. To block a Japanese thrust from Wewak, elements of the 163rd RCT set up a defensive position on the Driniumor River 15 miles east of Aitape, where IJA 18th Army Commanding General Adachi sent 20,000 troops from the Madang and Wewak garrisons, which broke through the American defensive perimeter despite Lieutenant General Krueger inserting reinforcements. After a month of gruesome fighting, the Japanese withdrew, with heavy losses on both sides. (*NARA*)

(**Above**) A camouflaged, entrenched Japanese 20mm twin AA gun pit at Vila Airfield on the south-eastern tip of Kolombangara Island (see Map 2) is shown. Halsey did not want to attack the 10,000 Japanese defenders on Kolombangara Island, as he had at Munda Airfield on New Georgia from July to August 1943, requiring 50,000 American troops, with 1,000 killed and over 4,000 wounded, so he bypassed it and headed northwest, to Vella Lavella. From 28 September to 7 October 1943, mass evacuation of Japanese forces on Kolombangara Island occurred, as Halsey's strategy to bypass the island was successful. (NARA)

(**Opposite, above**) At Cape Torokina in Bougainville's Empress Augusta Bay, a 3rd Marine Division 0.75-ton utility truck loaded with munitions moves across uncontested for the front lines and inland storage soon after the 1 November 1943 invasion (see Map 2). Although the Japanese commanders on Bougainville suspected, after finding American debris at beach locales prior the invasion, that Torokina was a potential landing site, only one company of the IJA 23rd Infantry Regiment of General Kanda's 6th Division maintained defensive positions on D-Day. Fearing the usual Japanese air and naval responses, one third of Major General Allen Turnage's 3rd Marine Division landing force assisted with unloading supplies from Rear Admiral Theodore Wilkinson's cargo ships. (NARA)

(**Opposite, below**) Marine Vought F4U Corsairs on the Marston-matted Torokina fighter strip after the first AirSols fighter sweep against Rabaul on 17 December. Eighty fighters from New Georgia staged through the Piva Fighter Strip. Medium Dauntless dive-bombers and Avenger torpedo bombers of the USN and MAW were needed against Rabaul as B-17s and B-24s were unable to destroy the bastion solely from high-altitude bombing. A bomber strip, Piva Uncle, first needed completion as USN Construction Battalions ('Seabees') started construction on 29 November, and by 19 December, the first medium bomber plane flew off the 8,000ft Marston-matted runway for a Rabaul bombing sortie. Another fighter strip, Piva Yoke, was ready for sorties on 9 January 1944. (NARA)

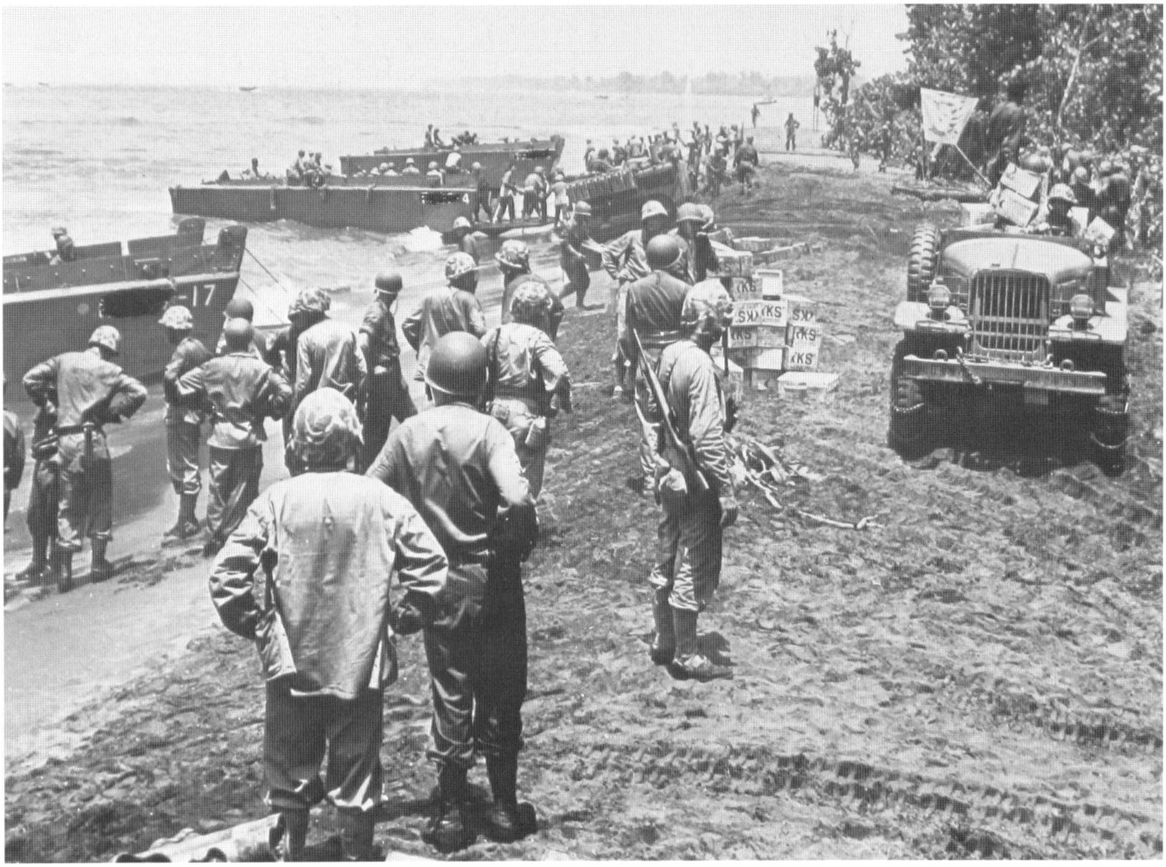

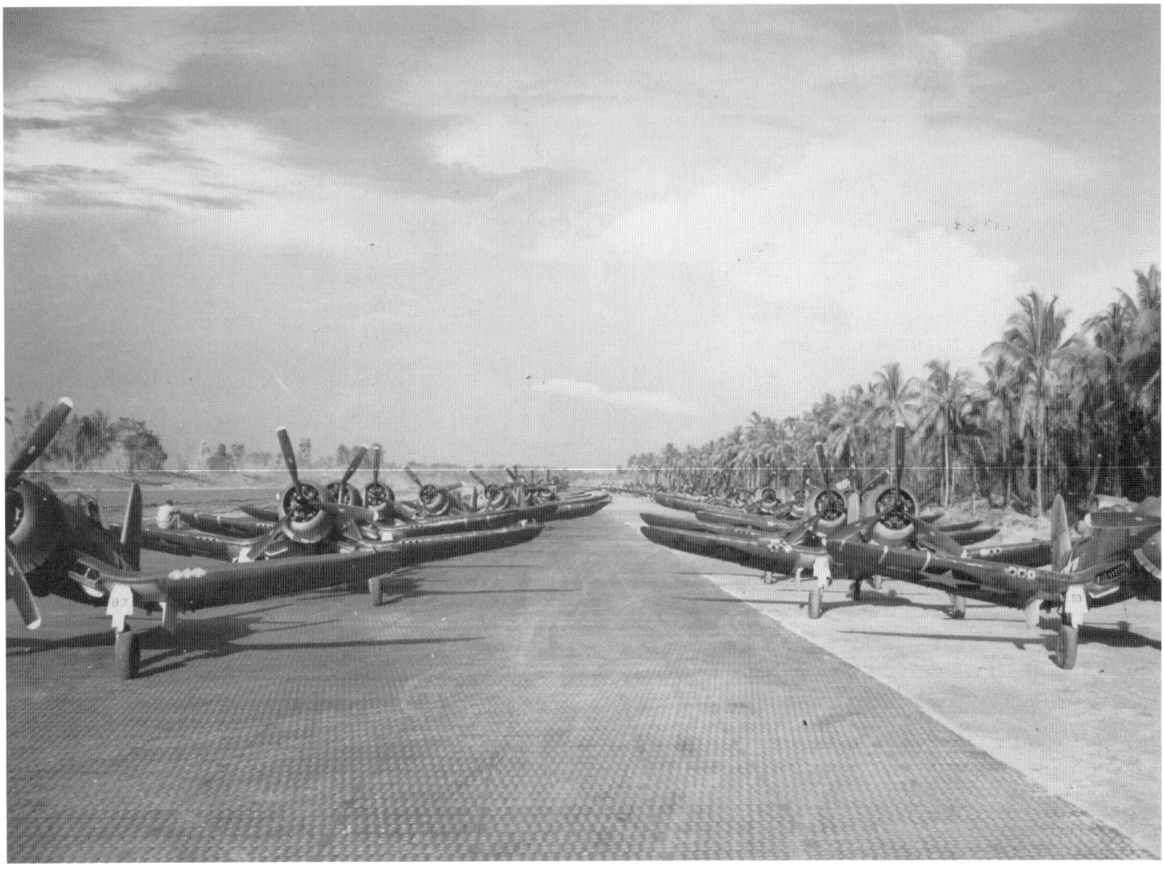

Chapter Two

Battle of the Bismarck Sea (2–5 March 1943) and the Air War over New Guinea

From June to September 1943, the Allies drove with overland and amphibious advances on Japanese garrisons at Salamaua and Lae near North-East New Guinea's Huon Peninsula (see Map 3) to acquire Japanese airfields there and at Finschhafen, allowing 5th USAAF aircraft to reach Rabaul without flying over Papua's Owen Stanley Range from Port Moresby. The Japanese regarded Wau, an Australian air base in New Guinea's interior, as a threat to the Huon Gulf. However, Japanese troop strength, supplies and equipment were insufficient for an offensive against Wau. IJA Eighth Area Army CG, General Imamura, on Rabaul, and its naval commander, Vice Admiral Jinichi Kusaka, decided to move by sea 6,900 troops of the IJA 18th Army to Lae to reinforce the existing garrison of only 3,500 men. They planned a huge Japanese fighter escort during favourable weather to hamper Allied aircraft from sighting a sixteen-ship convoy, comprising eight transports and eight destroyers, assembled in Rabaul's Simpson Harbour at the end of February 1943. Rear Admiral Masatomi Kimura, the destroyers' commander with his flag aboard *Shirayuki*, would depart Rabaul at midnight on 28 February, while on board the destroyer *Tokitsukaze* was Lieutenant General Adachi, CO IJA 18th Army, and his staff. Lieutenant General Nakano, with the IJA 51st Division staff, was on the destroyer *Yukikaze*. All transports were combat-packed for rapid unloading of troops within six hours of landing, and supplies and materiel within forty-eight hours of reaching Lae. Supplies and men were divided evenly, such that if half the transports were lost at sea, a balanced force could be set ashore. There was no precaution taken for the loss of the total convoy, designated 'Operation 81'.

Battle of the Bismarck Sea, 2–5 March 1943

The IJN convoy that left Simpson Harbour steered south under storm clouds entering the Bismarck Sea (see Map 2) and by 1600hrs on 1 March 1943, it approached Dampier Strait, at New Britain's western end near

Cape Gloucester (see Map 3). There the convoy was spotted by a 5th USAAF Force B-24, which alerted the 200 Allied bombers and 130 fighters at Papua's Dobodura, Gili Gili and Port Moresby airfields. Japanese fighters from Rabaul, Gasmata and Lae would have limited fuel for complete convoy protection.

Major Paul I. ('Pappy') Gunn of the 90th Bombardment Squadron/3rd Bombardment Group, a subordinate officer in Lieutenant General George Kenney's 5th USAAF, re-equipped the noses of the North American B-25 Mitchell medium bomber with four single forward-firing 0.50-inch calibre machine guns replacing the bombardier for strafing, along with two forward-firing 0.50-inch calibre MGs on either side of the forward fuselage. He also similarly rearmed Douglas A-20 Havoc bombers as 'strafers'. The B-25 strafers carried 500lb bombs armed with a five-second delay fuse, permitting a 200–250ft above sea level (mast height) drop without danger from their own bombs' explosions. Kenney promoted Captain Edward Larner of the 89th Bombardment Squadron to command the 90th BS, which received twelve modified B-25 strafers for the new mast-height attack bombing method without a bombardier. Additionally, an RAAF squadron with twin-engine Bristol Beaufighters was trained for low-level attacks. Kenney banked on the modified B-25 strafers to destroy the Japanese convoy sailing to reinforce Lae from Rabaul.

Major William Benn, another Kenney protégé, commanding the 63rd Bombardment Squadron/43rd Bombardment Group, devised a method for his B-17Fs attacking at mast height to drop their five-second fuse-delayed bombs, which would either explode in the water alongside the enemy ship and create a 'mining effect' to damage the enemy ship's hull or hit the water and 'skip' over the water's surface, and with its delayed fuse hit the ship and explode on impact. B-17s recently tried this 'skip bombing' technique on ships in Simpson Harbour and now it would be used on seagoing vessels.

At 1015 hours on 2 March, twenty-nine Allied heavy bombers arrived over the IJN convoy approaching Dampier Strait and made horizontal bombing runs from 5,000 feet, despite Japanese CAP from two dozen Rabaul-based fighters and ship AA fire, and sunk by noon the 5,500-ton *Kyokusei Maru*, while the 6,900-ton *Teiyō Maru* and 4,500-ton *Nojima* transports were damaged. The IJN destroyers *Yukikaze* and *Asagumo* rescued 900 survivors from *Kyokusei Maru* and rapidly steamed into Lae after dark to unload the men and rejoin the convoy. An Australian PBY Catalina then followed the convoy overnight.

On 3 March, with forty Japanese fighters too high as CAP to get low-flying, skip-bombing Allied aircraft bombed the convoy exiting Vitiaz Strait, accompanied by sixteen P-38 Lightning and P-40 Warhawk fighters, which kept the Japanese air cover occupied. Out of 37 500lb bombs, 28 scored hits on the Japanese ships and by noon, over 200 bombs were dropped. Over a dozen RAAF Beaufighters swept in at mast height for strafing runs. Over Lae, three dozen Allied fighters interdicted Japanese aircraft, forcing their retirement. All eight Japanese transports were sunk, along with four of their eight escorting destroyers, as only *Shikinami*, *Yukikaze*, *Asagumo* and *Uranami* escaped destruction, rescued survivors and fled northwards. Tons of equipment, supplies and reinforcements for the Lae garrison and airfield never arrived and more than 3,000 soldiers and sailors perished. Only 900 IJA troops reached Lae.

Of the 335 Allied planes engaged, only 2 bombers and 3 fighters were lost. The Japanese never again sent a large-scale convoy to North-East New Guinea nor risked a transport larger than a small coaster or barge. The planned Wau offensive ended as supplies and reinforcements for Lae and Salamaua were delivered from Cape Gloucester by barge or by submarines at night.

Air War over New Guinea as a Prelude to Rabaul Aerial Offensive

From 16 June to 15 September 1943, as the Allies campaigned for Lae and Salamaua, the IJAAF Fourth Air Army moved a large number of aircraft out of range of Allied fighters to the major aerodrome at Wewak, 400 miles west of the Huon Peninsula, and its satellite airfields of Boram, Dagua and But. Farther west, Hollandia and Tadji were staging and dispersal areas for the Wewak and Madang aerodromes. Although under heavy attack since August, these airfields were threatening to the Allies as 5th USAAF fighters from Dobodura lacked range to reach Wewak and long-range unescorted bomber raids were too risky.

After receiving appeals from the Lae commander, Lieutenant General Adachi, the IJA 18th CG with HQ at Madang since 19 April 1943, established a barge run carrying reinforcements from New Britain to the Huon Peninsula's threatened bases of Lae, Salamaua and Finschhafen, which MacArthur contemporaneously decided to seize; however, he needed local air superiority. The Lae and Salamaua airstrips under regular 5th USAAF bombing were not a threat since April 1943, but the Wewak and Madang aerodromes were. SWPA planners had to build new interior airfields for Kenney's aircraft to fly deep into the Japanese perimeter to maul the airfields at Wewak and Madang while continuously bombing Lae, Salamaua and Finschhafen.

In August 1943, the IJA Fourth Air Army in New Guinea received 250 planes from Rabaul with orders to attack Allied air bases and Papuan coastal convoys. On Wewak's four airstrips, IJA aircraft were parked wing to wing, believing the distance from Dobodura in Papua would protect them from Allied aerial assault. On 14 August, the Japanese attacked an Allied emergency airfield at Marilinan, built in mid-June 1943 by US Army engineers near Morobe (see Map 3), south of Lae and Salamaua, so Kenney decided to neutralize the new Japanese air offensive at Wewak, from 17 to 21 August. On 17 August, Kenney amassed over 150 B-25 Mitchell strafers with a P-38 Lightning fighter escort and destroyed 70 Japanese planes at Wewak's airfields. Over one-third of the Japanese air capacity at Wewak was shattered overnight and a follow-up attack the next day augmented the Japanese losses to over 100 planes, nullifying a continued Japanese air offensive.

Kenney's 5th USAAF conducted large bombing missions against Madang on 1 September 1943 and Wewak on 2 September. The Japanese, having suffered from August's previous raids on Wewak, left few targets on the battered airfields, so Allied pilots focused on shipping in Wewak harbour.

B-17 four-engine heavy bombers are seen in flight (above), from a Flying Fortress's waist gunner's window, en route to strike the Japanese convoy at the Battle of the Bismarck Sea after the enemy convoy of destroyers, transports and merchant vessels was sighted on 2 March 1943 heading from the Bismarck Sea towards Dampier Strait, near Cape Gloucester. A force of twenty-nine heavy bombers struck from 5,000 feet that morning, sinking a large transport, the *Kyokusei Maru*, and damaging two vessels. The B-17s were attacked by thirty Japanese fighters, which shot down three Flying Fortresses. Ten other B-17s, riddled with Japanese fighter gunfire, all returned to Port Moresby. During the night of 2/3 March, the convoy passed through the Vitiaz Strait for the main 3–4 March air-sea battle in the Solomon Sea east of Huon Bay. *(NARA)*

Aerial view of a Japanese transport approaching Dampier Strait with the *Kyokusei Maru* ablaze during the Battle of the Bismarck Sea, on 2 March 1943. Twenty-nine 5th USAAF heavy bombers made a horizontal high-altitude attack, setting the *Kyokusei Maru* on fire before it sank. The Japanese convoy continued its approach towards the Vitiaz Strait for its destination, Lae. The convoy was struck again on 3 March, with many ships sunk or damaged by new 5th USAAF bombing and strafing tactics. *(NARA)*

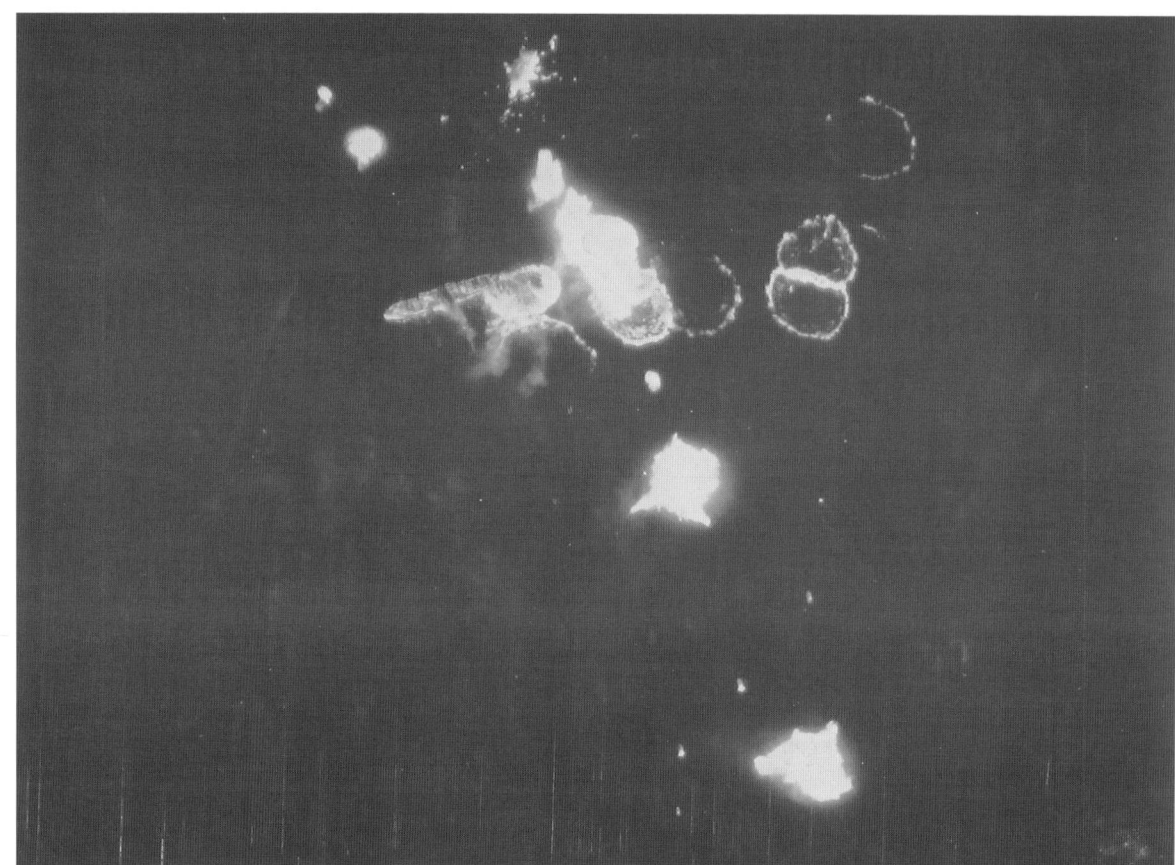

(**Above**) On 2 March 1943, twenty-nine 5th USAAF B-17s dropped 1,000lb bombs from 5,000 feet, resulting in the huge pools of water caused by the explosions bracketing and hitting the 5,500-ton *Kyokusei Maru* transport, causing it to sink near the Dampier Strait. A special service vessel carrying SNLF troops, the *Nojima*, and another transport, *Teiyō Maru*, were also attacked but not sunk. (NARA)

(**Opposite, above**) An aerial view of the IJN *Asashio*-class destroyer *Arashio*, dead in the water and leaking oil, after 5th USAAF B-25 bombers hit it with three 500lb bombs during the Battle of the Bismarck Sea on 3 March 1943. Bomb explosions in the water left of the destroyer are visible. IJN Destroyer Squadron 3's eight destroyers, commanded by Rear Admiral Masatomi Kimura, were tasked with escorting the eight Japanese transports and merchant vessels (8 Transport Fleet) carrying the IJA 51st Division from Rabaul to Lae. Lieutenant General Adachi, CG IJA 18th Army, and his staff were aboard the *Kagerō*-class *Tokitsukaze* while Lieutenant General Hidemitsu Nakano and the staff of the IJA 51st Division sailed on the other *Kagerō*-class destroyer, *Yukikaze*. By morning's end on 3 March, all seven remaining transports and merchant vessels were crippled or sinking while three of the eight destroyers were out of action. The *Arashio* (above) eventually sank. (NARA)

(**Opposite, below**) An IJN destroyer passes a pool of foam from an Allied bomb's near miss on 3 March 1943. The convoy, shadowed by a B-24 and then by an RAAF PBY Catalina, the latter dropping an occasional bomb, during the night of 2/3 March headed west past Dampier Strait for the larger and more manoeuvrable Vitiaz Strait, which placed the convoy closer to Lae's airfields and fighter cover. At 1730 hours on 2 March, the *Yukikaze* and the *Asagumo*, an *Asashio*-class destroyer, both left the convoy, steaming to Lae at a speed of 21 knots to deliver Lieutenant General Nakano, his staff, and the troops rescued from the *Kyokusei Maru*, sunk earlier that day. (NARA)

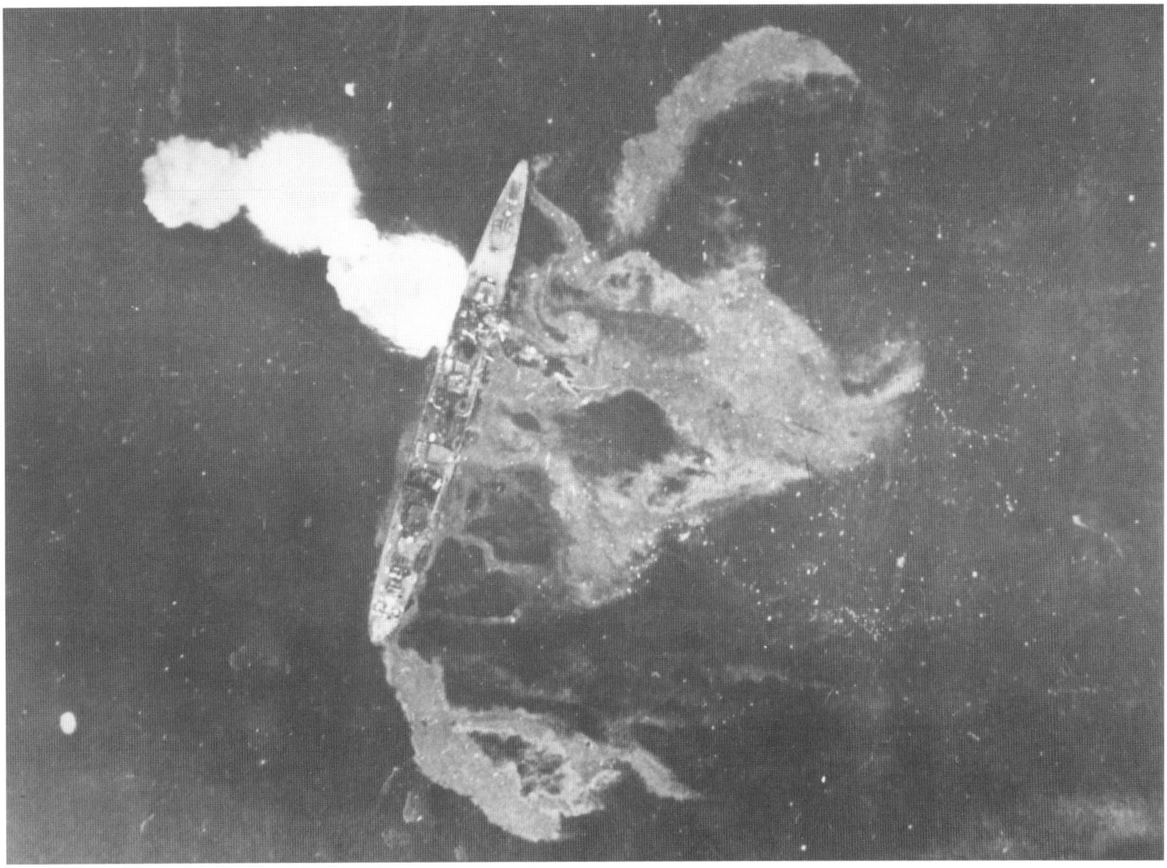

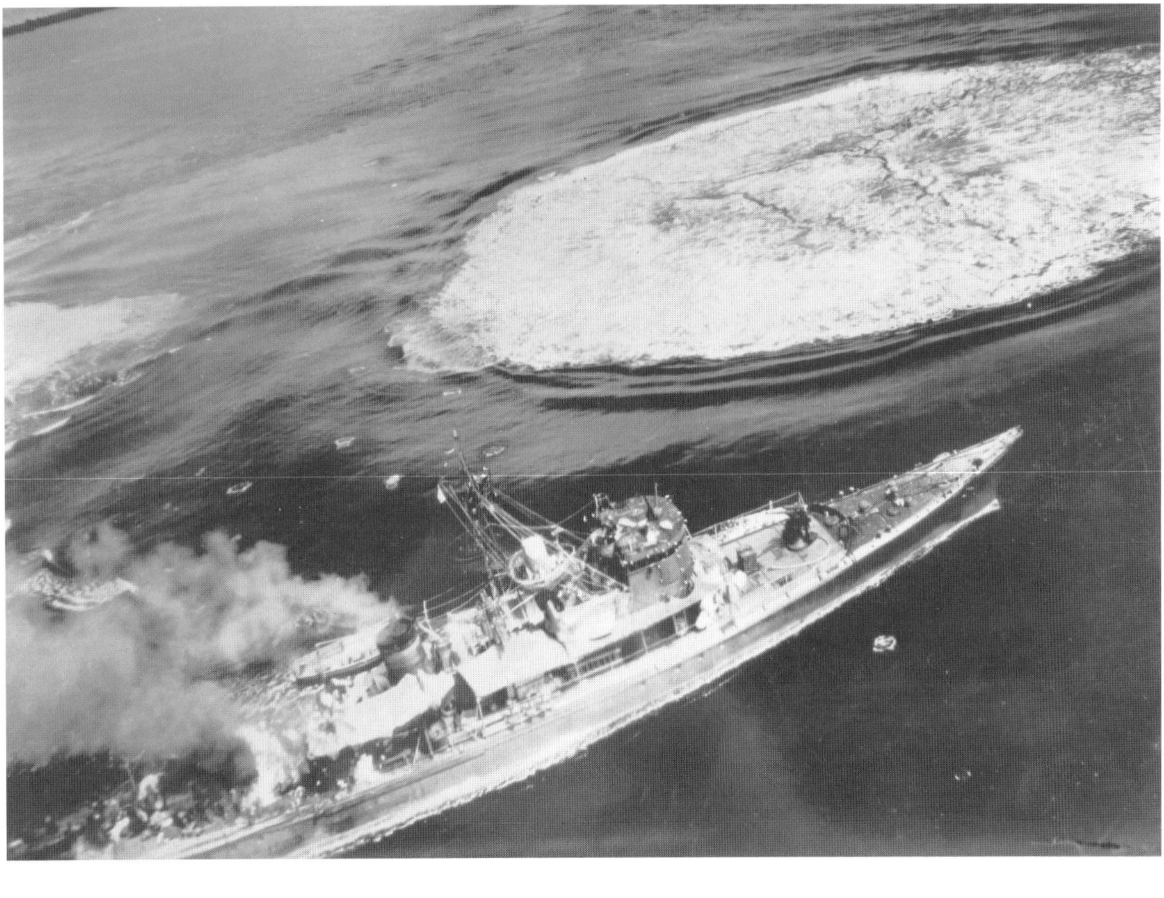

(**Opposite**) The IJN destroyer *Shirayuki*, a *Fubuki*-class destroyer, is attacked and photographed by a B-25 gunner flying at mast height on 3 March 1943, the battle's main day. This destroyer, the flagship of Destroyer Squadron 3, had Rear Admiral Kimura on board. B-25 machine-gun fire raked the destroyer's length, killing many IJN aboard and wounding Kimura. A bomb struck the rear portion of the destroyer, blowing off its stern, crippling the vessel in the first wave of attacks and eventually sinking it. The *Shikinami*, another *Fubuki*-class destroyer, rescued survivors and the wounded admiral. (*NARA*)

(**Above**) A B-25 attacks an IJN destroyer at mast height near New Hanover Island in the Bismarck Archipelago (see Map 2) on 24 February 1944. The dropped 500lb bomb is visible between the B-25 and the destroyer. This tactic, employed at the Battle of Bismarck Sea, caused the bomb to either directly hit the IJN vessel or the bomb's explosion in the adjacent water created a mine effect below the hull, damaging the ship's plating. At the Battle of Bismarck Sea on 3 March 1943, each B-25 strafer made two passes at a Japanese ship, sinking the *Asashio*-class *Arashio* destroyer and the transport *Nojima* carrying the SNLF troops. The next IJN destroyer hit and eventually sunk was the *Fubuki*-class *Shirayuki*, Destroyer Squadron 3's flagship. The *Kagerō*-class destroyer was attacked by two B-25s, hitting the ship with several bombs, one in the engine room, stopping the ship dead in the water, like the *Arashio* prior to it. Lieutenant General Adachi and most of the crew were evacuated by the *Yukikaze*, with the *Tokitsukaze* sinking later that day. (*NARA*)

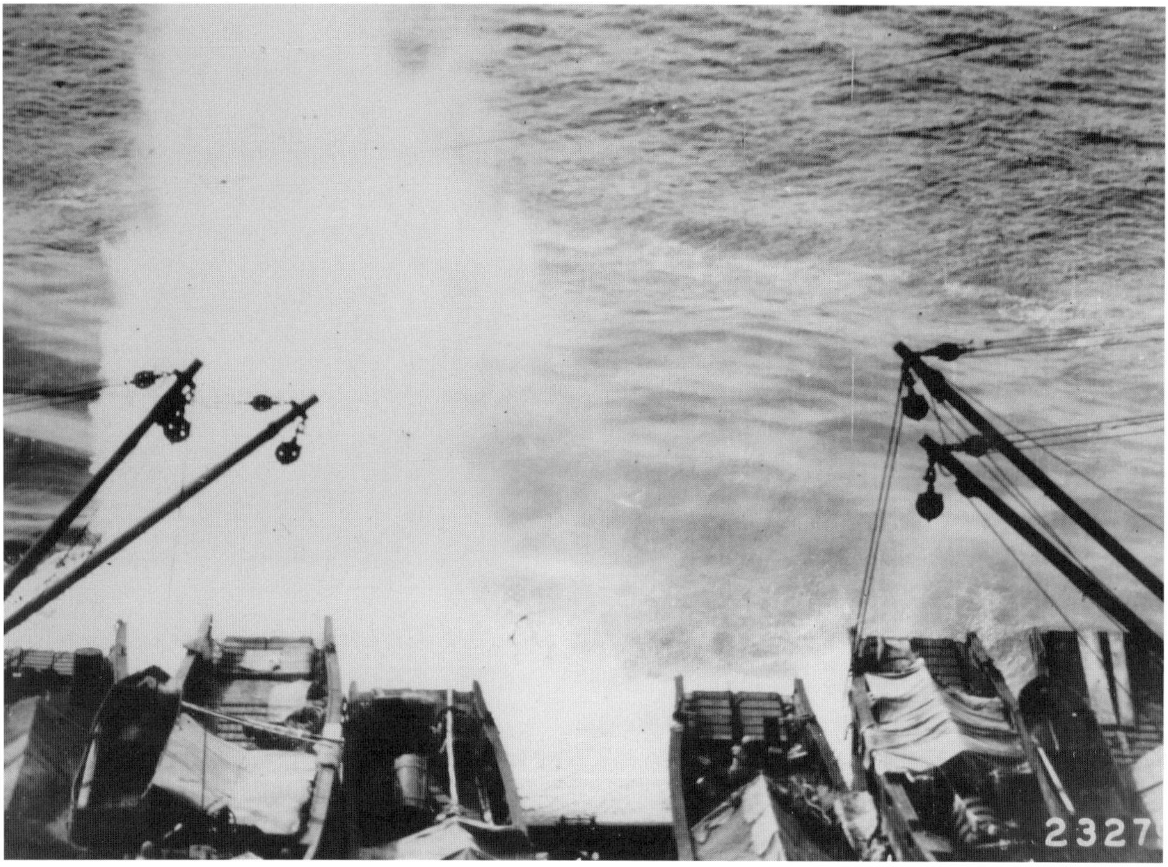
2327

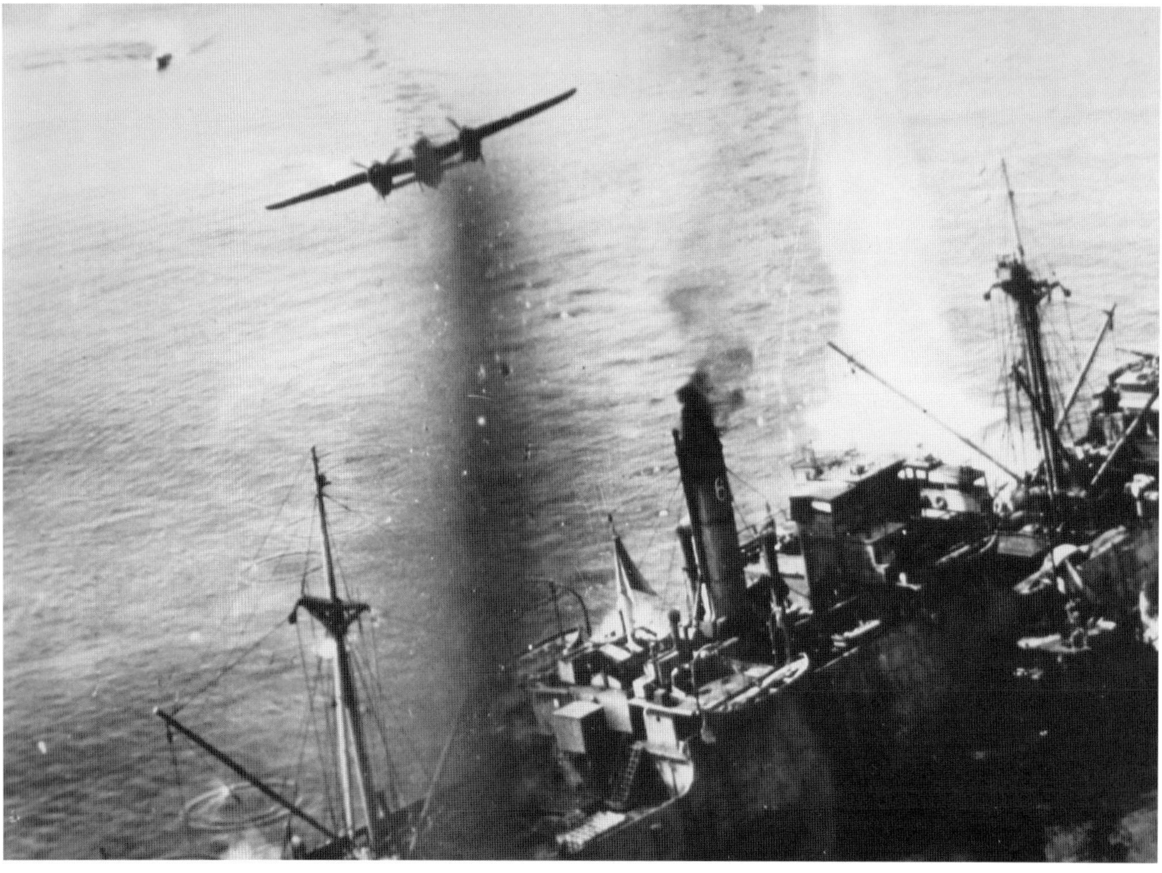

(**Opposite, above**) An IJN transport is attacked in the Vitiaz Strait off the Huon Peninsula (see Map 3) on 3 March 1943, with troop landing barges on the deck. Additionally, a 400-man SNLF was to be transported on a special service vessel, the *Nojima*. The convoy's troops, equipment, provisions and ammunition were carried by six transports and merchant vessels. On this day, the *Aiyo Maru* and *Oigawa Maru* were each hit by bombs at 1005 hours. Within minutes, the *Shinai Maru*, *Taimei Maru* and *Teiyo Maru* each took four bomb hits. The eighth merchant vessel, *Kembu Maru*, which carried aviation fuel for Lae's aircraft, exploded. (*NARA*)

(**Opposite, below**) A B-25 skip-bombs a Japanese freighter during the 3 March thirty-minute morning attacks that sunk or crippled seven transport and merchant vessels, with only the *Oigawa Maru* still afloat by nightfall. All eight transports and merchant vessels eventually sank. B-25 Mitchell and A-20 Havoc strafers attacked to suppress Japanese AA gunfire. Three IJN destroyers were sunk or left sinking as 2,700 soldiers and sailors were saved by the IJN destroyers *Uranami*, *Shikinami*, *Asagumo* and *Yukikaze*. These vessels rapidly withdrew back up the Vitiaz Strait. The *Asashio* stayed behind to assist the crippled *Arashio*, the latter still afloat. On 4 March, the wrecks of the *Arashio* and *Tokitsukaze* were sunk by 5th USAAF bombs. (*NARA*)

(**Above**) Two B-25s attack *Oigawa Maru* early on 4 March 1943 at mast height after the convoy's destroyer escort raced back towards Rabaul with survivors rescued from the water on 3 March. The B-25s attacked in pairs as one suppressed deck AA gunfire with strafing machine-gun fire while the other aircraft skip-bombed the target. (*NARA*)

(**Above**) The 2,883-ton *Taimei Maru* is attacked at mast height by an RAAF Bristol Beaufighter on 3 March 1943 during the height of the Battle of the Bismarck Sea, with bombs bracketing the freighter, which had its deck loaded with armaments and supplies. Thirteen Beaufighters from RAAF No. 30 Squadron participated in the battle. These aircraft were powerfully armed with four 20mm automatic cannons mounted in the lower fuselage and six machine guns in the wings, enabling it to destroy lightly armoured IJN vessels. The squadron proved adept at low-level attacks, especially by suppressing the AA from Japanese ships, contributing to their 46 per cent bomb hit rate. *(NARA)*

(**Opposite, above**) Japanese sailors and troops swim and cling to the wreckage of their sunken transport at the Battle of the Bismarck Sea on 3 March 1943, which, after the carnage, thousands of Japanese sailors and soldiers were still afloat in the Solomon Sea as night fell. Japanese submarines and destroyers saved more than 2,700 men from the convoy but over 3,000 were missing. The four IJN destroyers that headed back up the Vitiaz Strait – *Uranami*, *Shikinami*, *Asagumo* and *Yukikaze* – rendezvoused with the IJN destroyer *Hatsuyuki* during the evening of 4 March to unload 1,400 sailors. Three of the four IJN destroyers refuelled and returned to the Solomon Sea under the cover of darkness to recover more survivors of the destroyers *Arashio* and *Tokitsukaze* with the *Hatsuyuki* and *Uranami*, reaching New Ireland's Kavieng (see Map 2). Two IJN submarines recovered another 275 soldiers between 3 and 5 March. On the night of 3 March, ten USN PT boats from New Guinea arrived to sweep through the Huon Bay during darkness, killing survivors in boats, rafts or wreckages, preventing them from swimming to join the Lae garrison. On 4 March, American fighters mercilessly strafed any enemy on the water's surface. *(NARA)*

(**Opposite, below**) The main runway at Lae is pummelled by 5th USAAF bombers in May 1943, with destroyed and strewn IJAAF aircraft visible. Bombers of every type participated in the Lae raids, particularly RAAF Beaufighters, interdicting Japanese air traffic. With the successful invasion and capture of Lae by the Allies on 15 September 1943 and the Australian seizure of Finschhafen a few weeks later, these new Allied air bases sealed the fate for Wewak's airfields, and later, Hollandia's. The Allies repaired the Lae airfield as a fighter strip. *(NARA)*

C-25909 A.C.

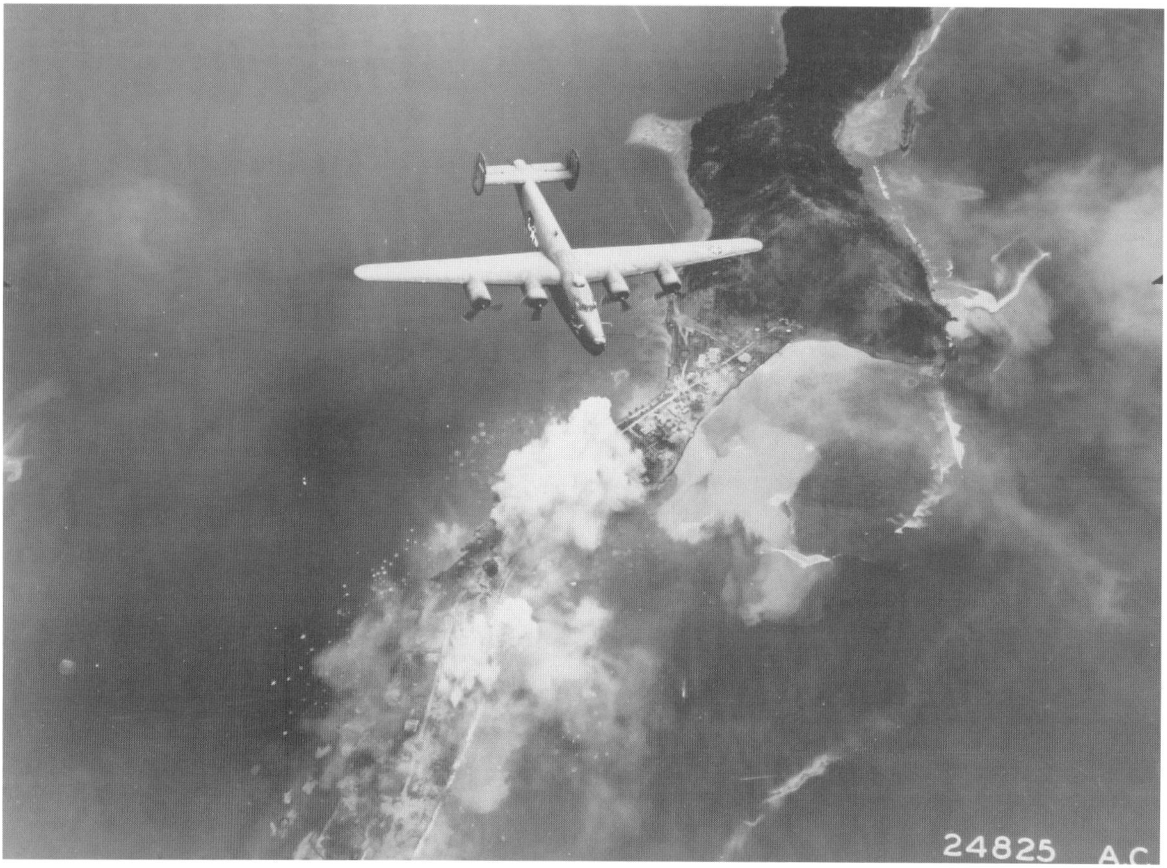
24825 AC

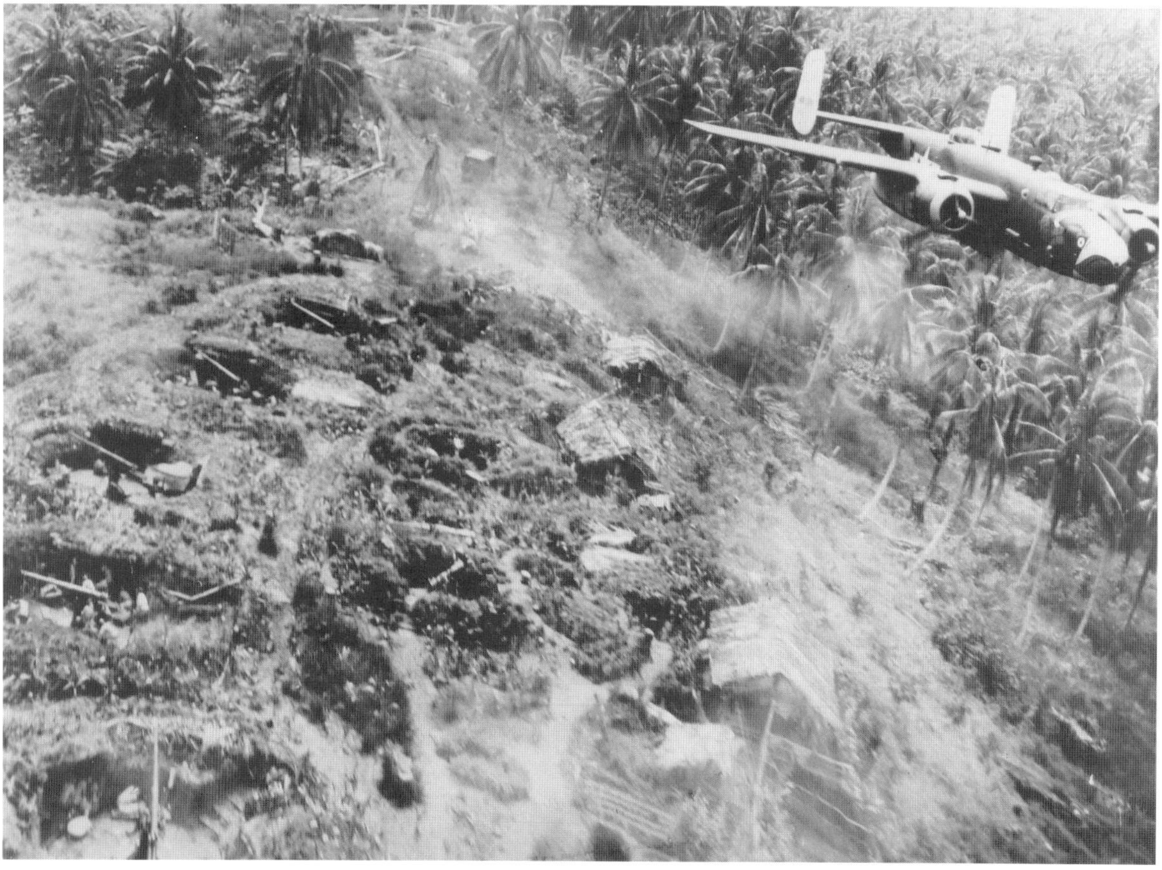

(**Opposite, above**) A Consolidated B-24 Liberator four-engine heavy bomber pounds the airfield at Salamaua, a principal Allied target to capture. In early 1943, the airfields at Lae and Salamaua (see Map 3) became targets as Rabaul sent air reinforcements to both sites. After Salamaua was captured by Australian troops on 11 September, Allied engineers decided that the shredded airfield there was not worth rebuilding except as an emergency strip. (*NARA*)

(**Opposite, below**) A B-25D 'Red Wrath' strafer of the 498th Bombardment Squadron, 345th Bombardment Group ('Air Apaches') makes a low-level attack with 100lb bombs alongside Japanese DP 75mm artillery positions on 16 October 1943 at Boram aerodrome, east of Wewak, as enemy gunners take cover in their redoubts. Tokyo reinforced the IJAAF on New Guinea after Buna fell on 2 January 1943, with the major aircraft build-up at Wewak, northwest of Lae and Madang. The Wewak air complex had several nearby dispersal strips, separated by a few miles: at Boram (located to the east of Wewak), But Drome (referred to as But West by the Japanese), Dagua (also known as But East to the Japanese), and Wewak itself, the latter activated with the IJAAF Fourth Air Army in June 1943, having a 2,000ft-long field with seventy revetments. On 12–14 August, the IJAAF's Fourth Air Army conducted a wave of raids on Allied air bases at Marilinan, Mount Hagen, Bena Bena and Wau. After only small Allied raids against Wewak, the 5th USAAF mounted its first major attack there and against its three satellite fields on 17 August. Other large-scale attacks occurred on 18 August and 20–21 August. (*NARA*)

(**Above**) At Boram Airfield, Japanese gunners crouch within reinforced AA gun positions (right foreground) during a late August 1943 'parafrag' bombing attack, a tactic Lieutenant General Kenney himself helped develop pre-war. The parafrag was a 23lb fragmentation bomb parachuted at less than 100 feet with its slow descent allowing Allied aircrew to escape the explosions. To quickly drop many parafrag bombs, A-20 Havoc and B-25D Mitchell strafers had special racks field-engineered by Major Paul 'Pappy' Gunn in Australia. Factory production improved Gunn's prototypes and thousands of parafrag bombs and racks were sent to the 5th USAAF. The offensive that destroyed Japanese airpower in New Guinea began in mid-August 1943 as the 5th USAAF received new units and aircraft earlier in the summer of 1943, just as the IJAAF at Wewak's airfields was also reinforced. (*NARA*)

Low-flying B-25 strafers attack Boram Airfield on 17 August 1943, destroying sixty Japanese planes warming up in close proximity. During the Lae campaign, when Allied aircraft neutralized the Japanese airfield there on 3 May 1943, the IJAAF Fourth Air Army moved many aircraft to Wewak's airfields. 5th USAAF HQ moved against the IJAAF at Wewak and its satellite fields at Boram, But and Dagua in late August 1943, since the Allied 4–5 September 1943 scheduled landings at Lae would be within range of these Japanese air bases. The Japanese assumed Wewak was outside Allied fighter range so their merchant ships entered Wewak harbour with men and materiel to finish Wewak area's airstrips as well as Hollandia to the west. However, Australian engineers built a new Allied fighter strip at Tsili Tsili, a few miles northwest of the Australian inland base at Wau in the Markham River valley (see Map 3). As the newly built fighter airfield at Tsili Tsili received it first fighter units, Kenney was assured of fighter support and an emergency strip for his large bomber airstrikes on Wewak and its satellite fields on 17–18 August and 20–21 August, concurrent just after the arrival of substantial IJAAF units. (NARA)

An IJN destroyer attacked (upper panel) and sunk (lower panel) by a 5th USAAF B-25 strafer in the Bismarck Archipelago. The strafer flying at mast height resembled a torpedo attack so the Japanese destroyer captain defensively turned the vessel 'bow-on' (above), making the B-25 skip bombing (as depicted by the accurate trail of the foam pools) and strafing more effective as not all Japanese AA guns could be utilized against the bomber, especially as the deck's crew was being decimated by the Mitchell's concentrated firepower. (NARA)

(**Above**) IJAAF planes in their revetments at the Dagua Airfield, to Wewak's west, subjected to low-level precision parafrag bombing by Allied medium bombers on 21 August 1943. Wewak, and its satellite dispersal fields, had too few taxiways leading from the revetments so when a scramble order came, Japanese aircraft movement to the runway was delayed. Also, as soon as 5th USAAF heavy demolition bombs disabled the runway, the Japanese aircraft take-off was further hindered, especially after successive raids. (NARA)

(**Opposite, above**) A late August 1943 parafrag bombing attack against Wewak airfield shows parachutes precisely descending onto Kawasaki Ki-45 twin-engine, two-seat Toryu ('Nick') fighters hit in their shallow revetments. This aircraft, designed as a long-range escort fighter, evolved into an interceptor and fighter-bomber. (NARA)

(**Opposite, below**) Dagua Airfield, situated on New Guinea's northern coast, undergoes a low-level HE bombing run by B-25 medium bombers on 13 August 1943 as a lead-up to the devastating raids of 17–18 August. The IJAAF began building this airfield in January 1943 and by the end of February, it was operational for Japanese bombers. As Dagua was important for missions against Allied targets in New Guinea, it was resupplied with replacement aircraft from Hollandia to the west (see Map 5), along the Netherlands New Guinea coast. (NARA)

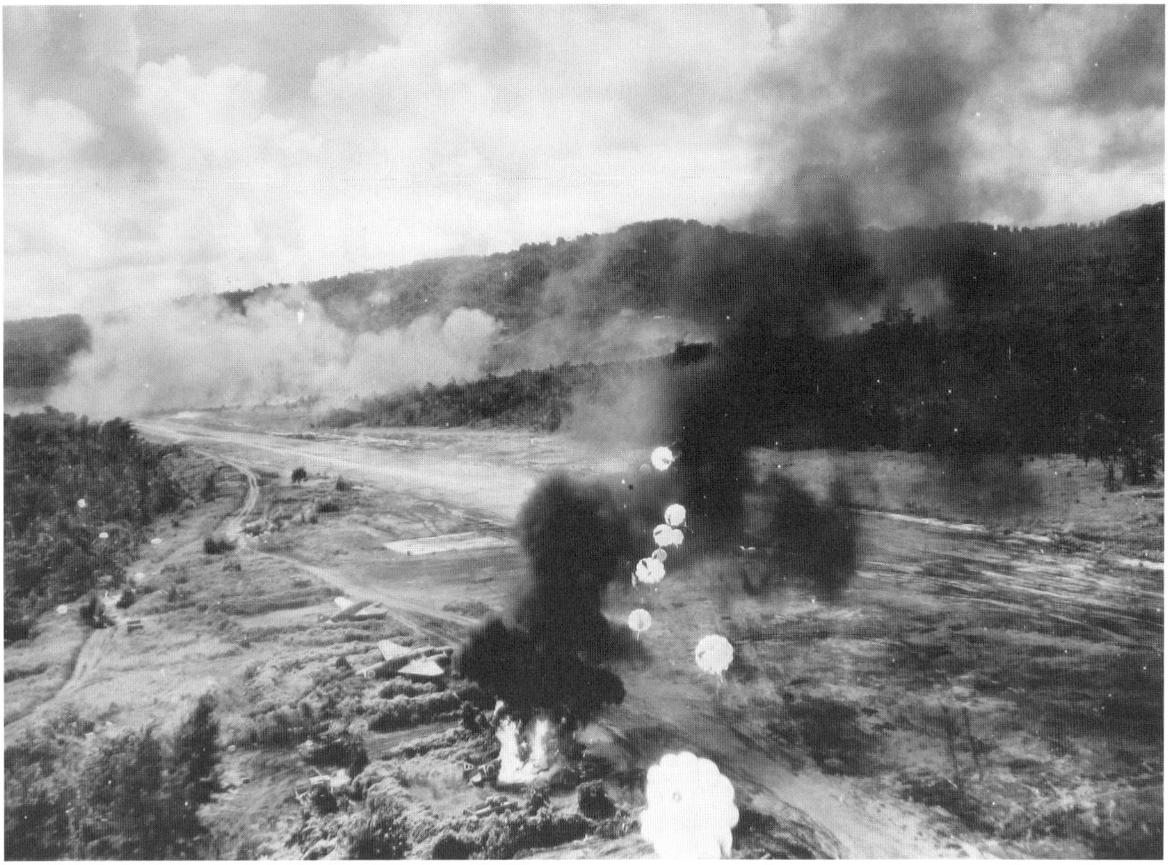

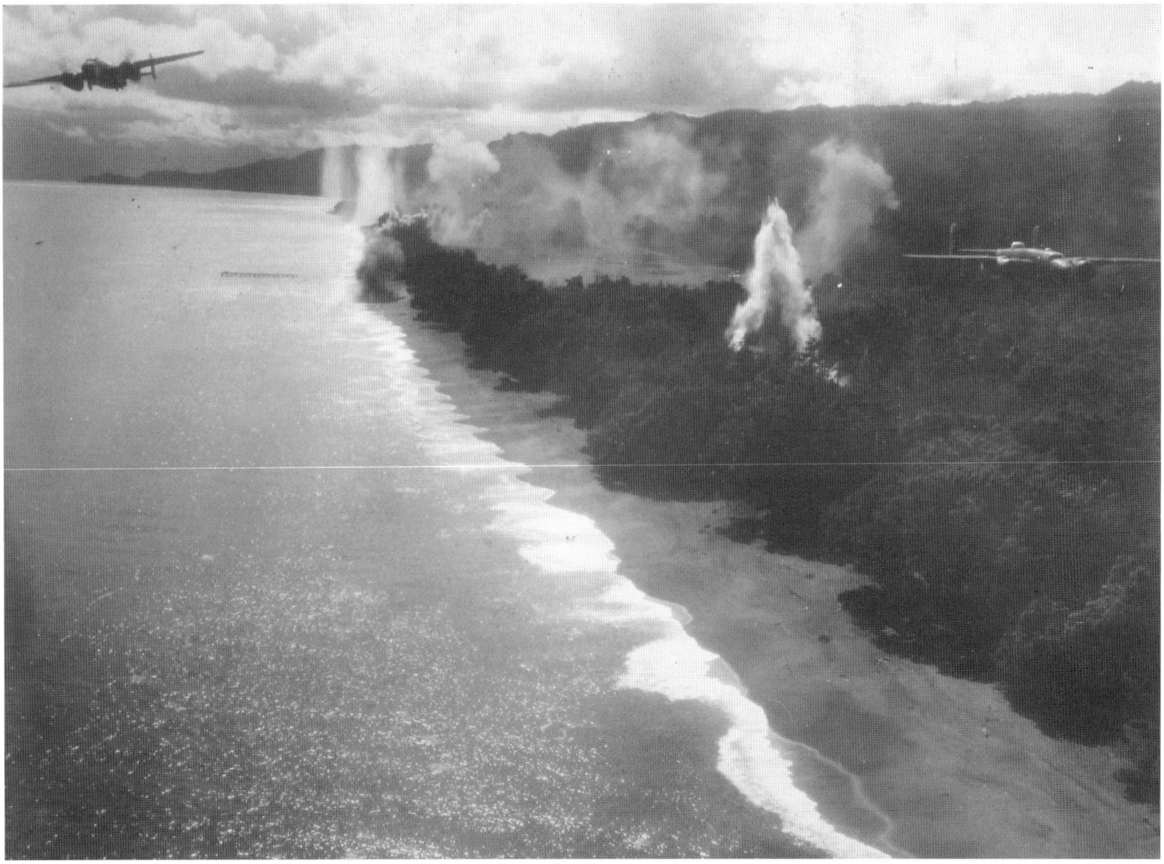

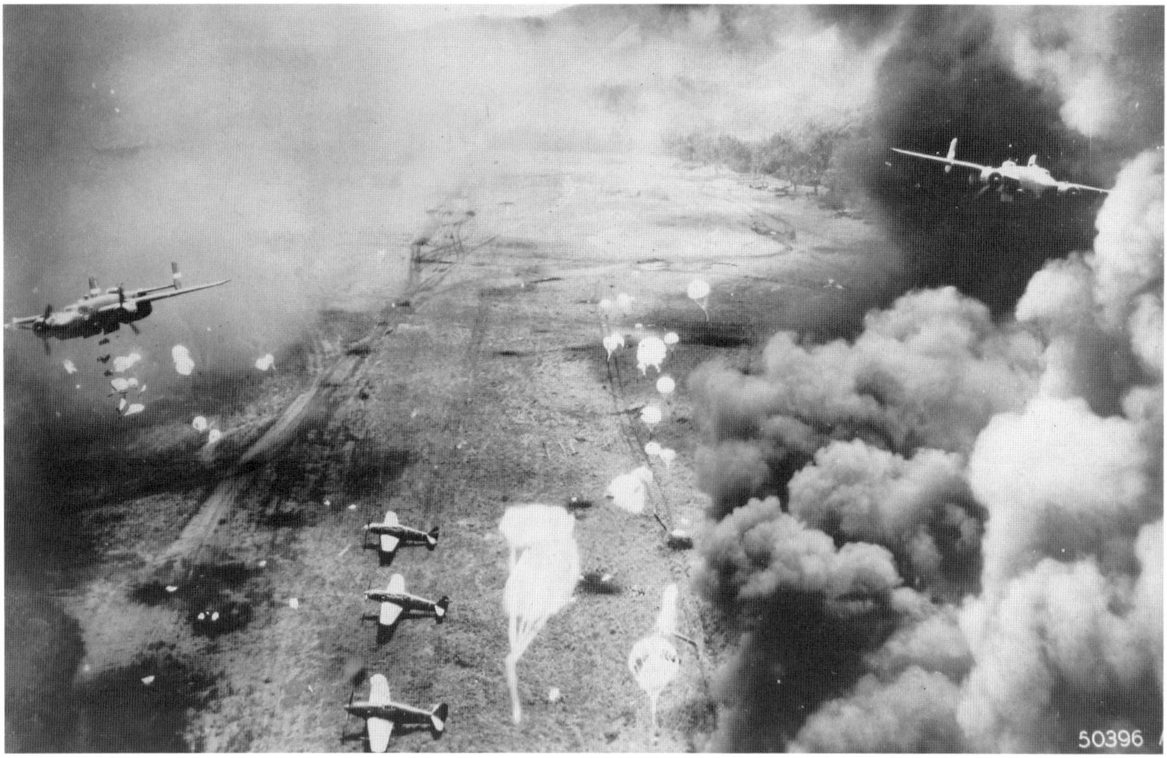
50396

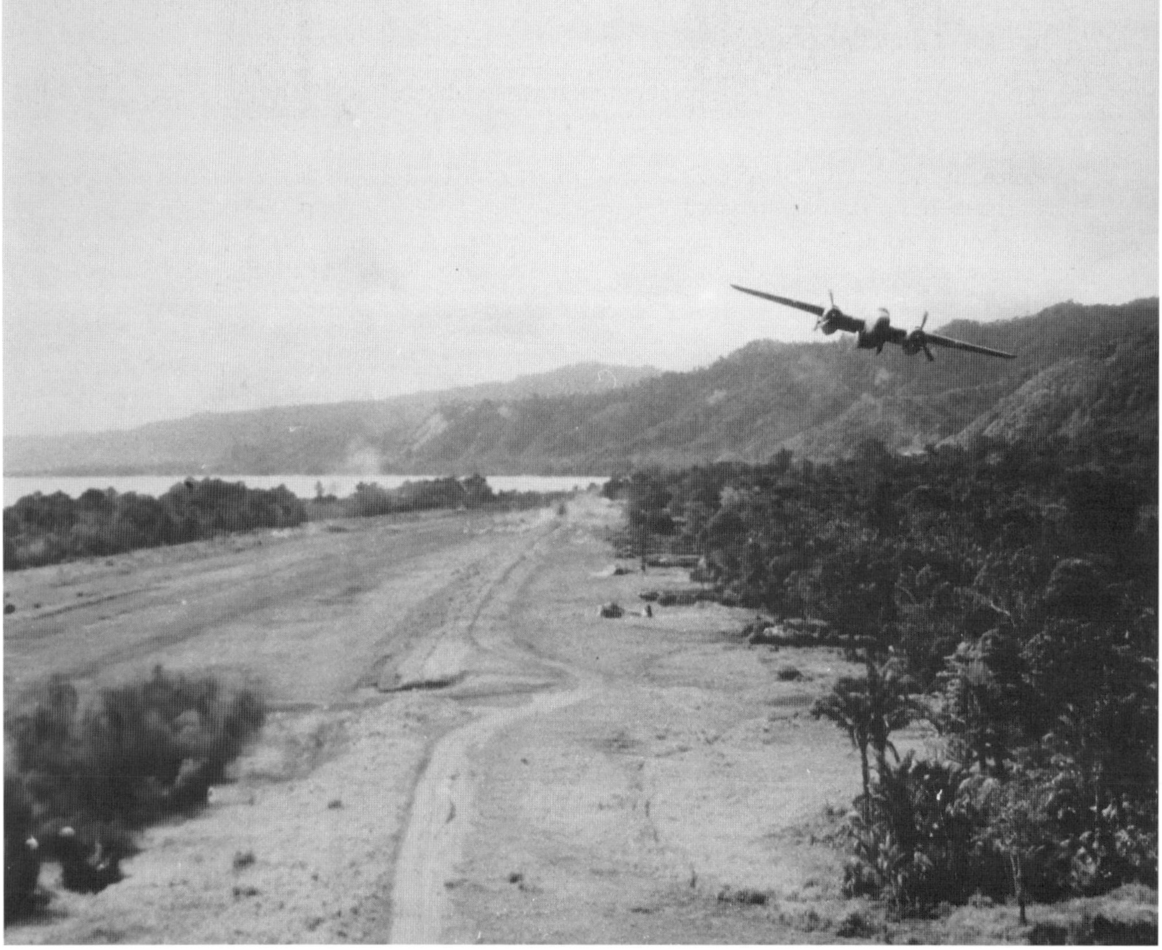

(**Opposite, above**) A 5th USAAF B-25 bombing mission against Dagua Airfield with Japanese single-engine fighters lined up wingtip to wingtip, making them easy targets for the parafrag bombs dropped low level by parachutes. By early April 1944, Dagua Airfield's runways were not operational and the aerodrome was bypassed by SWPA ground forces' landings on 22 April 1944 at Aitape and Hollandia, west of Wewak. (NARA)

(**Opposite, below**) A Douglas A-20 Havoc medium bomber flies low as a strafer over But Drome's runway as parafrag bombs explode on it (lower left). This aircraft served with the RAF (called the 'Boston'). The A-20's American combat debut as the 'Havoc' was in North Africa. RAAF No. 22 Squadron Bostons took part in the Battle of the Bismarck Sea along with 5th USAAF A-20 Havocs. The A-20 saw its initial combat in the 89th Bombardment Squadron, 3rd Bombardment Group, during New Guinea operations on 31 August 1942, and after conversion to a strafer role, with the bombardier removed and replaced by additional machine guns in the nose, it was instrumental for pinpoint strikes against aircraft, hangars and supply dumps at Japanese airfields and installations. (NARA)

(**Above**) Heavily bombed runway and revetment areas at But Drome on 26 August 1943 after the four-day aerial offensive by 5th USAAF on Wewak and its satellite fields. Heavy bombers damaged the airfields' runways, making the lighter Japanese fighters manoeuvre around them to get airborne. The craters did prevent the heavier IJAAF bombers from taking off. Japanese ground crews worked hard to repair the cratered runways, often making a riddled airfield somewhat operational the next day. (NARA)

(**Above**) A low-flying B-25 strafer attacks over Wewak's main airfield in December 1943. Wewak, like the other satellite airfields, was raided repeatedly. The initial major assault on 17 August 1943 comprised almost a total long-range effort by the 5th USAAF, with 200 aircraft utilizing B-24 heavy bombers in the first wave. The second wave of B-25 strafers destroyed scores of IJAAF aircraft on the ground. This raid and the other late August attacks reduced the number of Wewak's operational aircraft from a peak of 250 to 160 in three weeks, with IJAAF reinforcements from Rabaul and Hollandia rebuilding its strength to 200 aircraft until the 5th USAAF renewed attacks in November 1943. A final 5th USAAF assault during January–February 1944 reduced the total number of IJAAF planes to fewer than 100. By April, the IJAAF Fourth Air Army abandoned Wewak as its 6th Air Division was destroyed. (NARA)

(**Opposite, above**) The aftermath of a B-25 strafer and parafrag bombing mission on Wewak Drome on 27 November 1943, with many Japanese planes ablaze (middle). A large number of wrecked planes (left foreground) are among others undergoing parafrag bombing. Similar tactics of an advance B-24 attack targeting runways followed by B-25 parafrag precision bombing and strafing of planes and AA batteries were used. (NARA)

(**Opposite, below**) Pinpoint precision parafrag bombing of Japanese planes parked on one of the four Hollandia area airfields (Hollandia, Sentani, Cyclops and Tami) on 3 April 1944, next to a cratered runway and taxiway. From 30 March to 3 April, the 5th USAAF conducted a series of bombing raids on Hollandia's airfields, destroying 340 enemy planes on the ground and 60 shot down in aerial combat, before the 22 April amphibious invasion along Dutch New Guinea's northern coast at Humboldt Bay and the nearby airfields' capture on 26 April, which removed the last major Japanese New Guinea airbase to threaten Allied forces on the ground or in the air. The 3 April raid was the largest, with sixty-six B-24s and ninety-six A-20 Havocs with escorting fighters, with the extensive enemy aircraft destruction leading to the success of the Hollandia, Aitape and Tanamerah Bay landings by assaulting units of the I Corps' 41st and 24th Divisions, enabling MacArthur's bypassing of the strongest IJA 18th Army garrisons at Madang and Wewak to expedite his advance to the Vogelkop Peninsula (see Map 5) by several months. (NARA)

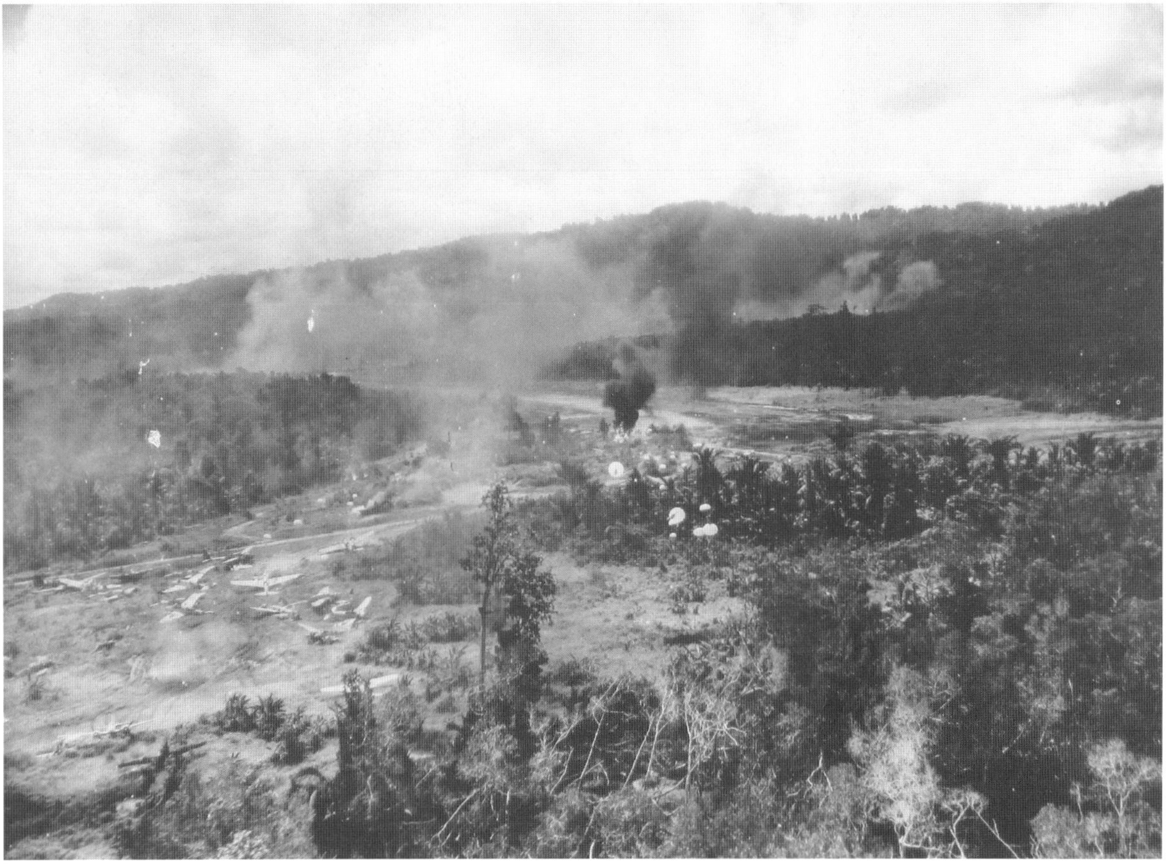

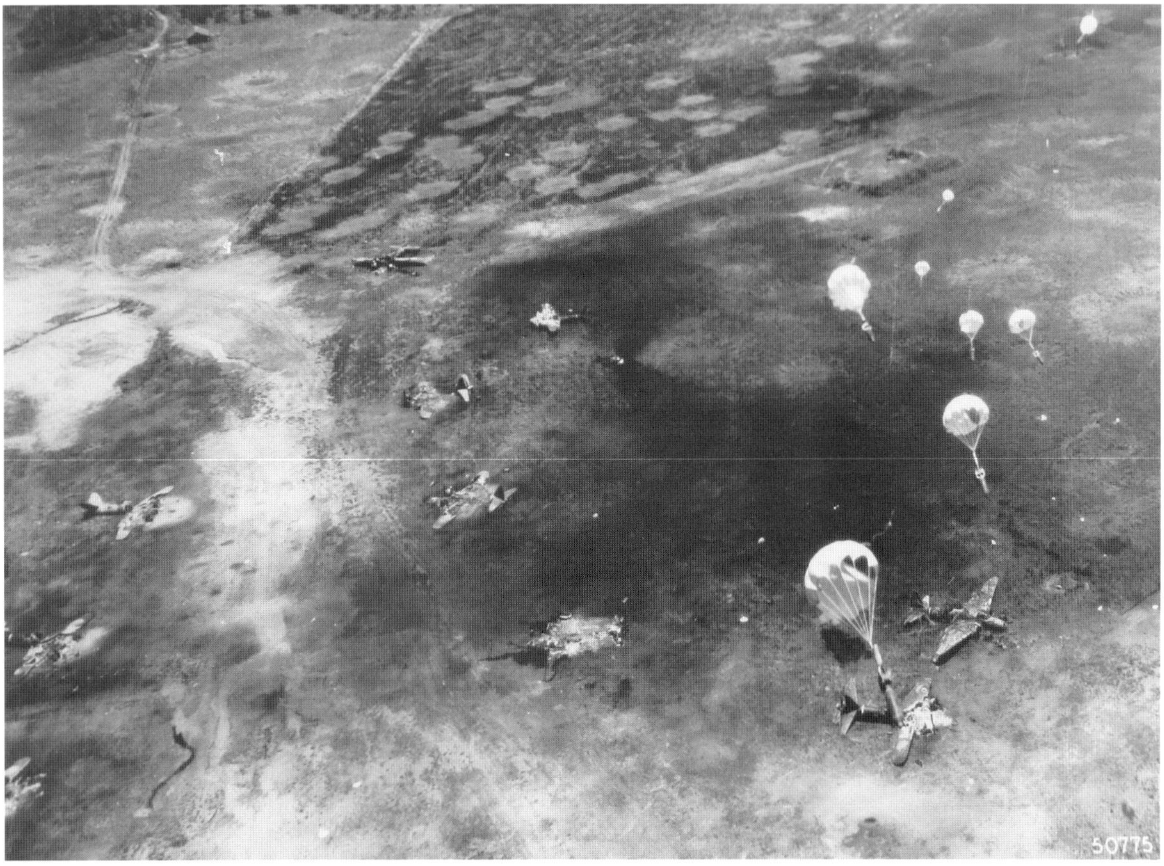
50775

(**Above**) An A-20 Havoc bombs Humboldt Bay in April 1944 as a prelude to MacArthur's 22 April combined amphibious assault at Hollandia, Aitape and Tanahmerah Bay. From early 1943, the A-20 Havocs attacked land targets in New Guinea with time-delayed 500lb bombs. These were replaced with parafrag bombs, which were better suited to destroy Japanese aircraft parked in the open or in revetments. (NARA)

(**Opposite**) Flak (top frame, upper right) was one of the most serious dangers facing Allied strafers when attacking land or naval targets. This series of three consecutive photographs taken from another attacking aircraft (top frame) demonstrates the destruction of one (middle frame, right, trailing smoke) of a pair of 5th USAAF A-20 Havocs (bomb bay doors still open) by enemy AA batteries while bombing the waterfront at Kakas in Dutch New Guinea on 15 September 1944. (NARA)

An A-20 Havoc misses a Japanese 4,000-ton troopship 10 miles offshore of Wewak on 19 March 1944 in a skip-bombing mission to interdict IJA reinforcement of northern New Guinea. The Allies scheduled a late April operation against Hansa Bay, midway between Madang to the southeast and Wewak to the northwest; however, SWPA HQ chose instead to leap 500 miles westwards to capture the major Japanese air and supply base at Hollandia (see Map 5). MacArthur and Krueger knew that they would meet strong opposition at Hansa Bay, since the Japanese anticipated such an Allied move on an excellent natural harbour 150 miles west of Saidor (captured on 2 January 1944) and moved two IJA divisions to that anchorage. (NARA)

A B-25 strafer at less than 500ft altitude has two of its bombs 'skip' over the water's surface towards Japanese shipping in Wewak Harbour in January 1944. With five-second time-delayed fuses, an Allied strafer could have its bombs directly hit the enemy ship and detonate below deck, causing engine destruction or igniting ammunition magazines. If the bomb missed and exploded underwater near the vessel, the hull's steel plates could rupture ('mining effect'), causing seawater to rush in. (NARA)

A low-level B-25 strafer narrowly misses a Japanese freighter on a skip-bombing run in Wewak Harbour on 18 September 1943, with enemy flak above the bomber. Interdiction of Japanese naval resupply of Wewak doomed the IJA Fourth Air Fleet, formed initially in Rabaul and then sent to Wewak. From May 1943 to April 1944, 800 Japanese planes were lost; they were not replaced, due to lower aircraft production, and ferrying and shipping losses. *(NARA)*

B-25J strafers of the 42nd Bombardment Group lined up on Mar Strip at Sansapor on Dutch New Guinea's Vogelkop Peninsula in September 1944. These aircraft possessed two 0.50-inch calibre machine guns in blisters on the side of each fuselage below the pilot in addition to the nose, waist (manned by radio operator), dorsal turret (manned by flight engineer) MGs and a gunner firing the twin tail MGs. Other B-25J crewmen included the pilot and co-pilot, with the navigator doubling as bombardier. *(NARA)*

John 'Jack' Fox, the NAA senior technical representative in SWPA, stands by one of the first field-modified B-25s, named *Lil Fox*, after him. His head is beneath a T-13E1 M5 75mm cannon in addition to the four nose-mounted 0.50-inch calibre machine guns. A dedicated 'cannoneer' loaded shells into the 75mm howitzer as each strafer carried twenty rounds for anti-shipping and ground attack roles. *(NARA)*

(**Above**) In the waters off the Boram Airfield near Wewak, a Japanese merchant ship takes a direct hit from the 75mm cannon of a strafing B-25 flying at 500ft altitude on 27 November 1943. In the B-25G modification with the 75mm gun, the navigator/radio operator doubled as the cannoneer, loading shells into the howitzer. Evidence of skip bombing is on either side of the vessel. The B-25 carried four M64 500lb bombs, which could seriously damage an unarmoured transport or an IJN warship up to the size of a light cruiser. (NARA)

(**Opposite, above**) An RAAF Consolidated PBY Catalina flying boat shown on its return from a mission. Extremely slow (200mph maximum speed) but reliable with good endurance, having a range of 1,900 miles, the PBY Catalina flew night missions against Japanese shipping and warships. It had up to six machine guns and could carry an external bomb load of 4500lb. These planes rescued downed Allied flyers in the waters off New Guinea, New Britain and New Ireland. As an amphibian, a main use was long-range reconnaissance. (NARA)

(**Opposite, below**) A USN PT boat patrols off the New Guinea coast in the summer of 1943. During the aftermath of the carnage at the Battle of the Bismarck Sea on 2–5 March 1943, ten PT boats armed with a pair of torpedoes, light 20mm cannon and machine guns were dispatched to the Solomon Sea. Two PT boats saw the wreckage of the *Oigawa Maru* ablaze on the night of 4 March. Each fired a torpedo, sinking the Japanese ship. Other PT boasts attacked rafts, boats or landing craft found during the morning hours of 5 March, preventing any surviving Japanese from reaching Lae. (NARA)

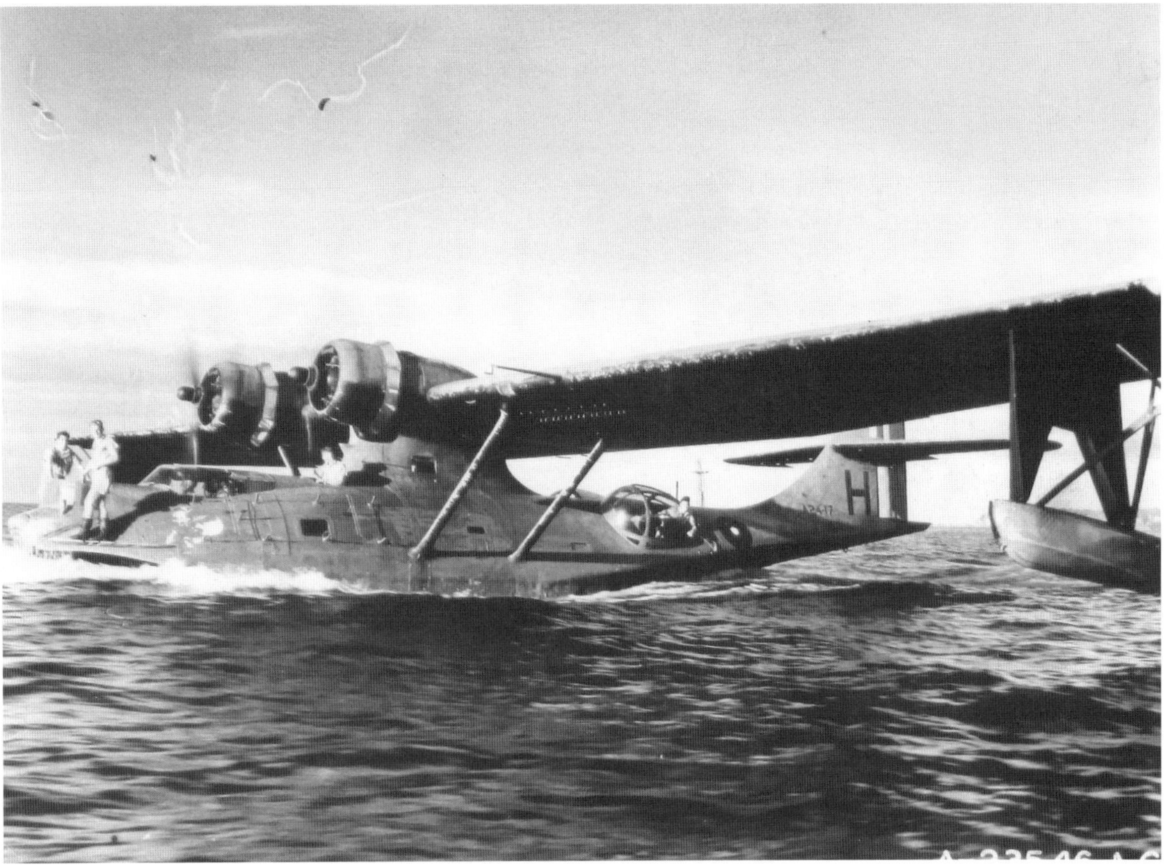

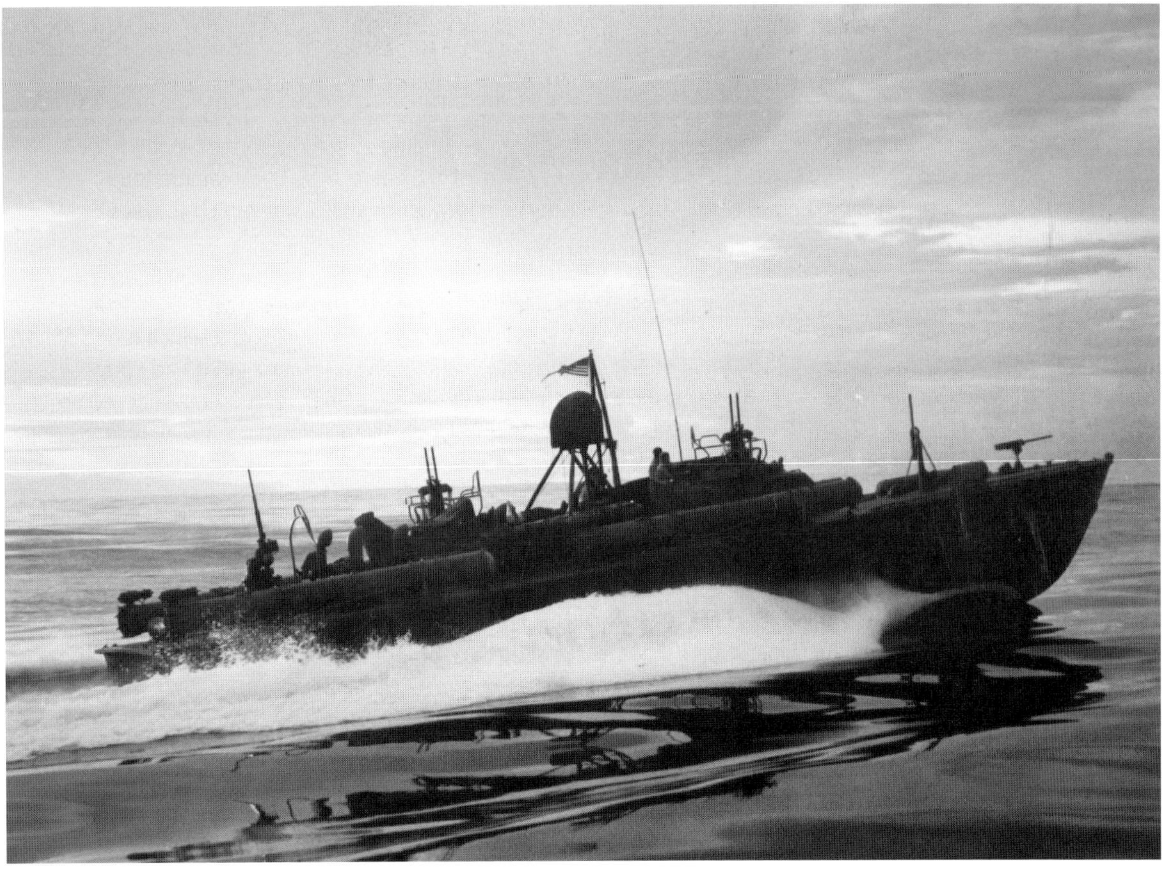

(**Above**) A Douglas C-47 Skytrain or Dakota (a DC-3 commercially) of the 6th Troop Carrier Squadron flies over Papua's Owen Stanley Range from Ward's Drome at Port Moresby to Wau, near the Huon Peninsula, in April 1943, escorted by a flight of US Army Bell P-39 Airacobras with extra 'belly' fuel tanks. The C-47 had a 1,600-mile range coupled with unparalleled transport capability, evolving into paratroop and glider-towing functions. The Bell P-39 Airacobra was a single-seat fighter and fighter-bomber. The engine was behind the cockpit, nearer the fuselage's centre of gravity, leaving the nose free for two machine guns, in addition to one 37mm fixed forward-firing cannon and four MGs in the leading edges of the wing. The plane carried an external bomb load of 500lb. *(NARA)*

(**Opposite, above**) On 5 September 1943, 1,700 paratroopers of the US 503rd PIR, partially concealed by smoke, parachuted unopposed onto an old Australian airfield at Nadzab in the Markham River Valley (see Map 3) in a *coup de main* seizure as part of the Lae operation. The C-47 pilots of the eighty-one transports descended to less than 1,000 feet for the airdrop as MacArthur observed from overhead in a B-17. The three paratroop battalions fanned out to their assigned blocking locations and to work on the airfield. The operation cost three dead and thirty-three wounded from accidents. That day, Australian units reached Nadzab after an overland and river trek down the Watut River, a tributary of the Markham River, to help throughout the night prepare the airfield for a 6 September arrival of the HQ, AIF 7th Division and the Australian 25th Brigade for the ground assault on Lae. Within two weeks, American and Australian engineers constructed two 6,000ft parallel airstrips and started work on six others. The Nadzab complex would be a vital air link in all subsequent SWPA operations. *(NARA)*

(**Opposite, below**) A flight of Bristol Beaufighters searching New Guinea's mountains for strafing targets near Finschhafen in April 1943. The Beaufighter, designed as an interceptor, had extraordinary destructive forward-firing armament, including four 20mm cannons and six machine guns. *(NARA)*

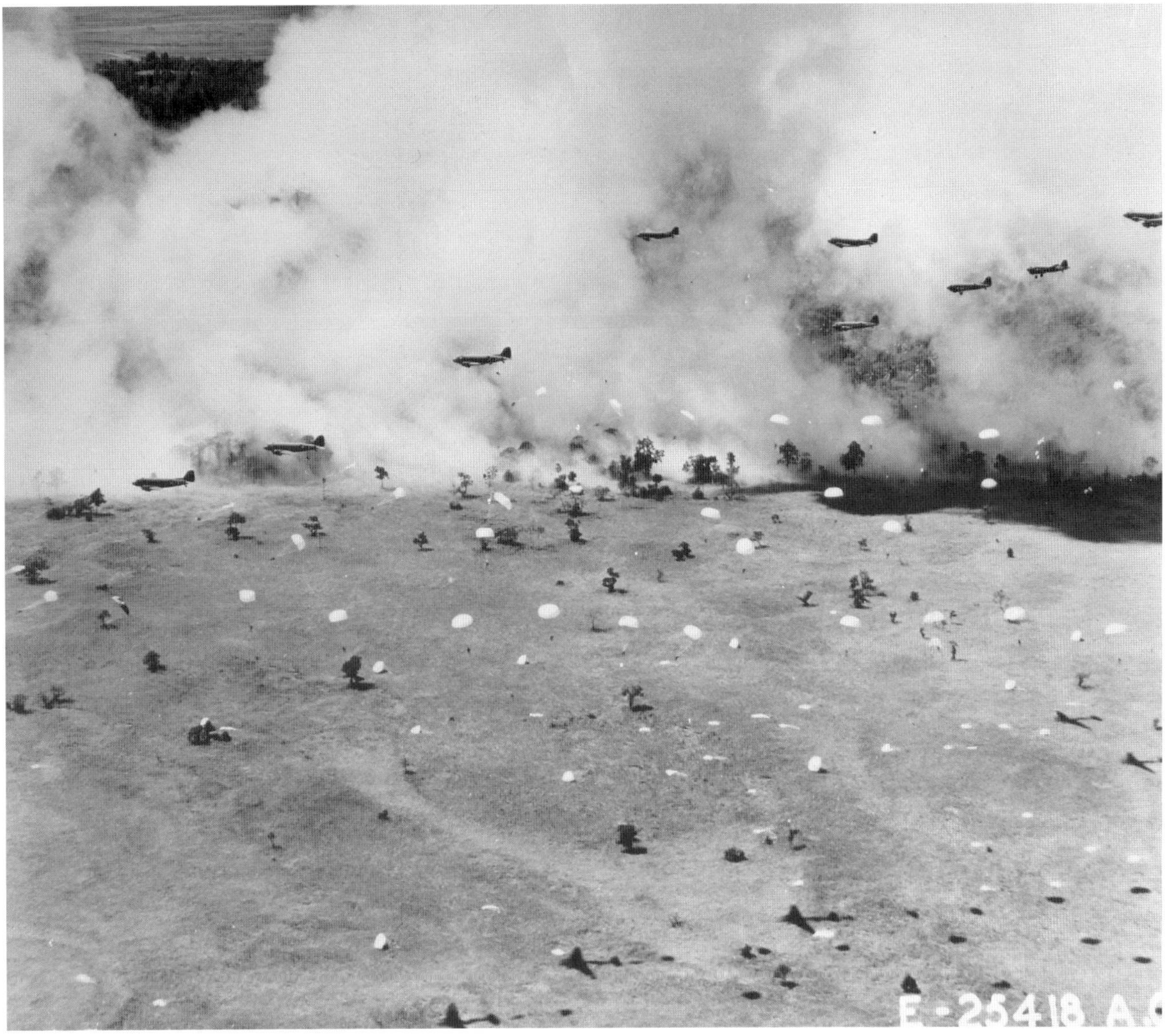
E-25418 A.

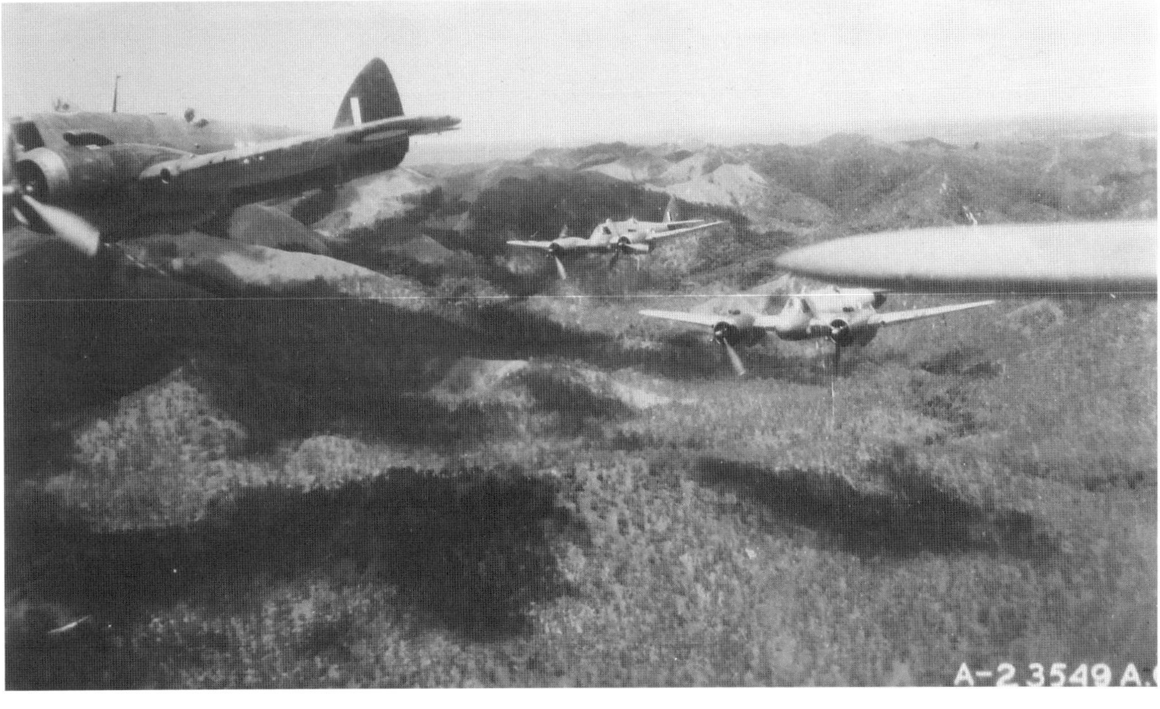
A-23549 A.

(**Above**) A 5th USAAF's 7th Fighter Group Curtiss P-40 Warhawk at a Dobodura airfield in May 1943 has its wing machine guns rearmed as another ground crewman wipes splattered oil from an exploded Japanese fighter from the cockpit's windscreen. The P-40 was an adequate and most numerous single-seat fighter early in the Second World War, but became a better fighter-bomber with six 0.50-inch calibre MGs, making it better armed than the Japanese A6M3 Zero as well as sturdier, with self-sealing fuel tanks and more pilot armour. When the P-40's guns fired properly, it could obliterate a Zero without need of a cannon. (NARA)

(**Opposite, above**) A burning P-38 Lightning of the 9th Fighter Squadron was hit by Japanese bombers on Air Strip 4 (the main runway) at Dobodura's complex of fifteen runways near Port Moresby on 11 March 1943. Allied aircraft at Dobodura were within range of Japanese planes operating from Gasmata, on the southern coast of New Britain, and secondary airfields at the western tip of the island at Cape Gloucester. (NARA)

(**Opposite, below**) A newer version of an IJNAF Mitsubishi A6M3 Reisen or Zero fighter abandoned at one of the two Cape Gloucester airfields on 29 December 1943. During the period of March 1939 to March 1942, over 800 Zeros were manufactured. In mid-1943, Mitsubishi produced 1,700 Zeros, sufficient to keep units up to strength in the SPA and SWPA but not enough to build new air units. The Zero was an excellent bomber escort as well as the premier carrier-based fighter until introduction of the USN F6F Hellcat in late 1943. Mitsubishi was unable to do extensive upgrades due to Japanese economic conditions and this aircraft was outclassed by mid-1943. (NARA)

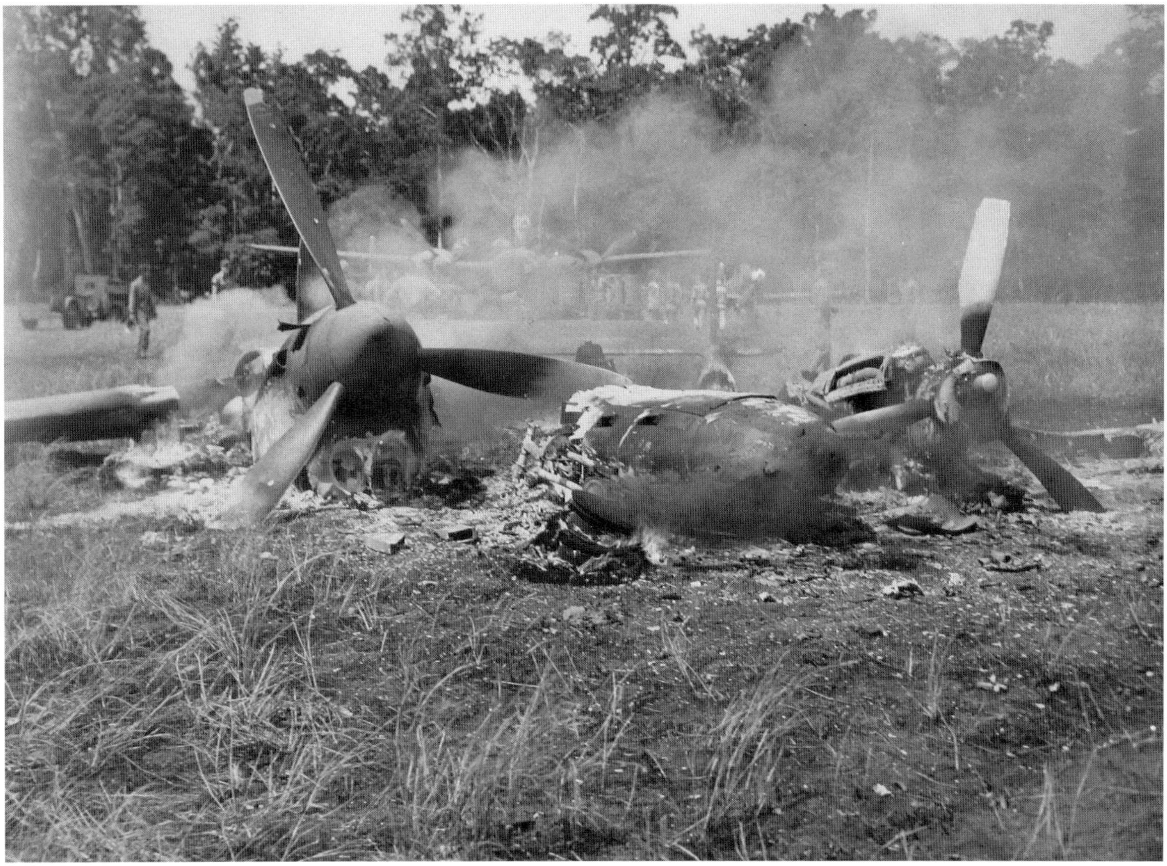

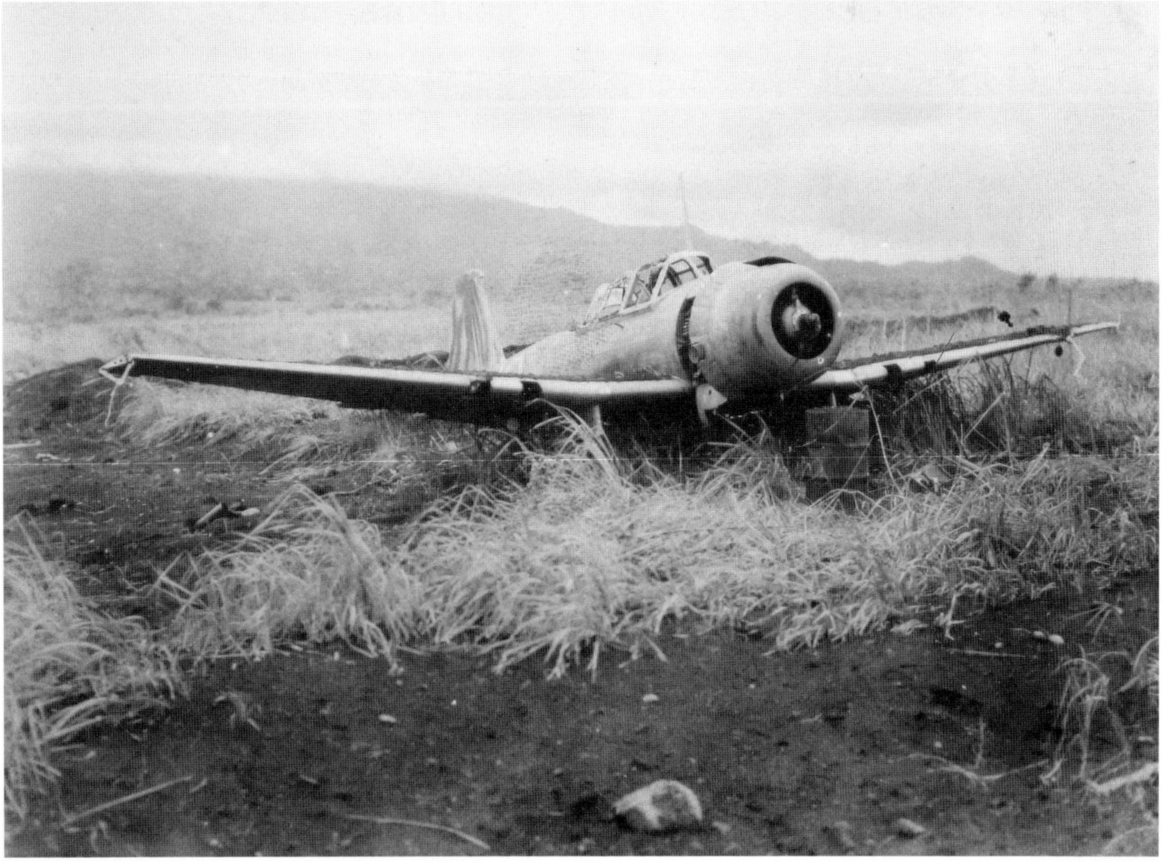

(**Above**) An IJAAF Mitsubishi Ki-21 Mk III 'Sally' twin-engine bomber flies over New Guinea jungle before being shot down by 5th USAAF B-25s on 27 December 1943. This was the best bomber available in significant numbers to the IJAAF. Mitsubishi opted for more speed and range at the expense of pilot protection, defensive armament and offensive payload. This medium bomber had either five or seven seats, with a range of almost 1,700 miles and a bomb load of 2,200lb. (*NARA*)

(**Opposite, above**) An IJAAF Nakajima Ki-49 Donryu 'Helen' 'heavy' twin-engine bomber is smoking on the ground at Dagua Airfield on 22 October 1943 after an Allied parafrag bombing attack. Its designation as a 'heavy' bomber is misleading, as it was barely able to carry more than 2,200lb of internal ordnance. Bombs stacked at the right of the smouldering fuselage suggest it was being prepared for a bombing sortie. Designed to carry out daylight bombing missions without the protection of escort fighters, it had a range of over 1,800 miles and was to replace the IJAAF Mitsubishi Ki-21 Sally, making its combat debut in February 1942 in a Darwin, Australia raid. The Ki-49 was frequently encountered over New Guinea and New Britain. Like most Japanese aircraft of the Second World War, it was under-armed and under-armoured. Only 800 were manufactured. (*NARA*)

(**Below**) An IJAAF Mitsubishi Ki-46 Type 100 Command Reconnaissance aircraft ('Dinah') lies partially destroyed at a Cape Gloucester airfield after its 29 December 1943 capture by the US 1st Marine Division. It was designed specifically as a high-altitude twin-engine, two-seat photographic reconnaissance aircraft with maximum service ceiling of 35,000 feet, a range of 1,500 miles and a speed of 375mph, and was introduced into service in July 1941. As the war progressed, the Ki-46 became vulnerable to fast-climbing Allied fighters. Over 1,700 were manufactured. *(NARA)*

Chapter Three

Commanders and Combatants

At the Casablanca Conference in January 1943, Admiral Ernest King, COMINCH and CNO, and Army COS George Marshall agreed to follow up the Midway victory and defeat the Japanese in Papua and on Guadalcanal. As only 15 per cent of the total Allied resources were employed in the Pacific and CBI theatres, they argued that this imbalance could cripple the war against Japan so troops and materiel from the ETO and MTO would be transferred to the SPA and SWPA for counter-offensives from Guadalcanal through the Solomons and from Papua into Northeastern New Guinea, ultimately to break through the Bismarck Archipelago and neutralize Rabaul (see Map 4).

General MacArthur's SWPA command received directives directly from the JCS via General Marshall just as Admiral Nimitz received his via Admiral King. Once the SWPA ground forces regained the offensive initiative during the first half of 1943, Rear Admiral Daniel Barbey's VII Amphibious Force transported them in coordination with US Sixth Army CG, Lieutenant General Walter Krueger. As Lieutenant General George Kenney's 5th USAAF was preoccupied with strategic bombing and Allied aerial troop transport, coordination with the USN and USMC air wings was not close until the second half of 1943.

Japan had a deified monarch: Emperor Hirohito, a figurehead under the Meiji Constitution, with the Imperial Japanese HQ the governmental power, or 'military autocracy', rigidly divided between Army and Navy branches. The Army branch consisted of the Army Minister and Chief of the Army General Staff, General Hideki Tojo. The naval branch included the Navy Minister, Admiral Shigetarō Shimada, and the Chief of the Naval General Staff, Admiral Osami Nagano.

When Hirohito inquired what was planned after the February 1943 Guadalcanal evacuation, Nagano was developing airfields at Munda on New Georgia and Vila on Kolombangara to aerially damage the Allied forces on Guadalcanal. This evolved into Operation I-GO under C-in-C of the Combined Japanese Fleet, Admiral Isoroku Yamamoto, who for the air offensive transferred his HQ to Rabaul in early April 1943 to personally honour his aircrews by observing each attack's departure from Rabaul's airfields. The naval branch of Imperial Japanese HQ issued directives to Yamamoto and later, Admiral Mineichi Koga.

General Douglas MacArthur, C-in-C SWPA

MacArthur was a US Military Academy graduate, COS of the 42nd ('Rainbow') Division in the First World War, Superintendent of the USMA, Army COS, FM Philippine Army, and then CG Filipino-American forces in the early months of the Second World War, for which he was awarded a Congressional Medal of Honor. On 21 February, Roosevelt ordered MacArthur from Corregidor to Australia. On 17 March, MacArthur, his family and retinue arrived south of Darwin after a PT boat trek to Mindanao followed by B-17 air transit, to assume SWPA command.

Lieutenant General Robert L. Eichelberger, CG I Corps

In Australia during the late spring and summer of 1942, the only American troops were the US 32nd and 41st Infantry Divisions (both National Guard units), comprising I Corps, under the commands of Major General Edwin Harding and Major General Horace Fuller, respectively. To train and lead the nascent I Corps, Marshall sent Lieutenant General Robert L. Eichelberger, a USMA graduate, Class of 1909. Previously, Marshall appointed his protégée, Eichelberger, as the Superintendent of West Point in October 1940, followed by US 3rd Division's assistant CG. After Pearl Harbor, Eichelberger, who trained the 77th Infantry Division, was promoted by Marshall to command I Corps for the upcoming Anglo-American invasion of Northwest Africa. However, with the Japanese South Seas Detachment's (Nankai Shitai) 1942 summer offensive from Buna closing in on Port Moresby (see Map 3), now Lieutenant General Eichelberger was ordered with his I Corps staff to Australia to ready for combat operations in Papua.

Lieutenant General George Kenney, CG Allied Air Forces and 5th USAAF

Kenney enlisted in the Aviation Section, US Signal Corps in 1917 and was awarded a DSC for First World War aerial combat on the Western Front. Commissioned into the Regular Army in 1920, he first attended and then taught at the USAAC's Tactical School, where he developed techniques to mount machine guns on aircraft wings. In 1937, reassigned back to the USAAC, Lieutenant Colonel Kenney commanded an observation squadron at New York's Mitchel Field. In 1938, he became Major General Henry H. Arnold's (CG, USAAC) troubleshooter in the Caribbean and then France in 1940 as Assistant Military Attaché for Air. In January 1941, Kenney was appointed assistant chief of the Materiel Division. After aircraft production reached 4,000 planes, Kenney was given command of the 4th USAAF, defending America's West Coast in March 1942. After reorganizing the 4th USAAF, he was given a combat command in the Middle East, but in early August 1942, he was assigned to MacArthur in SWPA, taking command of the Allied Air Forces in that theatre and becoming CG 5th USAAF. Before departing for Australia, now Lieutenant General Arnold gave Kenney fifty P-38 Lightning fighters he requested, along with fighter pilot Lieutenant Richard Bong. Kenney intended to build airfields in New Guinea despite deplorable conditions and the Japanese securing the initiative in Papuan skies. Two other noteworthy appointments followed, with Brigadier General Ennis C. Whitehead, a fighter commander, to run an Advanced HQ in Papua and assigning Lieutenant Colonel Paul Wurtsmith to Port Moresby to direct fighter operations there to seize the aerial advantage.

Admiral Ernest J. King, COMINCH US Fleet and CNO

In March 1942, King became the first and last to hold COMINCH US Fleet and CNO simultaneously, and the first qualified aviator to be CNO. As a JCS member, he staunchly defended the USN roles in both Atlantic and Pacific theatres. In July 1942, King learned of a Japanese airfield being built on Guadalcanal in the southern Solomon Islands and immersed the USN and USMC into a 7 August 1942 amphibious assault to capture and defend the airfield (renamed Henderson Field), employing the 1st Marine Division (Reinforced), along with aerial and naval assets, as one axis in the start of the Allied counteroffensive against Japan in the PTO (see Map 4). On 10 January 1943, as the Japanese were planning Guadalcanal's evacuation, King first suggested taking the Admiralty Islands and avoiding another costly land battle at Rabaul by neutralizing and bypassing the bastion.

Admiral Chester W. Nimitz, CINCPAC and CINCPOA

Nimitz, after the Pearl Harbor attack, restored shaken American morale and confidence with organizational skill and use of cryptoanalysis to decipher IJN plans. Nimitz was the leading USN authority on submarines and was Chief, Bureau of Navigation, in 1939, when he experimented in the underway refuelling of large ships, which proved to be a key element to the USN success in the vast Pacific Ocean during the war. After promotion to CINCPAC and CINCPOA, Nimitz had a joint staff with Army, Navy and Marine Corps officers in every section while local SPA and SWPA operations were planned by Halsey's or MacArthur's staffs after a joint conference in Nouméa or Brisbane, respectively.

Nimitz was a graduate and staff officer at the Naval War College and after strategic scrutiny on 15 January 1943, he also considered and rejected assaulting Rabaul as too exorbitant. At this time, Nimitz wanted Halsey to move against Munda on New Georgia, the next big objective after Guadalcanal, and eventually neutralize the Japanese presence in the entire Solomon Islands area. On 29 March 1943, tasks and command relations for 'breaking the Bismarcks Barrier', an essential condition of MacArthur's New Guinea–Mindanao axis of advance (see Map 4), were established. Nimitz controlled ships, planes and ground forces of the Pacific Fleet and POA while allowing MacArthur and Halsey to direct operation in SWPA and SPA, respectively. Thus, MacArthur retained strategic command; Halsey obtained tactical control up the Solomon Island chain, and Nimitz allocated fleet units subject to JCS rulings. Overseen by Nimitz, the relationship between MacArthur and Halsey was harmonious, built on mutual respect.

Admiral William F. Halsey, Jr., CO, SPA

Halsey was appointed SPA commander during the Guadalcanal campaign's crucial phase from October 1942 to February 1943. He served aboard destroyers against German submarines during the First World War, became a naval aviator in 1935 at age 52, and commanded the USS *Saratoga* in 1940, also receiving vice admiral rank that year and placed in charge of the Pacific Aircraft Battle Force. He served in Naval Intelligence and as Naval Attaché to the Weimar Republic in Berlin in 1922. In April 1942, Halsey commanded TF-16, built around USS *Hornet* and *Enterprise*, which carried sixteen USAAF twin-engine B-25B Mitchell medium bombers that took off from the *Hornet*'s deck (on the 'Doolittle Tokyo Raid'). Missing the Midway battle for health reasons, he replaced his friend Vice Admiral Robert Ghormley as commander SPA, arriving in Nouméa on 18 October 1942 to resupply, re-energize and reinforce American forces on Guadalcanal. Halsey worked cohesively with Major General Millard F. Harmon, Jr., who was appointed CG of USAAFs, South Pacific, an area that was under USN command. On 2 February 1943, with Guadalcanal secured, Harmon, still working with Halsey, was promoted to lieutenant general, becoming CG, Army Air Forces, Pacific Ocean Areas (AAFPOA) in September 1944.

Admiral Isoroku Yamamoto, Commander Combined Imperial Japanese Fleet

Yamamoto led the IJN's defence of the Solomon Islands after Guadalcanal's evacuation in February 1943. He moved 200 carrier planes to Rabaul on New Britain and to Buin (Kahili) Airfield, on Bougainville, in order to attack (Operation I-GO) the expanding American installations on Guadalcanal and Tulagi in April 1943, as well as strengthening his new airfields at Munda on New Georgia and at Vila on Kolombangara Island, in anticipation of Halsey's Central Solomons campaign. On the morning of 18 April 1943, Yamamoto's personal bomber, taking him to Bougainville and another offshore islet base at Ballale, was shot down by US Army P-38 Lightning fighters flying from Henderson Field on Guadalcanal.

Japanese Generals in SWPA and the Solomon Islands

Lieutenant General Hitoshi Imamura was made commander of the IJA Eighth Area Army with HQ at Rabaul in late 1942 after leading the 16th Army in the NEI. This new Area Army comprised Adachi's 18th Army and the 17th Army, under Lieutenant General Harukichi Hyakutake, the latter now committed solely to the campaign on Guadalcanal, with his HQ at Rabaul in the summer of 1942. Imamura was tasked by Tojo to recapture Guadalcanal, and as a second priority to hold Buna. Allied bomber interdiction prevented major Japanese reinforcements from reaching and reinforcing the northern Papuan coastal garrisons. While commander of the Eighth Area Army, Imamura was promoted to general in 1943 and served with Vice Admiral Jinichi Kusaka at Rabaul.

On 9 November 1942, Lieutenant General Hatazō Adachi was given command of the newly formed IJA 18th Army for operations on New Guinea's northern coast from 1942 to 1945, initially with HQ at Rabaul, where he was subordinate under Imamura but then at Madang and Wewak after holding combat commands in China. Adachi and his senior staff came under Allied air attack while en route from Rabaul to Lae in the Battle of the Bismarck Sea but he survived. The American landings, led by MacArthur, at Aitape and Hollandia from 22 to 27 April 1944, isolated the majority of Adachi's forces, which became prone to food and ammunition shortages. Of Adachi's original 140,000 men, only 13,000 were alive at the war's end when he surrendered near Wewak to the Australians.

Admiral Mineichi Koga, Combined Fleet Commander after Yamamoto

After Yamamoto's death, Admiral Mineichi Koga commanded the Combined Fleet at Truk, being responsible for reinforcing Rabaul. Koga's Operation RO, ordered on 28 October 1943, was to repeat April's Operation I-GO. Koga sent 173 IJN carrier planes from Truk to Rabaul for a 1 November arrival to combine with Kusaka's Eleventh Air Fleet's 200 land-based planes to strike against Solomon Island-based Allied airfields and supply routes to interdict a forthcoming Halsey advance. Instead of an air offensive, Operation RO became an ineffective struggle, first to defend Rabaul from Kenney's 5th USAAF attacks and then to challenge Halsey's 1 November Bougainville landings. Koga's Kawanishi H8K flying boat

('Emily') crashed during a typhoon between the Palau Islands and Davao on Mindanao on 31 March 1944 as he was overseeing the withdrawal of the Combined Fleet from its Palau anchorage HQ.

Vice Admiral Jinichi Kusaka

A graduate of the IJN Academy, Kusaka served on cruisers and battleships. In November 1940, he was promoted to vice admiral after commanding a battleship and serving as commandant of the Naval Gunnery School. On 28 September 1942, he took command of the Eleventh Air Fleet, located at Rabaul. Throughout the Guadalcanal campaign, Kusaka's air units battled the 'Cactus Air Force' based at Henderson Field for control of Guadalcanal's skies, which eventually Allied Air Forces won, as well as supporting Japanese campaigns in New Guinea. In late December 1942, all naval forces in New Guinea and the Solomon Islands were newly combined into the Southeast Area Fleet with Kusaka in command, making him responsible for the Eighth Fleet and for all naval forces in the Bismarck Archipelago, Solomon Islands, and New Guinea. With little help from the Combined Fleet or IJA, Kusaka strengthened Rabaul's air defences and sped up Munda and Vila airfields' development on New Georgia and Kolombangara, respectively (see Map 2). He directed IJN ships and combat personnel fighting the Allies advancing up the Solomon Islands chain, in New Guinea, and in early 1944 against American forces invading western New Britain advancing towards Rabaul. He surrendered IJN forces at Rabaul to the Allies on 6 September 1945, along with General Imamura.

5th USAAF, AirSols and ComAirSols

Rabaul was situated between SWPA under MacArthur and SPA under Halsey. The plan to neutralize Rabaul by an aerial campaign (Operation CARTWHEEL, 1943–44) involved cooperation between the 5th USAAF under Kenney in SWPA, and AirSols, which was active from April 1943 to June 1944. AirSols absorbed the 'Cactus Air Force', the Allied air units in the Solomons during 1942–43, 13th USAAF and USN, USMC, RNZAF formations. The USN furnished thirteen land-based and fourteen carrier-based naval squadrons along with thirty-three USMC squadrons. ComAirSols (Commander, Aircraft, Solomons) directed the combat operations of all land-based air forces in the Solomons (AirSols) during Operation CARTWHEEL. The commanders were rotated among the branches such that Major General Ralph J. Mitchell, USMC, took over the command of all land-based planes in AirSols on 20 November 1943 from the USAAF's Brigadier General Nathan Twining, who, in turn, succeeded Rear Admiral Marc Mitscher. USAAF Major General Hubert Harmon (brother of USAAF Lieutenant General Millard F. Harmon, Jr.) succeeded Mitchell on 15 March 1944.

Japanese Forces at Fortress Rabaul

As Japanese HQ in Tokyo chose a policy of active defence in the Solomon Islands and offensive action along New Guinea's northern coast after February 1943's Guadalcanal evacuation, by October 1943, IJA assets in Rabaul, including almost all IJA aircraft, left for New Guinea, leaving the bastion's aerial defence to be conducted almost exclusively by the IJN under Kusaka. The Japanese had nearly 300 land-based aircraft stationed on Rabaul when the Allied aerial campaign to neutralize the bastion intensified, beginning in October 1943. An additional 300 IJN carrier aircraft from Truk's Combined Fleet were available for transfer to Rabaul as needed, the former 700 miles directly north in the eastern Caroline Islands (see Map 4). Truk, acquired as a League of Nations mandate from the Germans after the First World War, would itself begin undergoing USN carrier raids on 17–18 February 1944, temporally coinciding with Nimitz and Spruance's landings on Eniwetok in the western Marshall Islands.

Yamamoto's Operation I-GO commenced on 1 April 1943 and lasted through to 19 April, a day after Yamamoto's death. For Operation I-GO, the air contingents of four IJN aircraft carriers and the remaining Mitsubishi G3M Nell and G4M Betty bomber squadrons were sent to Rabaul from Truk, raising the operation's air strength at Rabaul to over 350 aircraft. Operation I-GO's target was new American airfields in the Russell Islands, north of recently abandoned Guadalcanal. The operation resulted in heavy IJN aircraft losses and minor damage to the American bases.

Rabaul's defence was based on close cooperation between IJA and IJN forces patrolling the skies over New Britain's Gazelle Peninsula. However, losses in IJA aircraft in the skies over New Guinea during 1942 to 1943 forced a change in Rabaul's defence as IJA aircraft were transferred from New Britain to Wewak and Hollandia, especially after the 5th USAAF August–September 1943 Wewak area raids. Rabaul's largest weakness was its lack of replacements in aircraft, pilots and supplies.

In October 1943, there were five operational airfields in New Britain's Gazelle Peninsula to protect Rabaul and Simpson Harbour. The two Australian airfields captured in early 1942 were at Lakunai and Vunakanau and initially had grass runways, which the Japanese improved. Lakunai Airfield, adjacent to Simpson Harbour with a 4,300 × 650ft runway of coral and sand, possessed ninety IJN fighter and ten bomber revetments, support buildings, and 2 miles of taxiways. Vunakanau Airfield's larger runway (5,200 × 750ft) had a concrete central section and had ninety fighter and sixty bomber revetments, with over 5 miles of taxiways. Rapopo Airfield, an IJA bomber base 14 miles southeast of Rabaul, had ninety bomber and ten fighter revetments. Tobera Airfield, 20 miles south of

Rabaul, was a fighter strip with seventy-five fighter and two bomber revetments. Rapopo and Tobera airfields were added by the Japanese in 1942–43 and given concrete runways (4,600 × 630ft and 3,600 × 100ft, respectively). Keravat Airfield, 13 miles southwest of Rabaul, had an unpaved runway due to drainage issues and was a substitute landing field.

The Japanese believed that if one of Rabaul's airfields was disabled by an Allied air attack the others would remain operational. Also, New Britain had other Japanese airfields to Rabaul's southwest at Cape Gloucester, Arawe, Gasmata, Talasea and Cape Hoskins. Kavieng Airfield (Map 2), situated on the northwestern end of New Ireland, as well as heavily garrisoned airfields at Buin and Bonis on southern and northern Bougainville, and on Buka Island, all contributed to Rabaul's air operational strategy.

Japanese radar installations throughout the Gazelle Peninsula and at Kavieng could detect Allied aircraft formations 150 miles away and single aircraft 60 miles away, providing an alert of impending raids but not an integrated air defence system. The IJA defending Rabaul was well equipped with AAA, 75mm guns, 20mm AA guns and numerous machine guns throughout the Gazelle Peninsula. The IJN had 12.7cm guns along with 12cm dual-purpose guns, 75mm guns and 25mm AA guns ringing Blanche Bay to Simpson Harbour's southeast.

(**Opposite, above**) General Douglas MacArthur, CG SWPA, points at a map in his Brisbane, Australia, office on 27 March 1944 as Admiral Chester Nimitz, CINCPAC and CINCPOA, looks on. MacArthur's initial tasks were to defend Australia, retake Papua, and oversee the Allied offensive to break the Japanese hold on the Bismarck Archipelago. Following victory in Papua in January 1943, MacArthur did not want Australian General Thomas Blamey (in charge of Allied Land Forces) to directly command American troops, so he requested Lieutenant General Walter Krueger be assigned to command 'Alamo Force', a codename for the newly activated US Sixth Army, which MacArthur directly controlled, thus bypassing Blamey. On 30 June 1943, Alamo Force landed on Woodlark Island and Kiriwina Island, the latter the largest of the Trobriand Islands (see Map 2), and rapidly built airfields there. Then, MacArthur began to move his Australian-American forces methodically up the coast of Northeastern New Guinea, capturing Lae, Salamaua and Finschhafen. In December 1943, with Allied supremacy on the Huon Peninsula assured, US Sixth Army (Alamo Force) was primarily involved in the many subsequent amphibious operations while the Australian troops were given secondary roles. (NARA)

(**Opposite, below**) Admiral William Halsey, Jr., ComSoPac (centre) with Commander Joseph Clifton, CO USS *Saratoga*'s fighter groups, in Espiritu Santo on 15 December 1943, after the successful USN carrier-borne aircraft raids on Rabaul of 5 and 11 November 1943. After the Japanese evacuation from Guadalcanal victory in early February 1943, Halsey led the ground and naval forces in the SPA through the Solomon Islands campaign, notably at New Georgia, and with the Third Marine Division's amphibious Bougainville invasion at Empress Augusta Bay on 1 November 1943, to construct Allied airfields at Cape Torokina to begin pounding Rabaul and other targets in the Japanese-controlled Bismarck Archipelago. He was instrumental in the USN and USMC rapid invasion and conquest of Emirau Island in the St Matthias group in 1944, with the construction of an airfield there to bomb Kavieng on New Ireland. (NARA)

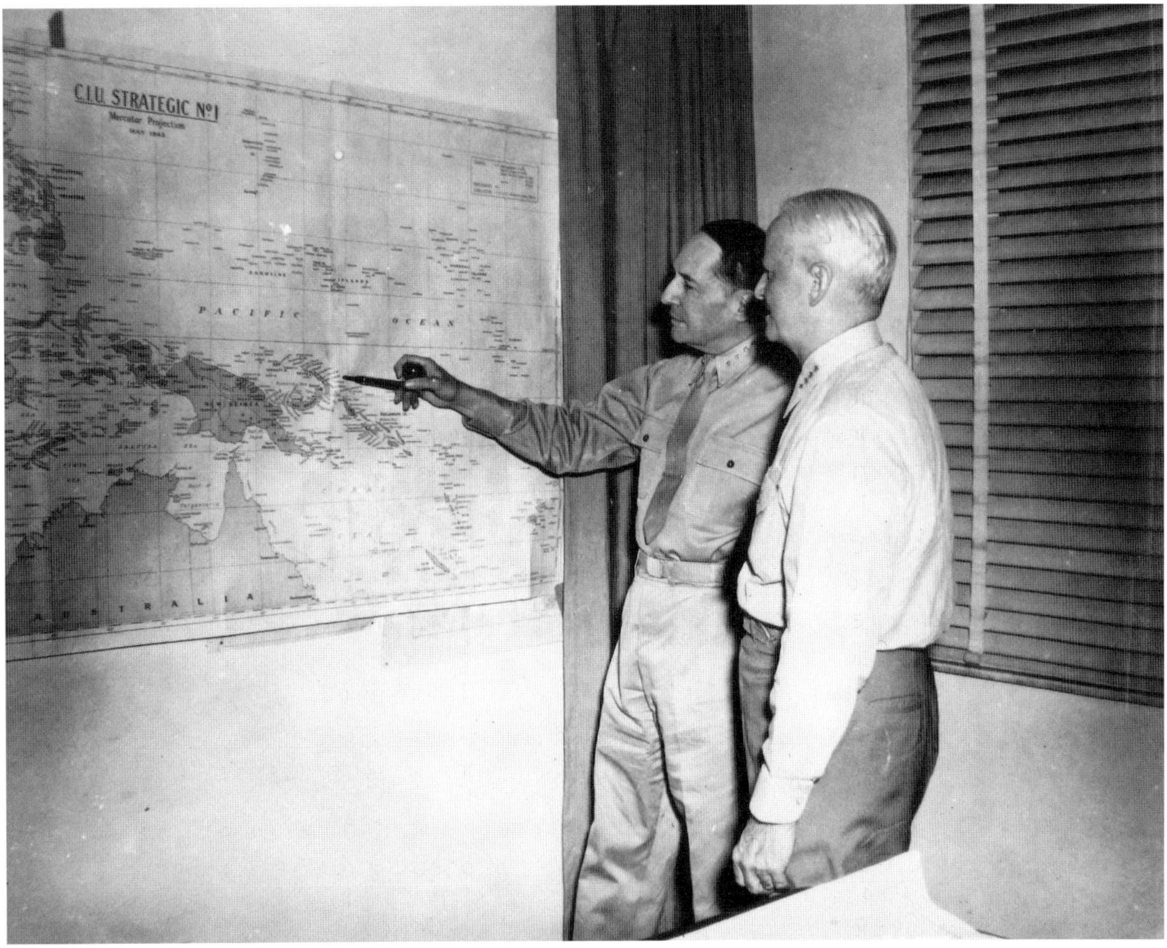
C.I.U. STRATEGIC Nº I
Mercator Projection
PACIFIC
OCEAN

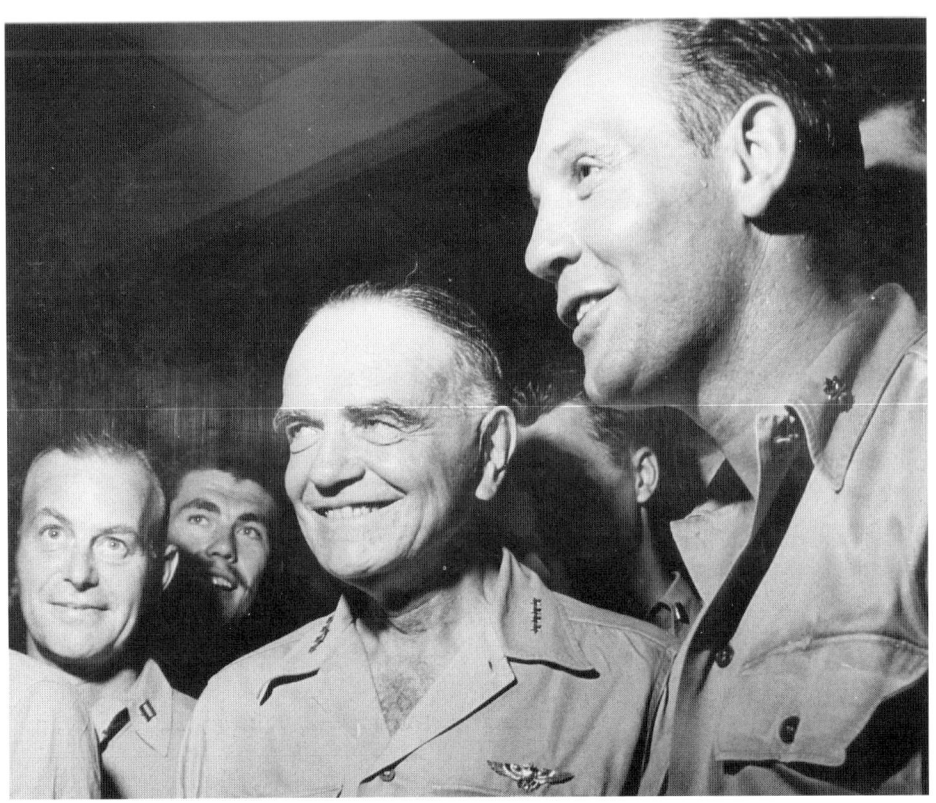

(**Opposite**) Lieutenant General George Kenney (right), 5th USAAF and Allied Air Forces CG in SWPA, stands and discusses plans with his deputy and forward New Guinea commander, Major Genral Ennis Whitehead, in Port Moresby. MacArthur, after arriving in Australia in March 1942, developed an antipathy to his air force commander, Lieutenant General George Brett, replacing him with then Major General Kenney, who reported on 30 July 1942. Whitehead assisted Kenney in setting up the initial airfields near Port Moresby and then eventually fifteen runways comprising the Dobodura complex inland and to Buna's south, creating an easier advanced bomber route, which did not require flight over the Owen Stanley Range to attack Rabaul, Lae and Salamaua as the Port Moresby fields' location necessitated. Whitehead facilitated the transport of some of the 32nd Division battalions in mid-October 1942 to Papua with Douglas C-47s. As Dobodura was too far from Lae and Salamaua for Allied fighters to reach, Kenney and Whitehead accepted an Allied reconnaissance report on a deserted gold miner's airstrip at Tsili Tsili near Marilinan, 40 miles inland from Lae and northwest of Wau. By 26 June, a new Allied fighter strip was operational. Whitehead was instrumental in planning and executing the 5th USAAF and RAAF attack at the Battle of the Bismarck Sea, which interdicted Japanese resupply of Lae in early March 1943 as well as destroying Lae-based Japanese aircraft on the ground. (NARA)

(**Above**) General George Kenney, CG Allied Far Eastern Air Force (left) and Brigadier General Paul Wurtsmith, the new CO of the 13th USAAF, discuss plans in 1945. In New Guinea, Kenney turned the 5th USAAF into a multidimensional unit including troop transport, supply and 'aerial artillery'. Wurtsmith enlisted in the USAAC in 1927 and was commissioned the following year, joining the 94th Pursuit Squadron. In December 1941, he commanded the 49th Pursuit Group defending Darwin, Australia, and was promoted to colonel in July 1942. During aerial combat over New Guinea, his fighter group downed more than ninety Japanese aircraft. On 11 November 1942, Wurtsmith took command of the 5th Fighter Group in New Guinea, being promoted in February 1943 to brigadier general. Kenney assigned Lieutenant Colonel Thomas Lynch and Captain Richard Bong, both at the time the top American fighter aces, to Wurtsmith's 5th Fighter Group staff. As CO 13th USAAF, Wurtsmith developed long-range fighter and bombardment tactics to strangle the Home Islands of raw materials. (NARA)

Lieutenant General Walter Krueger, CG US Sixth Army, with Major General Horace Fuller, CG 41st Infantry Division, at Hollandia on 12 May 1944 after the Allied victory there the previous month. MacArthur said of Krueger, 'He was swift and sure in attack; tenacious and determined in defence; modest and restrained in victory ... I don't know what he would have been in defeat because he was never defeated.' Krueger worked his way through the US Army, first as a private soldier fighting across the Luzon Plains during the Philippine Insurrection in 1898, earning a commission in 1901. Krueger served during Pershing's Mexican Punitive Expedition in 1916 and with the American Expeditionary Force in France during the First World War. After attending Fort Benning's Infantry School and commanding the 55th Infantry Division, he served in the Army War Plans Division and later as a corps commander. From February 1943 through to 1944, Krueger commanded Sixth Army from its Australian deployment to the recapture of Dutch New Guinea. His Sixth Army included I Corps' 32nd and 41st Divisions, the 1st Marine Division (under Army operational control), the 158th ('Bushmasters') Infantry Regiment, and the 503rd Parachute Infantry Regiment. The 24th Infantry and 1st Cavalry Divisions joined Sixth Army in May and July 1943, respectively. Fuller, a 1909 USMA graduate, commanded the 41st Infantry Division, comprising National Guardsmen from Idaho, Montana, Oregon, North Dakota and Washington. Due to a stalemate at Biak (see Map 5), Fuller requested relief of his command and with intervention by his former USMA classmate, Lieutenant General Eichelberger, Fuller was transferred to Burma, becoming Mountbatten's Deputy COS, SEAC. (NARA)

Lieutenant General Robert Eichelberger (left), Major General Frederick Irving, and Rear Admiral Daniel Barbey (far right), CO VII Amphibious Force. In the back are Colonel Frank Bowen and Brigadier General Clovis Byers. Eichelberger served in Siberia after the First World War, attended the Command and General Staff School in 1926, and knew MacArthur in 1935 when he was Secretary of the General Staff. MacArthur sent Eichelberger to Papua in late 1942 to lead the Australian-American effort there at the head of I Corps' 32nd Division and later the 41st Division. After capturing Buna and much recognition by the American press, Eichelberger was relegated back to Australia by MacArthur to retrain and refit I Corps for future Sixth Army New Guinea operations under Krueger. Rear Admiral Daniel Barbey arrived in SWPA in January 1943 and became one of the most successful amphibious commanders. MacArthur opined that he could not depend solely on air transport for the upcoming SWPA campaigns so Barbey established training bases and conducted the first amphibious operations in late June 1943, involving landings at Nassau Bay for the Lae-Salamaua campaign and the seizure of Kiriwina Island and Woodlark Island to secure airfields for operations against Rabaul. Barbey's VII Amphibious Force participated in MacArthur's landings along the northern coast of New Guinea, western New Britain and the Admiralty Islands. Brigadier General Clovis Byers (next to Barbey on the right) was another general wounded at Buna under Eichelberger. A USMA 1920 graduate, Byers, along with 77th Division staff officers, followed Eichelberger's I Corps to Australia in June 1942, playing an important role in the Biak campaign in Netherlands New Guinea in June 1944. Later, he became Eichelberger's Eighth Army's COS when its HQ was activated in New Guinea in August 1944. Major General Frederick Irving (next to Eichelberger) led the 24th Infantry Division during the Tanahmerah Bay invasion to seize Hollandia on 22 April 1944 and later with Major General Franklin Sibert's X Corps on Leyte. (NARA)

(**Above**) Major General William Rupertus, CG 1st Marine Division (left) discusses the 26 December 1943 invasion of Cape Gloucester with Colonel Julian Frisbie, CO 7th Marines, at the Oro Bay (see Map 3) embarkation site on 2 October 1943. Rupertus commanded the 1st Battalion, 4th Marines, in Shanghai under Japanese occupation in 1937. As brigadier general on Guadalcanal, he was the 1st Marine Division's ADC under Major General Alexander Vandegrift, becoming the division's CG on 8 July 1943, in charge of planning the New Britain campaign, under MacArthur and Krueger's operational control. The New Britain campaign was, at times, fierce, along with debilitating weather and disease. Frisbie's 7th Marines led the initial assault at Cape Gloucester, setting up a beachhead perimeter on 26 December 1943. His regiment remained in combat until relief by the 5th Marines on 15–18 January 1944. (NARA)

(**Opposite, above**) Rear Admiral Frederick C. Sherman (middle), CO of Task Force 38 during the 5 and 11 November 1943 carrier raids on Rabaul, is seen on the USS Saratoga, his flagship, on the latter date with Commander Joseph C. Clifton (right), CO of VF-12, Saratoga's fighter squadron, over Rabaul. Clifton's F6F Hellcat fighter escort downed twenty-four Japanese planes in the 11 November raid. (NARA)

(**Opposite, below**) Marine Major General Ralph Mitchell (left), ComAirSols from November 1943 to March 1944, and Marine Brigadier General Patrick Mulcahy (middle, with helmet), who commanded the 2nd Marine Air Wing of the 'Cactus Air Force'. In August 1943, Mulcahy moved from Guadalcanal to Munda Airfield on New Georgia to command air units operating from there. In September 1944, Mulcahy became CG, Aircraft, Fleet Marine Force. (NARA)

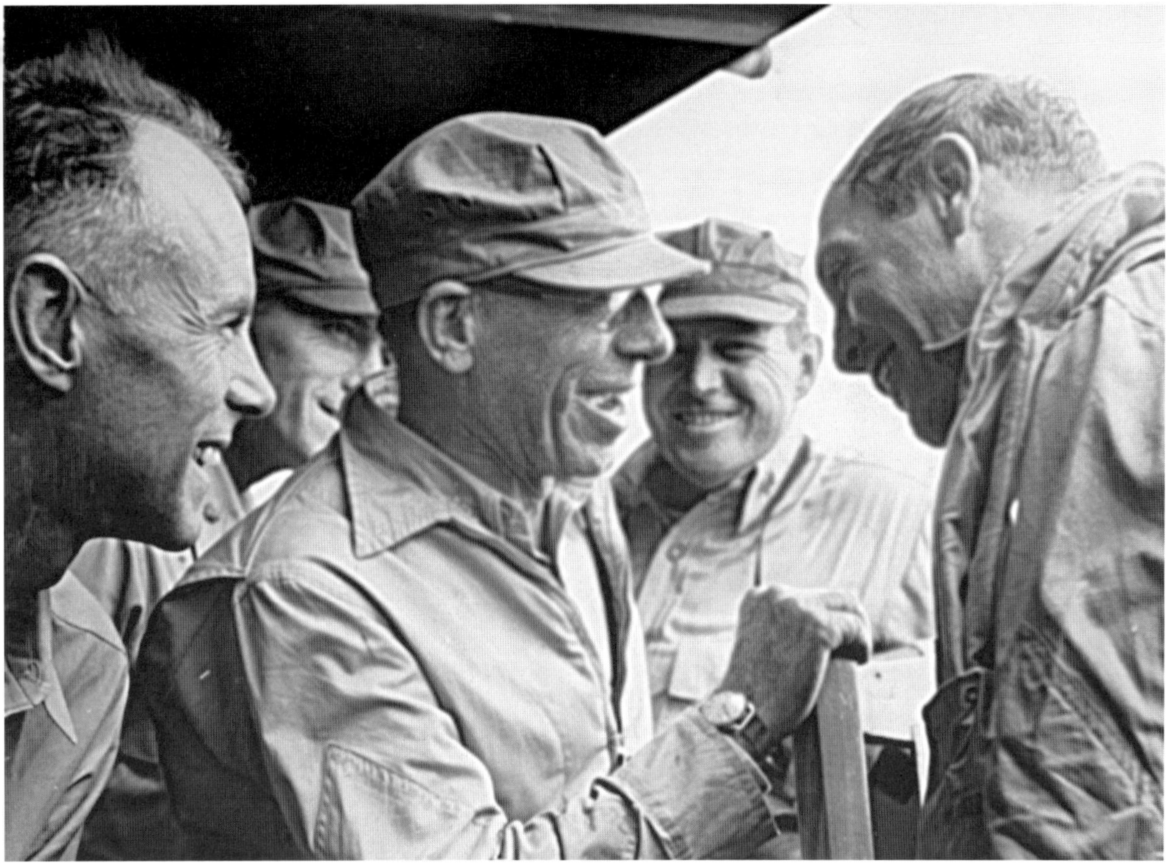

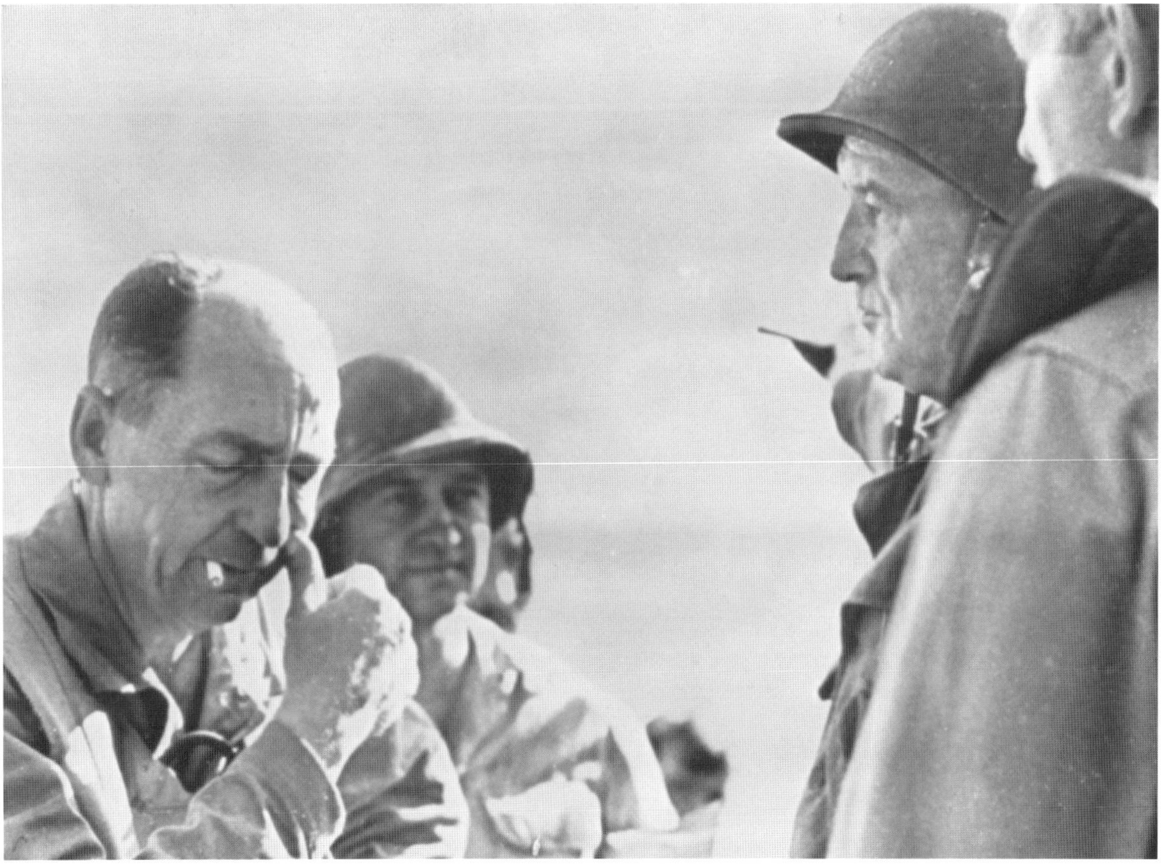

Major Paul 'Pappy' Gunn in the cockpit of his 5th USAAF 90th Bombardment Squadron/3rd Bombardment Group B-25C, *Pappy's 'Folly'*, with John 'Jack' Fox, the NAA senior technical representative in SWPA, holding a fuselage 0.50-calibre machine gun. This duo field modified the underperforming twin-engine A-20 Havoc and B-25 Mitchell, making them more destructive as low-level strafers that devastated Japanese shipping by removing the bombardiers and placing multiple forward-firing MGs in each aircraft. The A-20 carried extra fuel tanks in its forward bomb bay and up to forty small parafrag bombs in the rear compartment. In June 1942, Gunn made preliminary drawings of a B-25 that would have the low-level strafing capabilities of the A-20 Havoc as well as skip-bombing potential. The aim was a skip bomber that could overwhelm Japanese deck AA defences as the plane swooped in low to drop its bombs. Gunn joined the USN in 1918, trained as an aviation mechanic, and became an enlisted pilot, retiring in 1939 as a chief petty officer and flight instructor. He then became the operations manager and chief pilot for the Philippine Air Lines. After the Japanese attack on the Philippines, the USAAC requisitioned his planes and he was commissioned as an army captain; being older than 40, he was given the moniker 'Pappy', before escaping to Australia. (*Author's collection*)

Admiral Isoroku Yamamoto (standing left) and Vice Admiral Jinichi Kusaka (seated to Yamamoto's left) supervise IJN air operations at Rabaul for Operation I-GO from 1 to 16 April 1943. Yamamoto launched the Japanese air offensive against Allied forces in the Solomon Islands and New Guinea, shortly after the February 1943 Japanese evacuation of Guadalcanal. The offensive was aimed against Allied ships, aircraft and land installations in the southeast Solomon Islands and New Guinea locales, such as Port Moresby, Oro Bay and Milne Bay, to retard the Allied offensives into the Central Solomon Islands and to prepare a new set of defences in response to recent defeats at Guadalcanal, Buna, Gona and Wau, and the early March 1943 Battle of the Bismarck Sea. Yamamoto halted the operation under the belief that it was a success but it did not delay any Allied preparations for future advances. Yamamoto was killed shortly thereafter, on 18 April, while travelling to congratulate his IJN units that had participated in the operation. (Author's collection)

Admiral Mineichi Koga commanded the IJN Combined Fleet stationed at Truk after Yamamoto's death. In that capacity, Koga sent aircraft and warships to reinforce Rabaul's garrison, which precipitated Halsey's TF38 carrier aircraft raids of 5 and 11 November 1943, especially after the failed 1/2 November IJN surface engagement to dislodge the American landings at Empress Augusta Bay. (Author's collection)

General Hitoshi Imamura, photographed at Rabaul's 11th Division HQ in May 1945. Imamura was the GOC of the IJA Eighth Area Army headquartered at Rabaul and commanded IJA forces within Japan's Southeast Area, which included the IJA 17th Army in the Solomon Islands and the 18th Army on New Guinea. He remained on New Britain as senior Japanese officer after the large island was isolated, and surrendered the bastion to the Australians in September 1945. He was tried by an Australian military court in May 1947 for war crimes and sentenced to imprisonment for ten years at Sugamo Prison in Tokyo. (AWM)

IJA 18th Army CG Hatazō Adachi (left) surrenders to the AIF 6th Division at Cape Wom, near Wewak, on 13 September 1945. On 9 November 1942, Adachi was appointed CG IJA 18th Army on Rabaul to wage the New Guinea ground war. The 18th Army contained the IJA 20th and 41st Divisions, both of which arrived safely to New Guinea; however, the IJA 51st Division, including Adachi and his senior staff, came under Allied air attack attempting to reinforce Lae at the Battle of the Bismarck Sea, 2–5 March 1943. Only 2,427 men of the division were rescued, while 3,664 were lost at sea. MacArthur's Allied landings at Aitape, Hollandia and Tanamerah Bay essentially isolated the vast majority of Adachi's forces. By the end of the war, of Adachi's original 140,000 men, only 13,000 survived. He was tried for war crimes and on 12 July 1947, he was sentenced to life imprisonment, but committed suicide two months later on Rabaul. (AWM)

Brigadier General Hanford MacNider, the first American general to be wounded at Buna, later returned to the Philippines as CO, 158th Infantry Regiment ('Bushmasters'), an Arizona National Guard unit that participated in the combat at Arawe, New Britain, from mid-December 1943 to late January 1944. MacNider was Assistant Secretary of War from 1925 to 1928 and served in both world wars, being awarded three DSC medals, among other citations. *(NARA)*

(**Above**) Major Archibald Roosevelt (second from left), the son and fifth child of the late President Theodore Roosevelt, peers over offensive plans with other American officers at Nassau Bay, 10 miles south of the Japanese base at Salamaua along Huon Bay, south of the Huon Peninsula, in July 1943. Roosevelt, a wounded First World War veteran, commanded the 3rd Battalion, 162nd Infantry Regiment, 41st Infantry Division, at the hotly contested ridge line northwest of Tambu Bay, which was referred to as 'Roosevelt Ridge' in reports to Allied HQ and on maps. On 12 August, Roosevelt was wounded by a Japanese grenade in the same knee that had been injured in the First World War. He returned to active service in late 1944. (*NARA*)

(**Opposite, above**) Brigadier General Lemuel Shepherd, ADC 1st Marine Division, studies maps at Borgen Bay on Cape Gloucester on the Natamo Front on 26 January 1944. Shepherd, a 5th Marines' veteran in France in 1917, commanded the 9th Marines in March 1942 as part of the newly forming 3rd Marine Division. He was promoted to brigadier general in July 1943. In March 1944, he was awarded a Legion of Merit for meritorious command of operations in the Borgen Bay area. Shepherd became the twentieth person to be appointed Marine Corps Commandant. (*NARA*)

(**Opposite, below**) Colonel William Whaling, CO 1st Marines, with Captain George Hunt (middle) and Lieutenant William Watts (right) going over maps on Cape Gloucester on 26 December 1943. Intelligence reports estimated two full Japanese infantry battalions defending the aerodrome so Whaling delayed his infantry attack until 1100 on 28 December in order to bring forward two additional platoons of M4 medium tanks, which aided in reducing a Japanese strongpoint consisting of mutually supporting bunkers, manned rifle trenches supported by 75mm regimental guns, land mines and barbed wire. Whaling, an enlisted Marine, received a field commission during the First World War. He organized a scout sniper unit while a 1st Marine Division colonel on Guadalcanal and was CO, 29th Marines, on Okinawa in Major General Lemuel Shepherd's 6th Marine Division. (*NARA*)

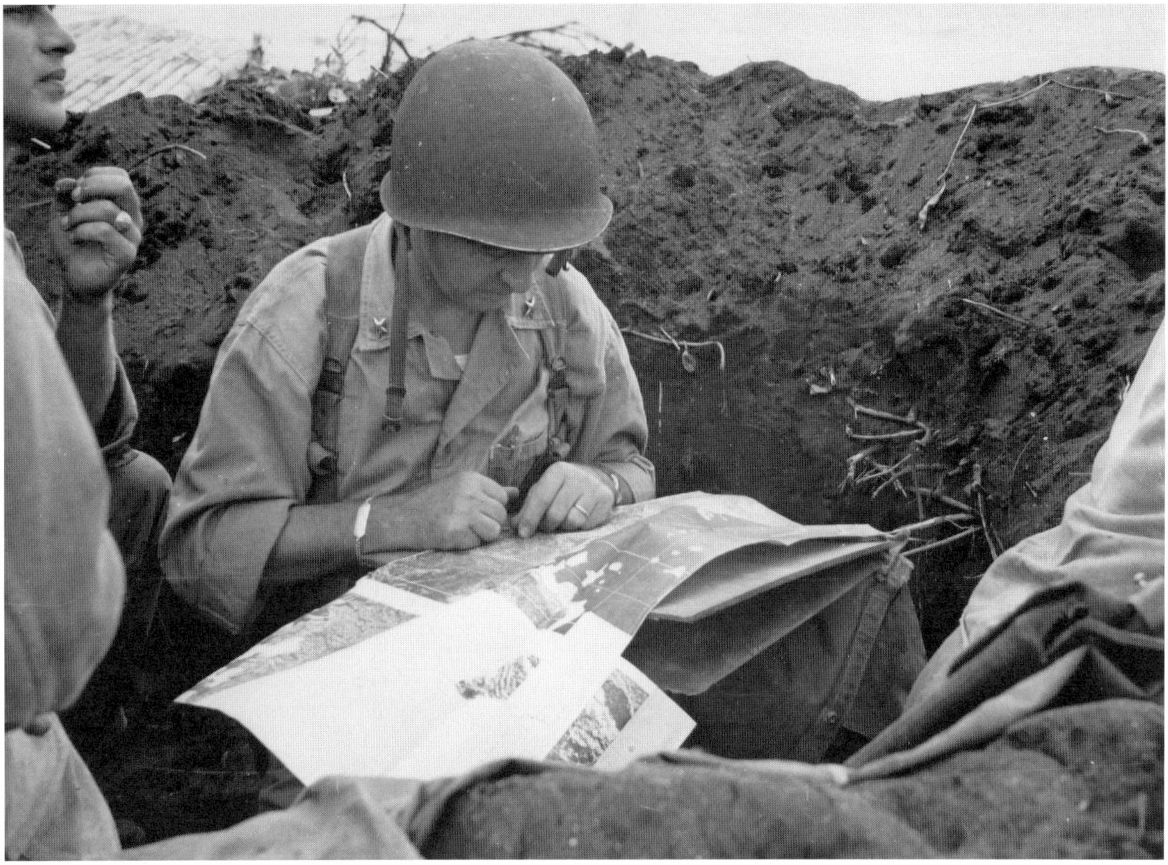

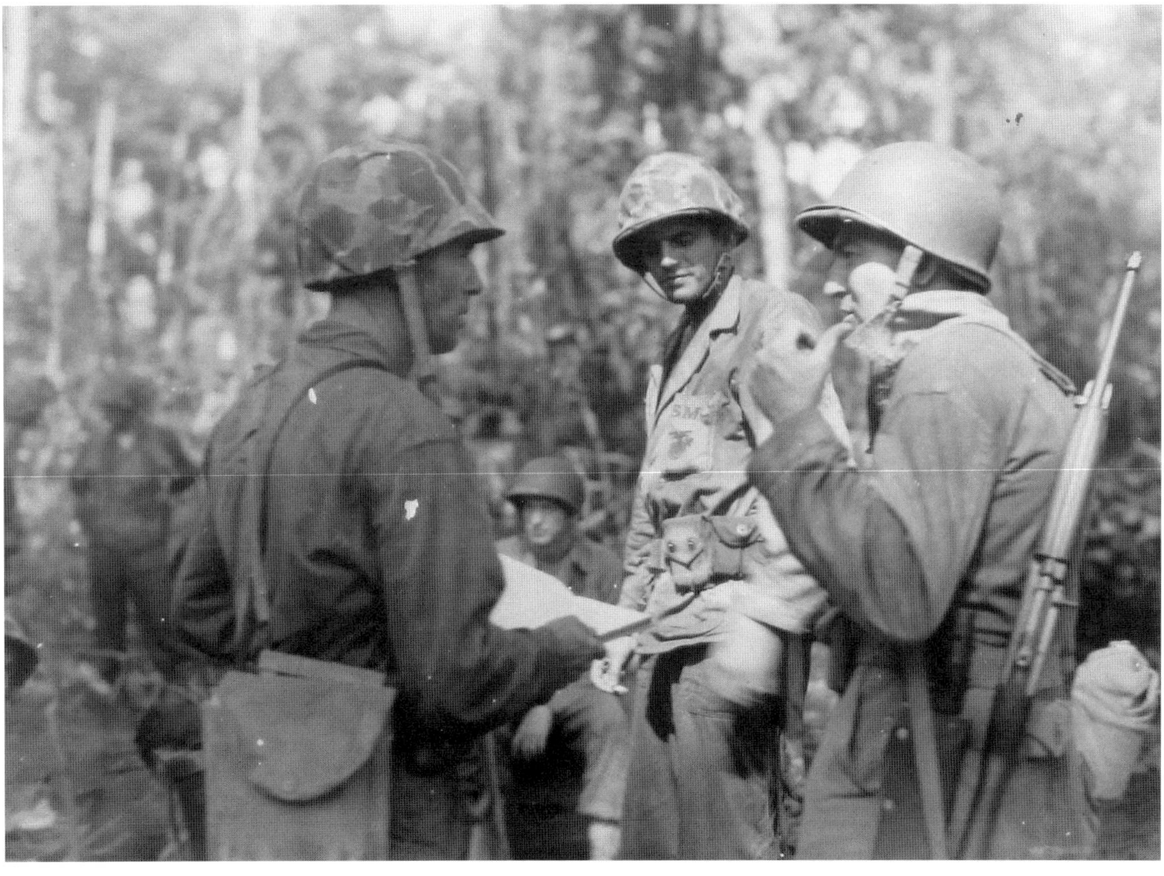

(**Above**) Colonel John Selden (left), CO 5th Marines, with Lieutenant Commander Richard Forsythe, USN MO, 5th Marines, stand in front of a destroyed Japanese aircraft at the Cape Gloucester airfield, captured on 29 December 1943. Selden worked closely with Brigadier General Shepherd on the Natamo Front at Borgen Bay in January 1944. In October 1942, Selden was transferred to the staff of the newly activated IMAC in New Caledonia and later participated in the Guadalcanal campaign. (NARA)

(**Opposite**) Colonel Harold Rosecrans (right), CO 17th Marines (Engineer), with Captain Francis Cooper (left), a regimental staff officer, on Cape Gloucester on 31 December 1943. During the Guadalcanal campaign, Lieutenant Colonel Rosecrans commanded the 2nd Battalion, 5th Marines, which along with Lieutenant Colonel Merritt Edson's 1st Marine Raider Battalion, amphibiously assaulted Tulagi Island, on 7 August 1942, and captured it the next day. On 21 January 1943, Rosecrans took command of the newly activated 17th Marines (Engineer) and was present at the November 1943 Goodenough Island meeting of MacArthur, Krueger and Rupertus to go over logistics for the 26 December 1943 Cape Gloucester assault. (NARA)

(**Right**) Lieutenant Colonel Lewis 'Chesty' Puller, XO 7th Marines, gives instructions on 28 January 1944 to Major William Piper for a two-week patrol into enemy territory on New Britain. Puller was a legendary Marine veteran of four Second World War campaigns, Korea, and pre-Second World War expeditionary service in China, Nicaragua and Haiti. He was one of the most decorated Marines and the only one to be awarded the Navy Cross five times for heroism and gallantry in action, as well as a DSC. At Cape Gloucester, he won his fourth Navy Cross. The 7th Marines rejoined the 1st Marine Division on 18 September 1942 on Guadalcanal, with Puller commanding the 1st Battalion and winning his third Navy Cross there. After Guadalcanal, he became XO, 7th Marines. On Cape Gloucester, when two battalion COs were wounded, Puller took over their units and moved through heavy machine-gun and mortar fire to reorganize them for an attack to take a fortified position. He was promoted to colonel on 1 February 1944, taking over the 1st Marines for the rest of the campaign. (NARA)

(**Opposite, above**) Lieutenant Colonel Thomas Hughes, CO 4th Battalion, 11th Marines (Artillery), stands by a 105mm howitzer and holds two artillery shell casings that were ripped apart after a Japanese air attack in January 1944. On 16 February, Hughes became the regimental XO. The 'Damp Flat', a swamp situated between and inland of the two Yellow landing beaches to the west of Silimati Point, Target Hill and Borgen Bay, posed a logistical problem for the 11th Marines. After landing from LSTs on Yellow Beaches 1 and 2 on 26 December, the artillerymen had to move their heavy ordnance and equipment through a 400-yard swamp to get into position to support the drive further west towards the aerodrome. Improvising, the howitzer crews used amphibious tractors for the first time as prime movers to cross the deep swamp. (NARA)

(**Opposite, below**) Major Gregory 'Pappy' Boyington, a Marine ace, instructs his VMF-214 'Black Sheep' Squadron's pilots about the initial AirSols fighter sweep on the Rabaul raid on 17 December 1943, a campaign lasting until 1 May 1944. AirSols aircraft were based from Guadalcanal to Bougainville. During the 17 December first AirSols strike, eighty aircraft under Boyington, comprising USN F6F Hellcats, Marine F4U Corsairs and RNZAF P-40 Kittyhawks, took off from airfields on Munda and Barakoma on New Georgia and Vella Lavella, respectively (see Map 2), and refuelled at Bougainville's Cape Torokina airstrip, deemed operational on 10 December, to reach Rabaul and return with reasonable reserves. The Allied pilots noted that Rabaul AA was heavy and accurate, more so than observed over the Japanese bases in the Solomon Islands; however, the tally for the 17–28 December raids was forty Japanese planes destroyed at a cost of fourteen AirSols aircraft. On the 3 January 1944 AirSols' Rabaul raid, Simpson Harbour had six destroyers, four submarines, thirty cargo ships and hundreds of barges. There were nearly 300 Japanese planes on four of Rabaul's airfields. During this 3 January raid, Boyington was shot down over Rabaul after making his twenty-sixth 'kill', tying him with ace Eddie Rickenbacker's First World War record. Boyington spent the rest of the war as a POW. Boyington would receive the Medal of Honor for his aerial combat score. His 'Black Sheep' squadron, VMF-214, downed 127 Japanese aircraft over the Solomons. (NARA)

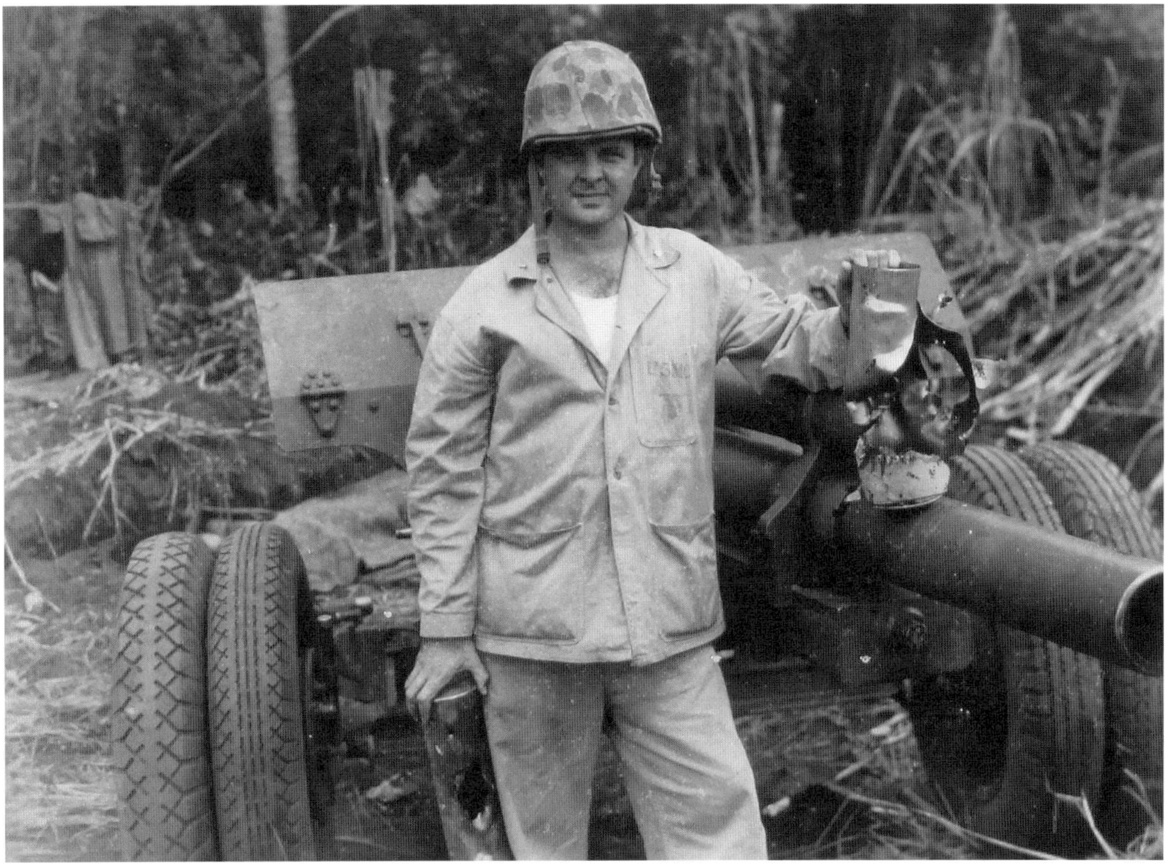

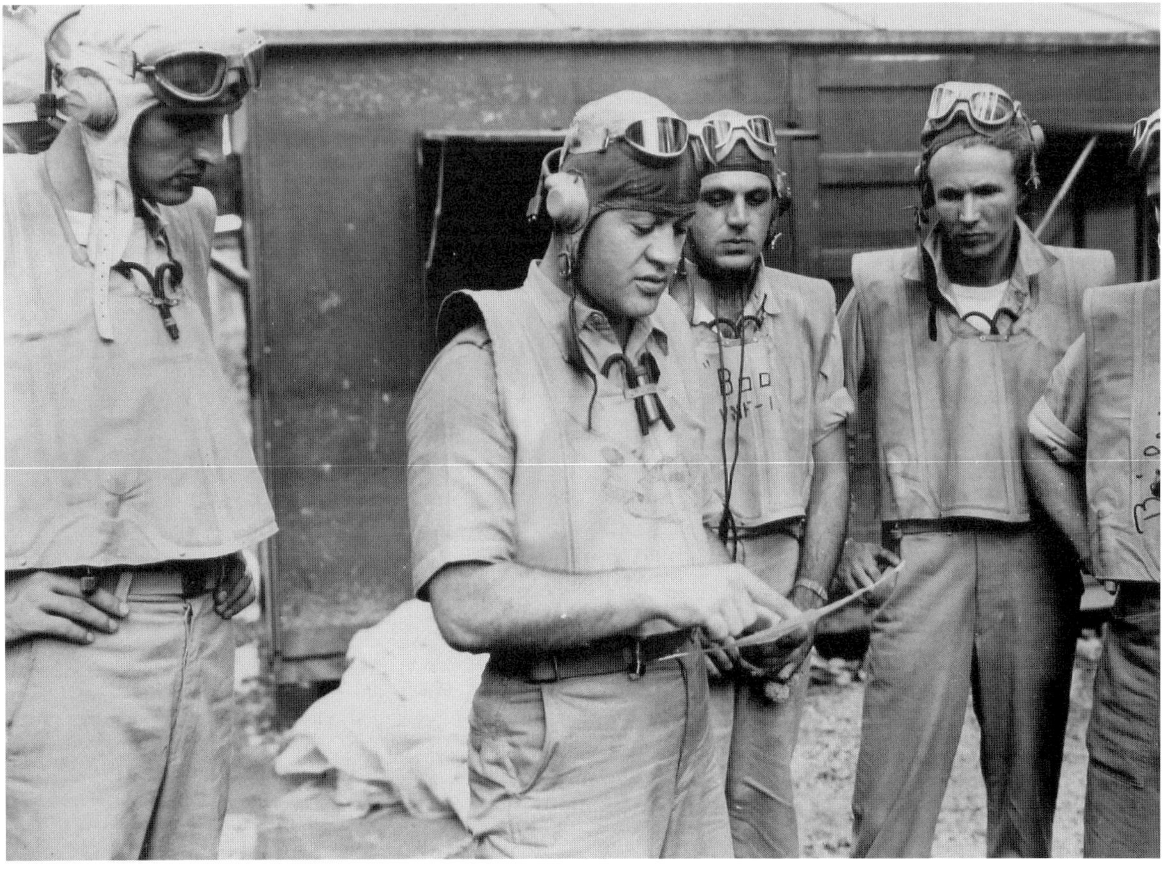

Marine Major Joseph Foss stands beside his land-based Grumman F4F Wildcat fighter, *The Sioux Chief*. Foss; a native of Sioux Falls, South Dakota, downed twenty-six enemy planes in combat flying the Marine F4F, becoming the Marines' highest-scoring ace during the Guadalcanal and SPA campaigns. Despite its extra rear weight and limited maximal ceiling (24,000 feet), the Wildcat could outdive the more manoeuvrable Mitsubishi A6M2 Reisen Zero. The F4F's six wing-mounted 0.50-inch calibre machine guns were vastly superior against Japanese fighters' ordnance. Foss was stricken with malaria and was sent to Australia for treatment. On 18 May 1943, President Roosevelt presented Captain Foss with the Medal of Honor, and he was promoted to major. He took command of Marine Fighter Squadron 115 (VMF-115), equipped with Vought F4U-1 Corsairs, which were stationed on 2 May 1944 at a new base at Emirau Island in the St Matthias group in the Bismarck Archipelago, flying combat missions the next day. Colonel Charles Lindbergh (a USAAC Reserve rank from 1927) visited Foss's squadron, flying four combat missions with VMF-115 from 26 to 30 May. Foss would become governor of his home state. (NARA)

Marine Captain Wallace Sigler, XO of a night-fighter squadron, VMF-(N)-542, stands by his plane in May 1944. Previously, he won an Air Medal and DFC for shooting down five Japanese planes and one probable in 1943 to become an ace as part of the 'Wolfpack Squadron', flying F4U Corsairs and F6F Hellcats from Guadalcanal's Henderson Field from February to November 1943. (NARA)

(**Above**) Lieutenant Richard Bong, a 5th USAAF fighter ace, in New Guinea on 11 March 1943. Arriving in SWPA in November 1942, Bong flew with the 9th Fighter Squadron, 49th Fighter Group. The 9th Fighter Squadron was one of two units in the 5th USAAF selected for conversion from the Curtiss P-40 Warhawk to the Lockheed P-38 Lightning, which were equipped with the newer twin-engine aircraft in January 1943. On 26 July 1943, Bong shot down four Japanese fighters over Lae, earning him a DSC and promotion to captain the next month. On 12 April 1944, he shot down his twenty-sixth and twenty-seventh Japanese aircraft, surpassing Eddie Rickenbacker's American record of twenty-six credited victories in the First World War. Soon thereafter, he was promoted to major. After an assignment to the Fifth Fighter Command (V FC) staff, under Wurtsmith, as an advanced gunnery instructor Bong was granted permission to go on missions but not to seek combat. Bong was America's greatest ace in any war, flying more than 300 missions to record his forty victories, all shot down with the Lockheed P-38 Lightning. His final rank was major and MacArthur presented him with the Medal of Honor in December 1944. Bong died testing a Lockheed P-80 jet fighter in California on 6 August 1945, at the age of 24. (*NARA*)

(**Opposite, above**) Captain Thomas Lynch at his New Guinea airbase by his Lockheed P-38 Lightning in March 1943. After joining the USAAC in 1940, Lynch flew the Bell P-39 Airacobra with the 39th Pursuit Squadron. That squadron was deployed to Port Moresby in early 1942. Lynch downed three Japanese planes flying the Airacobra, and in June 1942, the now redesignated 39th Fighter Squadron was selected to be the first 5th USAAF squadron to be re-equipped with the new Lockheed P-38 Lightning. Lynch had two more victories in late December 1942 to become an ace, shooting down two Nakajima Ki-43 Oscars over the Buna beachhead. He became commander of the 39th Fighter Squadron on 24 March 1943 after claiming a Mitsubishi Zero during the Battle of the Bismarck Sea early in that month. By October 1943, Lynch was the squadron's leading ace, with sixteen victories among five other squadron aces. In January 1944, he was assigned to V FC alongside fellow top-scoring ace, Richard Bong. On 28 February, Lynch covered Bong while he destroyed a Japanese transport possibly carrying senior officers on the Wewak runway. After this mission, Lynch was promoted to lieutenant colonel. He claimed two more downed Japanese planes on 3 March and his twentieth and last victory on 5 March. On 8 March 1944, Lynch and Bong strafed barges in Aitape harbour. Lynch's P-38 was hit in the engine by enemy AA fire and he bailed out too close to the ground for his parachute to deploy. (*NARA*)

(**Below**) 1st Marines' Major Martin Rockmore (left), Operations Officer, Lieutenant Colonel Harold Harris, XO (centre), and Captain George Hunt (right), Intelligence Officer, go over a map on a captured Japanese crate on Cape Gloucester on 30 December 1943. A lot of Japanese supplies and booty were captured at the Cape Gloucester aerodrome the day before this photograph was taken. (*NARA*)

(**Above**) At the command post of the 1st Battalion, 7th Marines, Lieutenant Colonel John Weber talks on the telephone with map on his knees. Colonel Kenshiro Katayama, CO of the IJA 141st Infantry Regiment, moved his forces to the Natamo area and assumed command of all Japanese combat troops in the Borgen Bay zone of action on 31 December 1943, and he was to hurl his forces at the Marine perimeter on 3 January 1944, situated on Target Hill, which was in the 1st Battalion, 7th Marines' zone of action. (NARA)

(**Opposite, above**) Marine Lieutenant Richard Greenwood (left) and Army Sergeant Kitoa Yamoda (right), a Japanese-American *Nisei* interpreter, go over a situation map on 27 December 1943, two days before the Cape Gloucester aerodrome capture. Seven *Nisei* soldiers served with the 1st Marine Division under Sergeant Jerry Yoshito Shibata. In 1944, MacArthur had in the Allied Translator and Interpreter Section (ATIS) 150 *Nisei* interpreters, receiving 4,000 Japanese POWs and translating 6,000 captured documents. Lieutenant General George Kenney was an avid consumer of ATIS reports as well as 'crash intelligence' from downed Japanese aircraft. For each combat operation, ATIS sent teams of enlisted *Nisei* led by Caucasian officers, sharing front-line hardships with the combat troops. Some fell ill with malaria, dysentery and other hazards of the tropics; some were killed in action or wounded. In addition, *Nisei* translators constantly risked being mistaken for the enemy and were regularly assigned bodyguards. For the Cape Gloucester landing, Moffett Ishikawa from California would meet with different units and tell them, 'Take a good look at me!' Ironically, the first *Nisei* interpreter to perish, Sergeant Ken Omura of Seattle, who served with the ATIS from September 1942, was not killed by enemy or friendly fire, but drowned on 19 March 1944 in the Admiralties' invasion. (NARA)

(**Below**) *Nisei* members of the US Sixth Infantry Division language team look over captured Japanese weapons at Arawe on New Britain on 28 January 1944, after coming ashore with the 112th Cavalry RCT on 15 December 1943. The team chief was Sergeant Yukitaka Terry Mizutari, a Hawaiian-born *Nisei* (second from right), while Sergeant Harry Fukuhara (left) holds a captured Japanese officer's *Samurai* sword. (*NARA*)

(**Above**) US Army amphibious engineers Private First Class Edward Andy (left), of the Yakima or Yakama Nation Confederated Tribes from Toppenish, WA, and Sergeant Roland Black, of the Quileute tribe of La Push, WA, on the way to the Arawe invasion at southwestern New Britain on 15 December 1943. Other Native Americans serving in SWPA included the Navajo, O'odham Pawnee and Pima. (NARA)

(**Opposite, above**) Navajo Indian Marine 'Code Talkers' of the 1st Marine Division kneel in their trench on Cape Gloucester. About 540 Navajos served as Marines, with approximately 400 trained 'Code Talkers' to send encrypted messages containing classified information in the Navajo language, preventing the Japanese from deciphering radio transmissions to discover operational plans. The Japanese never broke any of their coded messages. (NARA)

(**Below**) Soldiers of the 158th Infantry Regiment ('Bushmasters') in Krueger's Sixth Army await the signal to attack following the lifting of an artillery barrage and aerial bombardment during the Arawe operation from mid-December 1943 through to January 1944. The 158th IR ('Bushmasters') was made up predominantly of Mexican-Americans and members of the Pima and Navajo tribes from Arizona, as the regiment was a former Arizona National Guard Unit. As part of the Panama Mobile Force in 1942, the 158th IR was ordered to prepare for transfer to Australia in November 1942 to join US Sixth Army. Company G, 158th IR, embarked for Arawe on 15 December 1943 and was soon joined by the remaining battalions to begin combat duties after sailing from Finschhafen on the Huon Peninsula. (*NARA*)

(**Above**) An Australian RAAF Signals sergeant exits from a previous Japanese pillbox that was built into the root of a tree on Los Negros in the Admiralty Islands, near Momote Airfield on 23 March 1944. He carries his SMLE bolt-action rifle, the common weapon among British and Commonwealth forces. P-40 Kittyhawks of RAAF 76 and 77 Squadrons flew from Momote Airfield at the eastern end of the island soon after the 29 February 1944 invasion. (*NARA*)

(**Opposite, below**) US Army pilots are briefed by a Marine officer (centre) standing in front of a P-38 Lightning. The Army pilots were going to drop supplies from L5 Sentinel light aircraft to Marines of the 1st and 5th Regiments led by Lieutenant Colonel Puller on a search-and-destroy mission that began on 30 January 1944. B-17s from Dobodura proved inadequate to parachute supplies accurately to the Marine inland patrols. US Army LCMs and USN LCTs were also instrumental in getting supplies and heavy ordnance to support the more distant Marine movements, such as at Talasea on the eastern end of the Willaumez Peninsula. *(NARA)*

(**Above**) Marine Sergeant Theodore Cogswell, a Silver Star recipient as a corporal for heroism on Guadalcanal, holds a Japanese landmine that he unearthed on the track that the Marines moved inland on towards Talasea Airfield on 7 March 1944 in pursuit of Japanese General Matsuda's retreating forces. As if the muddy terrain was not tough enough to slow the advancing Marine riflemen and occasional M4 tank, landmines needed meticulous removal by Marines such as Cogswell to clear the path. *(NARA)*

(**Above**) US Signal Corps photographers attached to the US 41st Division film the American shelling of the ridge at Dot Inlet from atop 'Roosevelt Ridge' on 22 August 1944. US 41st Infantry Division troops landed at Nassau Bay in early July 1943 and began a drive north along the coast. By mid-July, the US 162nd Infantry Regiment came up against strong Japanese forces along a ridge overlooking Tambu Bay, which was later referred to as 'Roosevelt Ridge' after the regiment's 3rd Battalion CO. Over the course of July and August, the 162nd IR made several attempts to capture the ridge. (*NARA*)

(**Opposite, above**) Marine Private First Class George C. Miller shoulders the barrel of a M1917 Browning 0.30-inch calibre, water-cooled medium machine gun on Cape Gloucester in January 1944, after nineteen days of combat against the 2,500 to 3,000 Japanese defenders at the western end of New Britain. Miller's unit was instrumental in beating back the Japanese counterattack at Hill 660, near Borgen Bay, which was the last vantage point from which the Japanese could interfere with landing operations at the Yellow beaches. (*NARA*)

(**Opposite, below**) Four 1st Division Marines man a 0.30-inch calibre, water-cooled Browning M1917 medium machine gun in the jungle at Hill 660 on Cape Gloucester. The two other Marines have a 0.45-inch calibre Thompson submachine gun (left foreground) and an M1 0.3-inch-calibre carbine (right background), respectively. On 13 January 1944, the 3rd Battalion, 7th Marines clawed their way up Hill 660 against a determined Japanese machine-gun company, a 75mm gun crew and a company of IJA infantry. The 3rd Battalion gained the crest of the hill by 1830 hours on 14 January during a rainstorm and dug in. Not until 0530 hours on 16 January did the Japanese make any real effort to dispute the possession of Hill 660. This was in the form of a vociferous *banzai* attack by two companies of the IJA 141st IR. Lieutenant Colonel Henry Buse's 3rd Battalion Marines used machine guns, small arms, and 60mm and 81mm mortar fire to break up the attack, leaving 110 Japanese soldiers dead. (*NARA*)

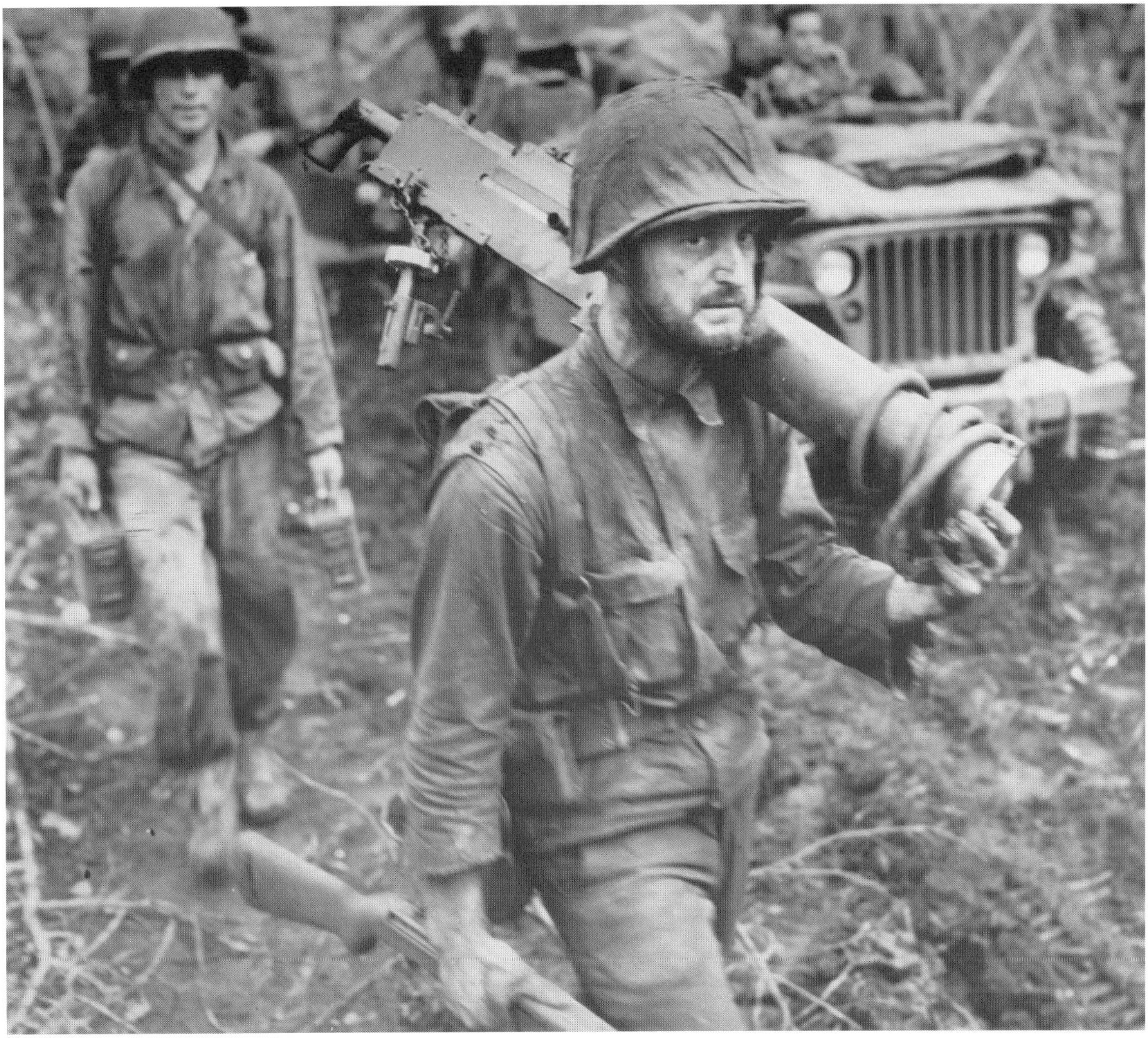

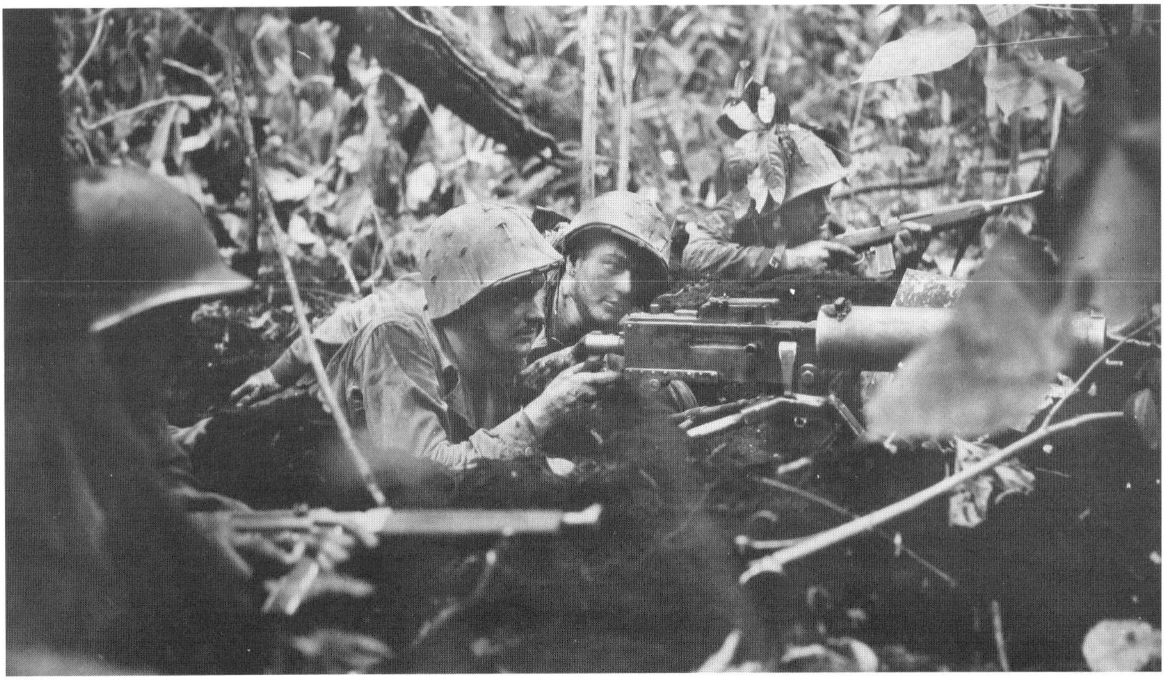

A Marine engineer, armed with his M9 'bazooka' or rocket launcher, marches along the muddy New Britain terrain. His engineer unit blasted several Japanese pillboxes on 3 January 1944, days after the Cape Gloucester aerodrome was captured by the 1st Marines on 29 December 1943. The bazooka, a nickname for a portable, recoilless AT rocket launcher, was among the first generation of rocket-propelled AT weapons used in infantry combat. Using a solid-propellant rocket for propulsion, it allowed an HE shaped charge to be delivered against armoured vehicles, machine-gun nests and fortified bunkers at ranges beyond that of a standard thrown grenade. In late 1943, a 2.36-inch rocket type was developed for the newly standardized M9 rocket launcher. (NARA)

A USN sailor mans his twin 0.50-inch calibre Browning machine guns in a rotating turret aboard a PT boat off the coast of New Guinea in 1943. These swift plywood craft played a vital role in interdiction of Japanese barge traffic off New Guinea and along the coast of western and central New Britain. They attacked Japanese seamen and troops that had abandoned their sinking IJN destroyers and transports at the Battle of the Bismarck Sea in early March 1943. (NARA)

Sergeant Vincent Zekas, 5th USAAF engineer/gunner, grins as he leaves his bomber in New Guinea after shooting down his first Japanese A6M Mitsubishi Zero fighter in aerial combat. Draped over his right shoulder is a belt of 0.50-inch calibre ammunition for his aircraft's Browning machine guns. *(NARA)*

Two 503rd Parachute Infantry Regiment paratroopers jump from their C-47 transport to participate in the capture of a Japanese airfield below in New Guinea in 1943. The paratroopers jump fully loaded with personal weapon, main parachute and an auxiliary one, personal gear, supplies and ammunition. The 503rd PIR was formed on 2 March 1942. The regiment landed in Cairns, Australia, on 2 December 1942 and expanded into an RCT later in 1944. During its three years in SWPA, the 503rd PIR served in five major combat missions. Among them, on 5 September 1943, the regiment jumped in the Markham River Valley onto a Japanese airfield at Nadzab, which forced the Japanese evacuation from Lae by a route that proved disastrous for them. Two battalions, the 1st and 3rd, of the 503rd PIR, jumped onto Noemfoor Island off the coast of Dutch New Guinea on 3–4 July 1944 at Kamiri Airfield and participated in the elimination of the island's Japanese garrison to re-establish the previously bombed airfield. The PIR's 2nd Battalion was amphibiously landed onto Noemfoor Island to reduce airborne-related casualties. (NARA)

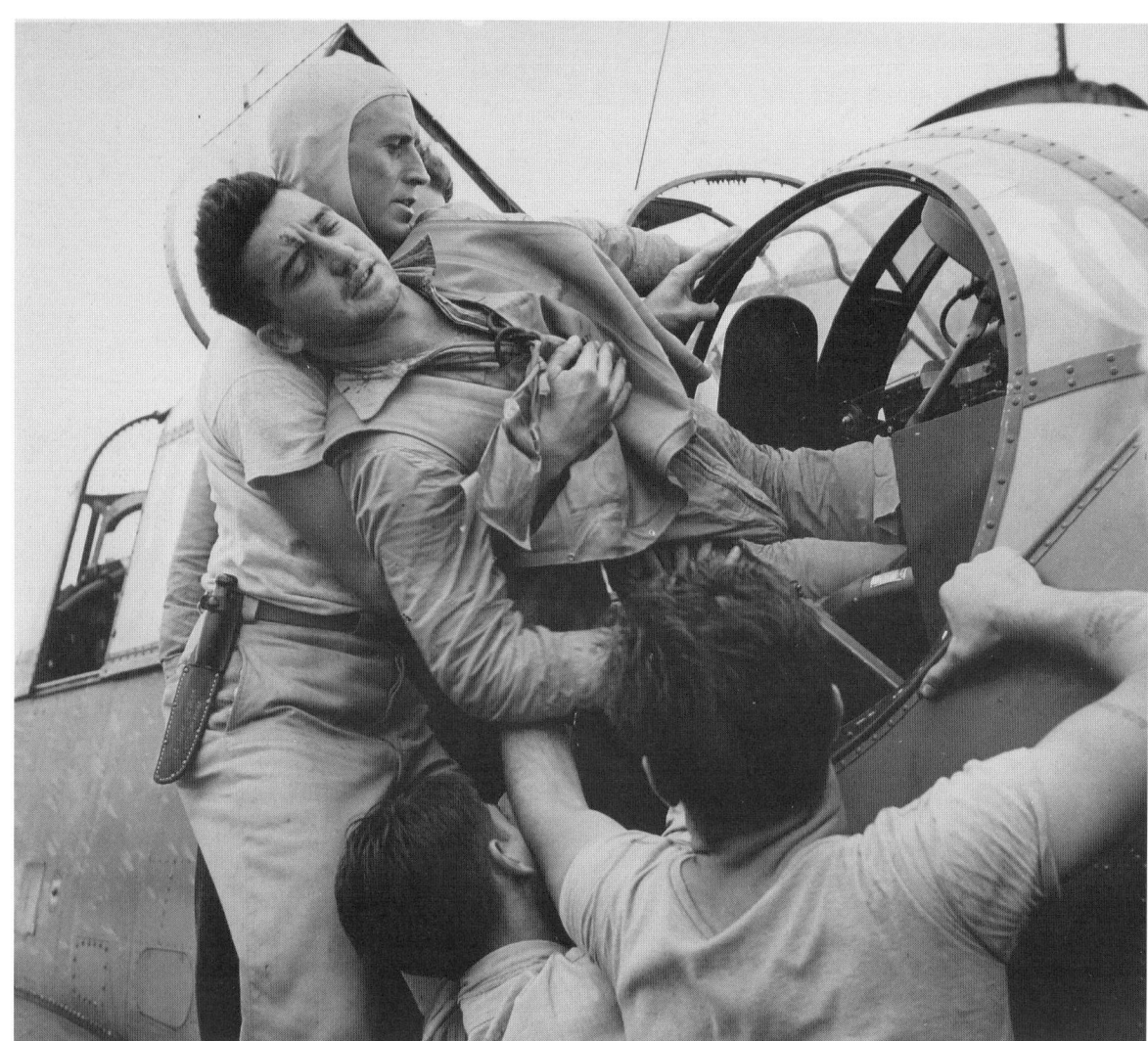

(**Above**) A wounded USN rear turret gunner, Aviation Ordnanceman (AOM) Kenneth Bratton, aboard a Grumman TBF Avenger torpedo bomber, is removed from his plane on its return to the USS *Saratoga* (CV-3) after the 5 November 1943 carrier raid on Rabaul's Simpson Harbour. Photographer's Mate First Class Paul Barnett was killed while photographing an A6M Mitsubishi Zero making a head-on attack on the TBF. Commander Caldwell, the Avenger pilot, made a one-wheel landing with no flaps, ailerons or radio and exited himself from the cockpit. The Avenger had a crew of three, with the rear gunner manning one 0.50-inch calibre Browning trainable rearward-firing machine gun in the dorsal turret. (*NARA*)

(**Opposite, above**) IJN A6M3 Mitsubishi Zero pilots are briefed at Rabaul for a mission over the Solomon Islands for Operation I-GO on 7 April 1943. Faulty intelligence led the IJN commanders at Rabaul to believe that the missions delayed the Allied advance up the Solomon Islands chain after the Japanese evacuated Guadalcanal in February 1943, but the Japanese air raids were unsuccessful. (*NARA*)

(**Opposite, below**) On Cape Gloucester, 1st Marine Division riflemen found dummy Japanese AA positions on 15 January 1944, constructed as decoys made up of a scarecrow gun crew and wooden poles to serve as the gun. This was an attempt to mislead the Marines about the strength of the Japanese forces in one area of Cape Gloucester. (*NARA*)

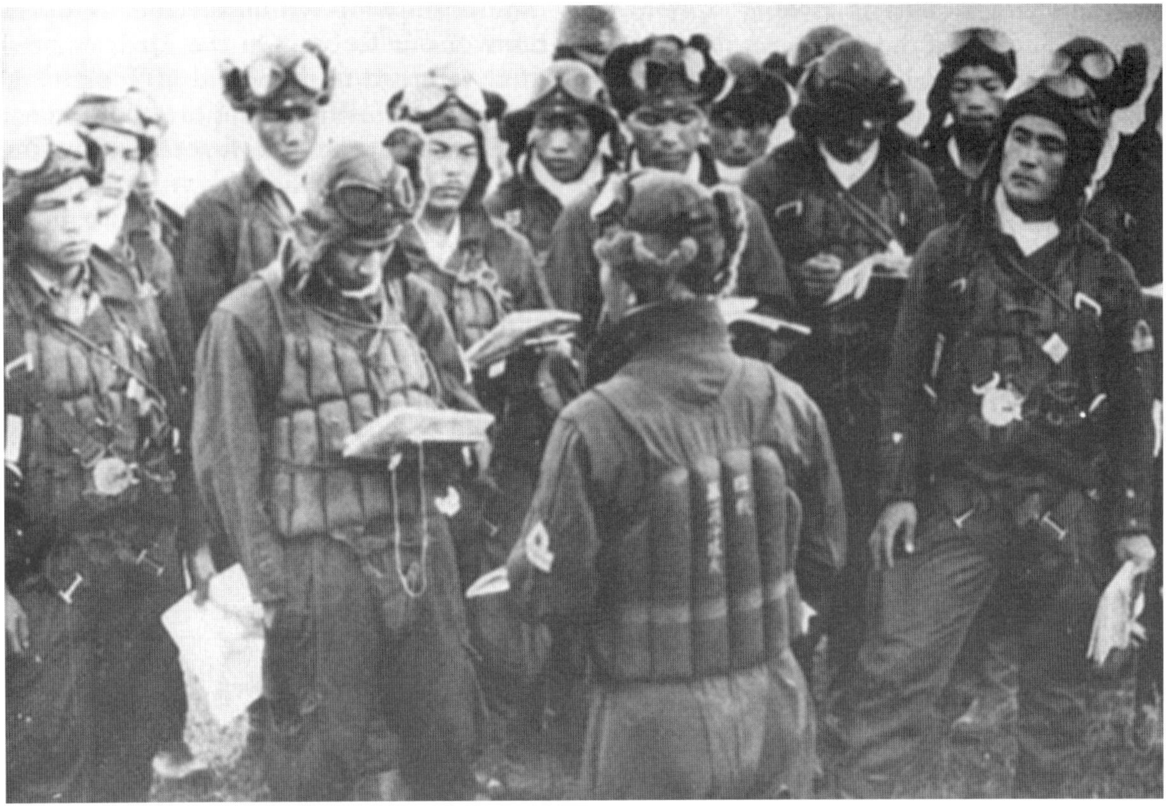

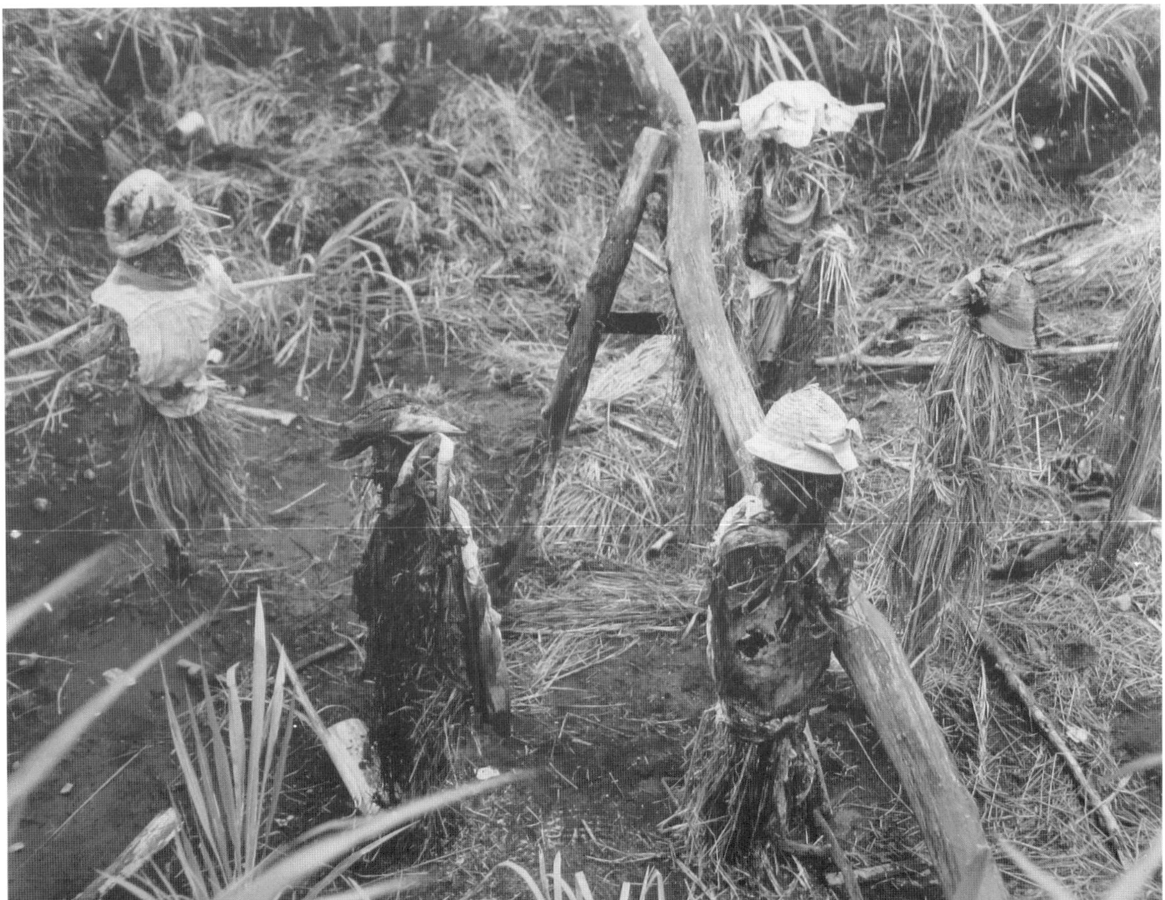

A well-appearing IJA officer of the 18th Army is interrogated under armed guard at Hollandia after the successful Allied amphibious landing there in Netherlands New Guinea on 22 April 1944. Throughout the war, POW interrogation by trained Army and USN military interrogators and interpreters played a crucial role in gathering valuable information about Japanese military operations and intentions. (NARA)

A gaunt, disheveled Japanese POW at Talasea on the eastern side of central New Britain's Willaumez Peninsula sits with a cigarette on 17 March 1944. As the Japanese were retreating eastwards across New Britain towards Gasmata and Rabaul, the IJA soldiers encountered in native villages were either dead or in various stages of dying from starvation, disease, or both. (NARA)

(**Above**) Cape Gloucester Marines return from the front lines in a truck to the beachhead sporting captured Japanese battle flags ('*hinomaru*') and other souvenirs after twenty-three days in action in January 1944. Some of these Marines exhibit the 'thousand yard stare' after prolonged combat as their faces tell of their ordeal in the 'Green Hell' or 'Green Inferno' of Cape Gloucester. (NARA)

(**Opposite**) Col (USAAC Reserve) Charles Lindbergh (left), the pilot of the *Spirit of St Louis*, which spanned the Atlantic in a solo thirty-three-hour monoplane flight from New York to Paris on 20–21 May 1927, meets Lieutenant General George C. Kenney in his Brisbane office on 12 July 1944. Lindbergh left for the South Pacific on 24 April 1944 to only observe combat as a civilian technical representative of Vought Aircraft Industries, the makers of the USN and USMC F4U Corsair fighter. The Roosevelt administration was unaware of Lindbergh's trip to the SPA. Once there, Lindbergh flew in thirty-five combat missions, including some against Japanese targets on New Ireland and New Britain, making strafing runs and bombing Japanese troops and installations at Kavieng and Rabaul, respectively. Most of the missions were with USN and Marine pilots with Corsairs, so he decided to move to the SWPA to observe P-38s in combat. He contacted his friend, Major General Ennis Whitehead, Kenney's deputy, who invited him to Hollandia, ultimately meeting with Whitehead at Nadzab on 1 July 1944. Lindbergh flew several missions with the 475th Fighter Group and the group's crew chief noticed that Lindbergh's P-38 returned with much more fuel than any of the other aircraft. Lindbergh explained that by raising manifold pressure and lowering engine revolutions, the P-38 would use much less fuel, increasing the plane's combat radius and aerial operation time. On 4 July 1944, Kenney heard from a war

correspondent that Lindbergh was in New Guinea and invited him to his Brisbane office. Lindbergh had obtained USN permission to visit the SPA but not the SWPA. So Kenney legitimized Lindbergh's presence in the SWPA by introducing him to MacArthur on 12 July 1944. MacArthur agreed that Lindbergh should help increase the operational radius of the P-38, but not fly combat missions. On his return to New Guinea and the 475th Fighter Group, Lindbergh did increase the P-38's operational radius from 400 to 600 miles. On 28 July 1944, Lindbergh shot down a Mitsubishi Ki-51 Sonia, a ground attack reconnaissance light bomber, which was relegated to *kamikaze* attacks by the end of the war. After nearly being shot down himself on 1 August 1944 near the Palau Islands, Lindbergh returned to the US in mid-August 1944. *(NARA)*

Chapter Four

MacArthur's Invasions of Arawe and Cape Gloucester (December 1943 to March 1944)

The New Britain operation to create a foothold at the western end of the island at Arawe and Cape Gloucester was planned for 15 and 26 December 1943, respectively. Western New Britain's seizure would give the Allies control of both the Dampier Strait and Vitiaz Strait as uncontested sea lanes into the Bismarck Sea to attack the Admiralty Islands, thereby covering SWPA's further westward advance along the northern coast of North-West New Guinea into Dutch New Guinea and the Vogelkop Peninsula (see Map 5) from Japanese air raids from the airfields of either Los Negros Island or Manus Island. The Allied capture of the Cape Gloucester aerodrome by US Marine forces would effectively sever the Japanese supply route between Rabaul and New Guinea.

Arawe on Cape Merkus

On 15 December 1943, US Sixth Army's 112th Cavalry Regiment was transported from New Guinea, landing in Marine amphibian tractors at Cape Merkus's western end, House Fireman Beach, across Arawe Passage, from the islet of Arawe, after naval and aerial bombardment with small diversionary rubber boat assaults at Pilelo Island and on the mainland at Umtingalu Village, the latter of which was repelled. The aims were to disrupt Japanese barge and small vessel traffic from moving IJA troops and supplies along New Britain's southern coast and to divert attention from the 26 December Cape Gloucester assault. The cavalrymen encountered little resistance by two companies of the IJA 51st Division, and once ashore they secured the Cape Merkus peninsula, but enemy reinforcements were en route. Japanese fighters and bombers from Rabaul's Eleventh Air Fleet attacked the Army and USN assault forces within two hours of the landing with sporadic attacks throughout December; however, the Allies dominated the skies over New Britain.

Major Shinjiro Komori, the Japanese commander of the 1st Battalion, 81st and 141st Infantry Regiments, arriving 25 and 29 December, respectively, at Arawe, believed that the 112th Cavalry's landing was to capture an abandoned airfield at Cape Merkus, but this was not in Kruger's plans. On 25 December, the Japanese forced the Americans to retreat from their outposts east of Arawe. The 112th Cavalry CO, Brigadier General Julian Cunningham, asked for reinforcements and received a company of the 158th Infantry Regiment (the 'Bushmasters'). Late December IJA attacks were repulsed. On 10 January 1944, F Company, 158th IR arrived and eighteen M5A1 light tanks of Company B, 1st Transport Battalion, 1st Marine Division, from Finschhafen, arrived on 12 January. An American two-platoon, tank-two company infantry attack on 16 January, with preliminary aerial and artillery bombardment, succeeded in destroying the Japanese bunkers by the end of the day, effectively ending the Arawe fighting. The Americans lost 118 dead, 352 wounded and 4 missing as their sacrifice kept two IJA infantry battalions away from the main western New Britain fighting at Cape Gloucester.

Major Komori ordered a retreat to the vicinity of the airstrip on which they dug in, but the Americans had no intention of attacking. With over 300 IJA casualties of all types, Major Komori received orders on 24 February to join in a general retreat from Western New Britain by Matsuda Force.

Invasion of Cape Gloucester by the 1st Marine Division

At 0746 hours on 26 December 1943, following Allied cruiser gunfire and heavy and medium bomber pre-invasion aerial attacks, the 1st Marine Division, under Major General William Rupertus's leadership with operational control by Krueger's Sixth Army, began its Cape Gloucester invasion. Two battalions of Colonel Julian Frisbie's 7th Marines landed at Yellow Beach 1 (3rd Battalion) and Yellow Beach 2 (1st Battalion), to the west of Silimati Point, separated by 1,000 yards of jungle over a shoreline of 700 yards, and headed inland. The Japanese mounted no defence, although the Marines' movements were observed by the enemy on Target Hill, inland from Silimati Point, which was captured by 7th Marines' units that afternoon. The Marines' main objective was capturing the Aerodrome's Strips 1 and 2 northwest of the Yellow landing beaches on the northern tip of Cape Gloucester.

The Marines began to encounter serious Japanese resistance from camouflaged log bunkers, impervious to bazooka rockets and 37mm AT gun rounds, so amphibious tractors and M4 medium tanks reduced the enemy strongpoint. With difficulty crossing a swamp just inland, the 11th Marines set up its artillery with the help of amphibious tractors carrying the lighter 75mm pack howitzers or towing the heavier 105mm guns. Japanese service troops, under the command of Major Shinichi Takabe, made a counterattack, which was repulsed by 37mm guns of Battery D, 1st Special Weapons Battalion.

On 28 December, the 7th Marines held the beachhead anchored on Target Hill while Colonel William Whaling's 1st Marines advanced westwards on the airfields to confront a maze of enemy trenches and bunkers stretching inland from a promontory called Hell's Point. M4 medium tanks collided with improved Japanese defences; a succession of jungle-camouflaged, mutually supporting positions protected by barbed wire and mines. The M4 medium tanks, protected by Marine riflemen, crushed the Japanese bunkers, killing over 260 Japanese at Hell's Point at the cost of 9 Marines killed and 36 wounded.

On the morning of 29 December, two 5th Marines battalions, the divisional reserve, came ashore to join the airfields advance. At dusk, the 1st Battalion, 1st Marines arrived at the edge of Airfield No. 2. On 30 December, the 1st and 2nd Battalions, 5th Marines, supported by tanks and artillery, attacked Colonel Kouki Sumiya's 53rd Infantry Regiment, which fell back to 'Razorback Hill', a ridge that ran diagonally across the southwestern approaches to the airfield, to defend Airfield No. 2. Sumiya's troops built sturdy bunkers, which did not impede the attacking 5th Marines as they repelled two separate *banzai* charges before M4 medium tanks again shattered the enemy bunkers. By dusk on 30 December, the Marines overran the airfields' defences and at noon on 31 December, Major General Rupertus raised the American flag beside the wreckage of a Japanese bomber at Airfield No. 2, the larger of the two airfields. Airfield No. 1 was thickly overgrown with tall kunai grass. Craters from US bombing runs pockmarked the surface of Airfield No. 2. US Army engineers worked ceaselessly to return Airfield No. 2 to operational status, taking until the end of January 1944. Then, 5th USAAF aircraft based there defended against enemy air attacks from Rabaul.

The Japanese in Western New Britain had the 1st and 8th Shipping Regiments, utilizing motor barges to move from Rabaul to Cape Merkus and Cape Gloucester. The Matsuda Force, established in September 1943 under Major General Iwao Matsuda, had units from the IJA 65th Infantry Brigade, 141st Infantry Regiment, plus artillery and AA units with HQ along the coastal trail to Mount Talawe's northwest within 5 miles of the airstrips. The force was nominally assigned to Lieutenant General Yasushi Sakai; CG of the survivors of the IJA 17th Division, most of whom were lost in sea transit from Shanghai and placed under Matsuda's tactical command.

A secondary landing on 26 December at Green Beach, off Dampier Strait, north of Tauali and south of Dorf Point, by the 2nd Battalion,

1st Marines and Company H, 11th Marines (Battalion Landing Team 21) encountered no resistance and carved out a 1,200-yard-wide beachhead extending 500 yards inland. Its objective was to sever the coastal trail that passed west of Mount Talawe to prevent the passage of Japanese reinforcements to the airfields. It was not until dawn of 30 December that the Japanese attacked the Green Beach force under cover of rain with reduced visibility, penetrating the Marines' lines, but an American counterattack drove the enemy off, costing the lives of six Marines killed with nearly ninety Japanese dead and seventeen wounded, with five surrendering. On 11 January 1944, Battalion Landing Team 21 began to rejoin the division via an overland march with heavy equipment and wounded Marines transported by landing craft.

On 1 January 1944, Brigadier General Lemuel Shepherd, ADC, moved to expand the 7th Marines' perimeter across Suicide Creek (west of Target Hill) and to secure Borgen Bay with Colonel Selden's newly arrived 3rd Battalion, 5th Marines. However, Colonel Kenshiro Katayama's IJA 141st Infantry Regiment's three reinforced battalions attacked the Marines at Target Hill on 2 January, and were repulsed. On 7 January, 3rd Battalion, 5th Marines moved on Aogiri Ridge (east of Suicide Creek and south of Target Hill), securing it two days later. On 10 January, the Japanese made five attacks on the Marine positions as 105mm howitzer fire contributed to repelling the counterattacks. Fifteen days of combat since the 26 December landings cost the 1st Marine Division 180 killed and 636 wounded in action.

Shepherd's next objective was Hill 660 (bordering Borgen Bay), which the 3rd Battalion, 7th Marines secured by 13 January 1944. Two companies of Japanese infantry counterattacked up Hill 660 on the 16th but were slaughtered by Marine mortar, artillery and small-arms fire. Marine possession of Hill 660 eliminated further potential Japanese counterattacks against the airfields. Next, on 20 January, the 1st Battalion, 5th Marines collided with a Japanese strongpoint armed with 20mm, 37mm and 75mm weapons at Borgen Bay's Natamo Point. Units of the 5th Marines, with M4 tanks arriving in landing craft, overran the enemy positions on 23 January. The surviving units of Katayama's 141st Infantry Regiment and other components of the Matsuda Force retreated eastwards via inland trails and villages, pursued by 5th and 7th Marines' separate patrols, resulting in some limited clashes through to 16 February. Matsuda's abandoned HQ near Mount Talawe yielded buried enemy documents as his retreat along New Britain's northern coast used the 500-man IJA 51st Reconnaissance Regiment as a rearguard. At Iboki Point, occupied by the 5th Marines on 24 February, only sick and wounded Japanese were found.

After the IJA 17th Division's CO, Lieutenant General Yasushi Sakai, decided not to defend Cape Hoskins; across Kimbe Bay from the Willaumez Peninsula, Matsuda's retreat became a two-week march of attrition towards Rabaul. However, a 600-man Japanese force built around the 1st Battalion, 54th Infantry Regiment, under Captain Kiyomatsu Terunuma's command, with mortars and artillery was prepared to defend Talasea and its crude airstrip on the east coast of the Willaumez Peninsula. This force was to hold long enough for the Matsuda Force to move past it towards Rabaul. On 6 March, the leading units of Matsuda's column arrived at the Willaumez Peninsula and Major Shinjiro Komori, after retreating from Cape Merkus, was now in the vanguard of 51st Reconnaissance Regiment's rearguard.

Also on 6 March 1944, the reinforced 5th Marines, now commanded by Colonel Oliver Smith, landed at Volupai, via amphibious tractors, on the west coast of the Willaumez Peninsula, midway between its tip and base. At Volupai, Marine M4s, brought ashore by LCMs, were rushed by suicidal Japanese with mines, and several dozen Japanese were killed. Japanese 90mm mortars killed nine and wounded twenty-nine artillerymen from the 2nd Battalion, 11th Marines setting up their 75mm howitzers on the open beach. On 8 March, 2nd Battalion, 5th Marines moved on Japanese positions at Bitokara Mission; however, the Japanese fell back first, allowing the Marines to capture Talasea and its abandoned airstrip. Other Marines patrols from the 2nd Battalion climbed up the steep slopes of Mount Schleuther and engaged Tenumuma's 1st Battalion, 54th Infantry Regiment force. Japanese 90mm mortar, 75mm field gun and small-arms fire claimed a score of Marines killed or wounded. At darkness, the Marines dug in at Bitokara Mission to allow the 11th Marines' artillery to pummel the Japanese positions during the night.

By the morning of 9 March, Colonel Smith's 5th Marines opened a new northwest–southeast route from Volupai across the Willaumez Peninsula to support further operations against Matsuda's line of retreat, killing 150 Japanese for a loss of 17 Marines killed and 114 wounded since 6 March. Talasea's grass airstrip was not long enough for fighters, but it accommodated the division's L5 Sentinel liaison planes. On 10 March, the American flag was raised over Bitokara. From 11 to 15 March, elements of the 3rd Battalion, 5th Marines fought a succession of sharp actions with the Japanese as they continued their retreat. The USN built a base on the Willaumez Peninsula for PT boats to harass any remaining Japanese barges. The retreating Japanese struggled onward towards Cape Hoskins, which like Talasea, had an abandoned airfield.

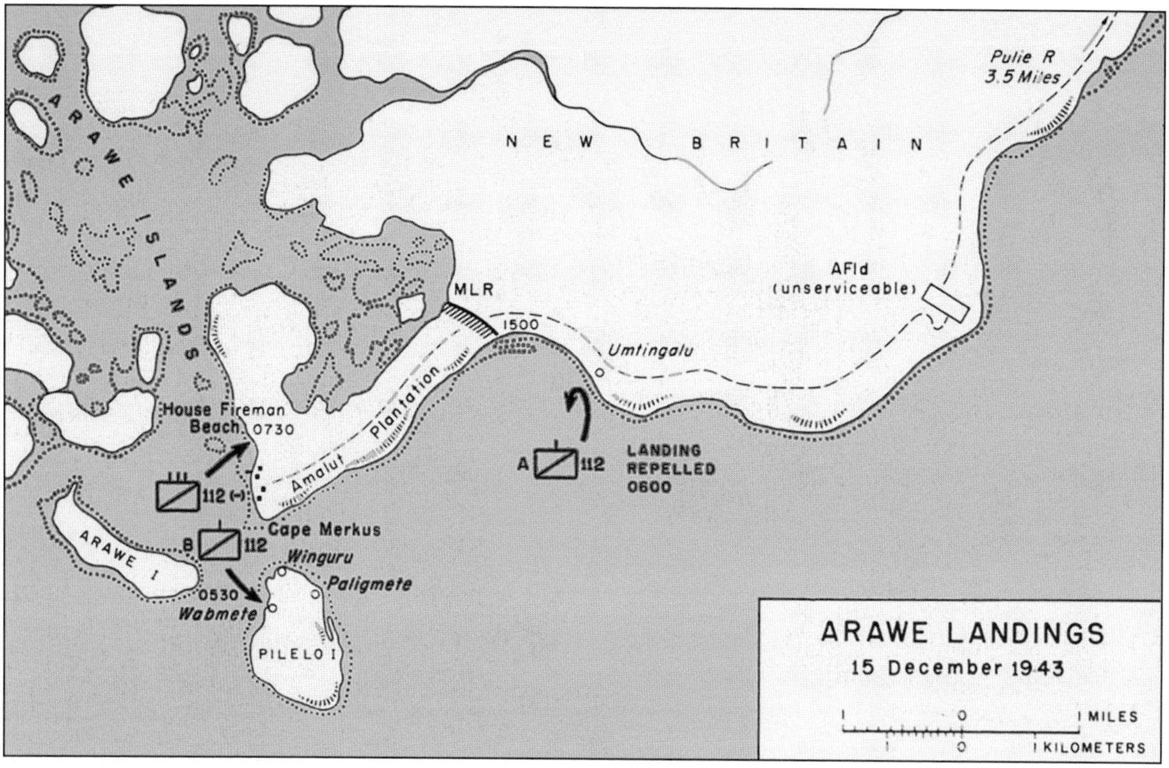

Map of the Cape Merkus peninsula, showing the sites of the 15 December 1943 Arawe landings by elements of the US 112th Cavalry Regiment. (US Army)

1st Cavalry Division, 112th Regiment of Krueger's 'Alamo Force', lined up on 13 December 1943 on Goodenough Island in 1st Marine Amphibian Tractor Battalion LVTs in cooperation with the Army's 532nd Engineer and Boat Regiment for the Arawe invasion two days later. (NARA)

The main landing at Arawe, conducted by Rear Admiral Daniel Barbey's VII Amphibious Force preceded by Allied destroyers' 5-inch guns bombardment with assault beach bombing and strafing by B-25s. The 2nd Squadron, 112th Cavalry led the assault in LVT(A) Buffaloes while the next three waves were in LCVPs (above) and the older LVT Alligators. Two IJA companies farther inland were overwhelmed. (NARA)

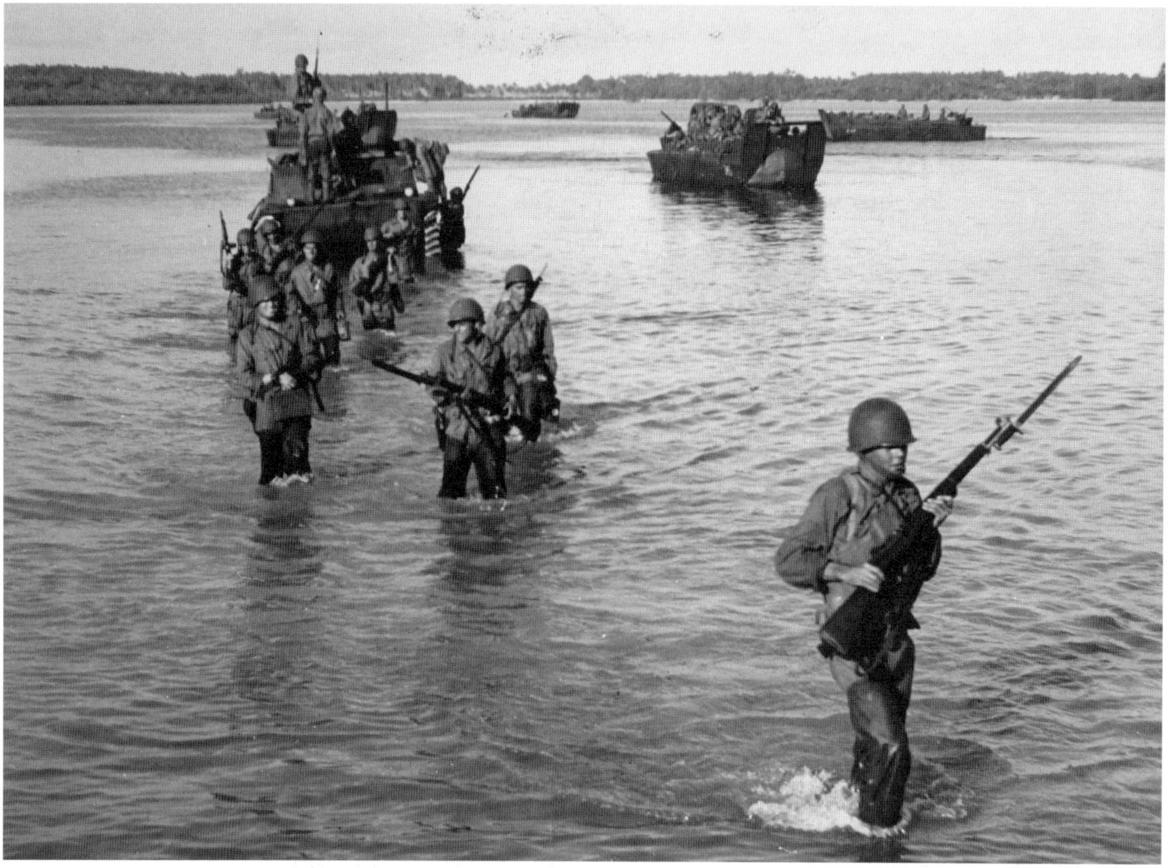

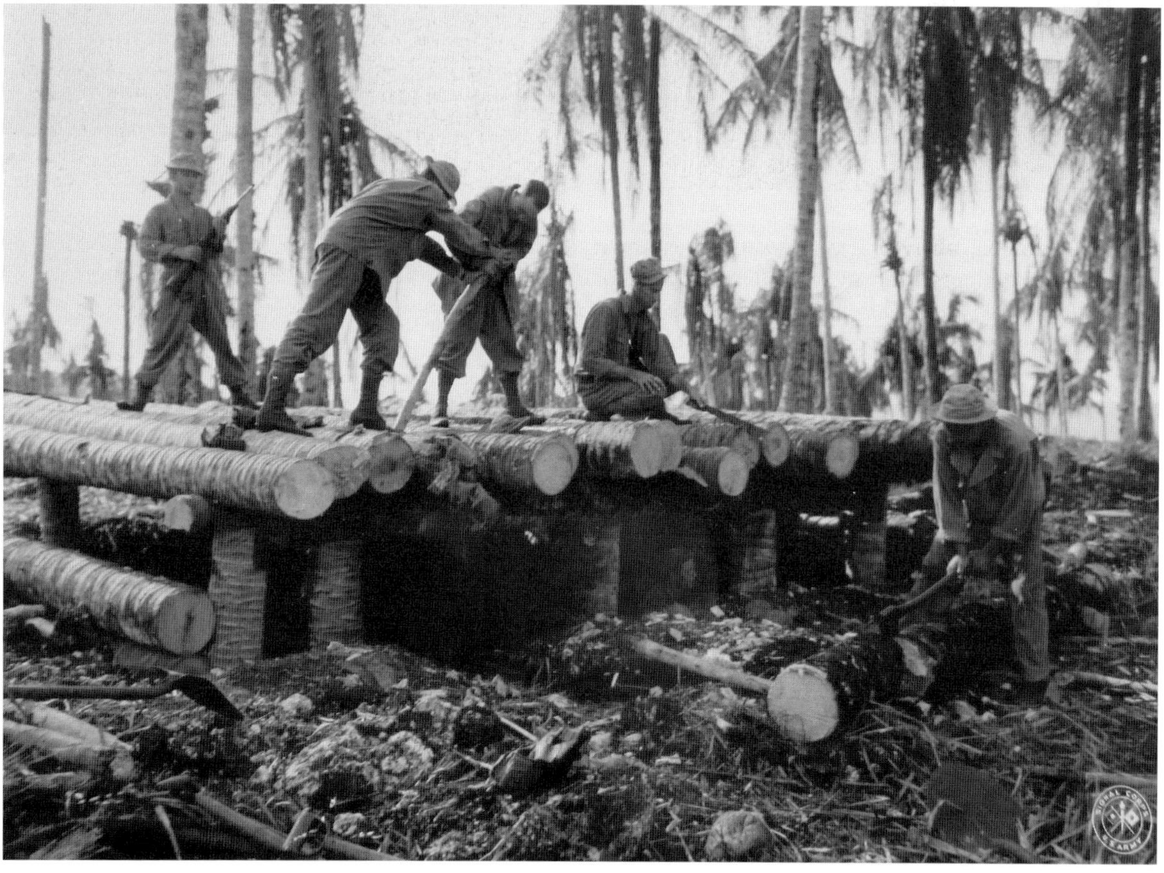

(**Opposite, above**) 2nd Squadron cavalrymen of the 112th Regiment, 1st Cavalry Division wade ashore at House Fireman Beach from an amphibious tractor on 15 December 1943. By mid-afternoon, 1,600 cavalrymen controlled the Cape Merkus peninsula, which was further consolidated as more troops and heavy weapons were landed. (*NARA*)

(**Above**) Two cavalrymen man a 0.50-inch calibre machine gun to protect a command post from Japanese aerial attack at Arawe soon after the 15 December 1943 invasion. Allied intelligence estimated only 500 IJA troops at Arawe. The concern was about aerial attacks from Rabaul and Wewak by the Japanese Eleventh Air Fleet and IJAAF 6th Air Division, respectively. On D-Day, thirty Japanese planes eluded the US fighter cover to attack the ships remaining on the beach or offshore. (*NARA*)

(**Opposite, below**) 112th Regiment cavalrymen work on an observation post 100 yards from Japanese lines at Arawe. The cavalrymen, under Brigadier General Julian Cunningham, constructed a main line of resistance 700 yards wide at Cape Merkus peninsula's base and were dug in with mortars and artillery for use against a Japanese attack by units of Major Komori's IJA units on 25 December 1943. (*NARA*)

(**Above**) Message runner Private First Class Wallace Grant (left), a Pima Indian from Arizona, crouches near his platoon command post as Private Stephen Lopez, a Papago Indian also from Arizona, phones in a report to the command post of F Company, 2nd Battalion, 158th Infantry Regiment (the 'Bushmasters'). During the interwar period, F Company was formed as an all-native American unit made up of alumni of the Phoenix Indian School. On 11 February, the 158th IR became a separate one from its previously 'square' US 45th Infantry Division. The moniker 'Bushmasters' refers to a venomous snake from the unit's earlier service in the Panama Canal Zone. In November 1942, the 158th IR was ordered to Australia and then served on the islands of Kiriwina, Goodenough and Woodlark off the Papuan coast in the Solomon Sea. G Co, 2nd Battalion, 158th IR arrived on Arawe on 27 December 1943 and F Company arrived 10 January 1944. *(NARA)*

(**Opposite, above**) An American M1917A 0.30-inch calibre machine gun fires on Japanese positions at Arawe in late December 1943. On 20 December, IJA 141st Infantry Regiment troops, under the command of Major Masamitsu Komori, landed in barges and by an overland march, and reached the Pulie River to Arawe's east. On 25 December, Komori's force attacked the US 112th Cavalry Regiment and drove back their advanced units' forward outposts, leading to the seizure of Lupin Airfield. Krueger reinforced his position with companies of the 158th IR (the 'Bushmasters'), by PT boats. Komori was reinforced with troops of the IJA 81st IR, and moved close to the Americans' main line of defence the next day. During the last week of December, Komori tried to dislodge the 112th Cavalry Regiment from its MLR, with American artillery and mortar fire taking a heavy toll on the attacking Japanese. *(NARA)*

(**Below**) F Company, 158th Infantry Regiment and 18 M5A1 light tanks of Company B, 1st TB, 1st Marine Division from Finschhafen advance on a 500-yard front through felled trees on 16 January 1944, following B-24 and B-25 bombing and mortar and artillery bombardment of Japanese positions. Earlier, on 29 December 1943, the 1st Battalion, IJA 81st IR joined the 1st Battalion, 141st IR (Komori Force) to defend Lupin Airfield, building foxholes and trenches to cover routes the Americans might take to reclaim the airfield. Initial attacks by the cavalrymen were beaten off, so Brigadier General Cunningham, 112th Cavalry Regiment CO, requested tank support. The tank infantry teams shattered the Japanese defences by mid-afternoon of 16 January, letting the remaining Japanese starve at Lupin Airfield, which Cunningham had no intention of capturing. On 24 February, IJA 17th Division HQ at Rabaul allowed Komori's surviving troops to withdraw to the middle of New Britain to join other Japanese forces covering Major General Iwao Matsuda's withdrawal from Cape Gloucester. (*NARA*)

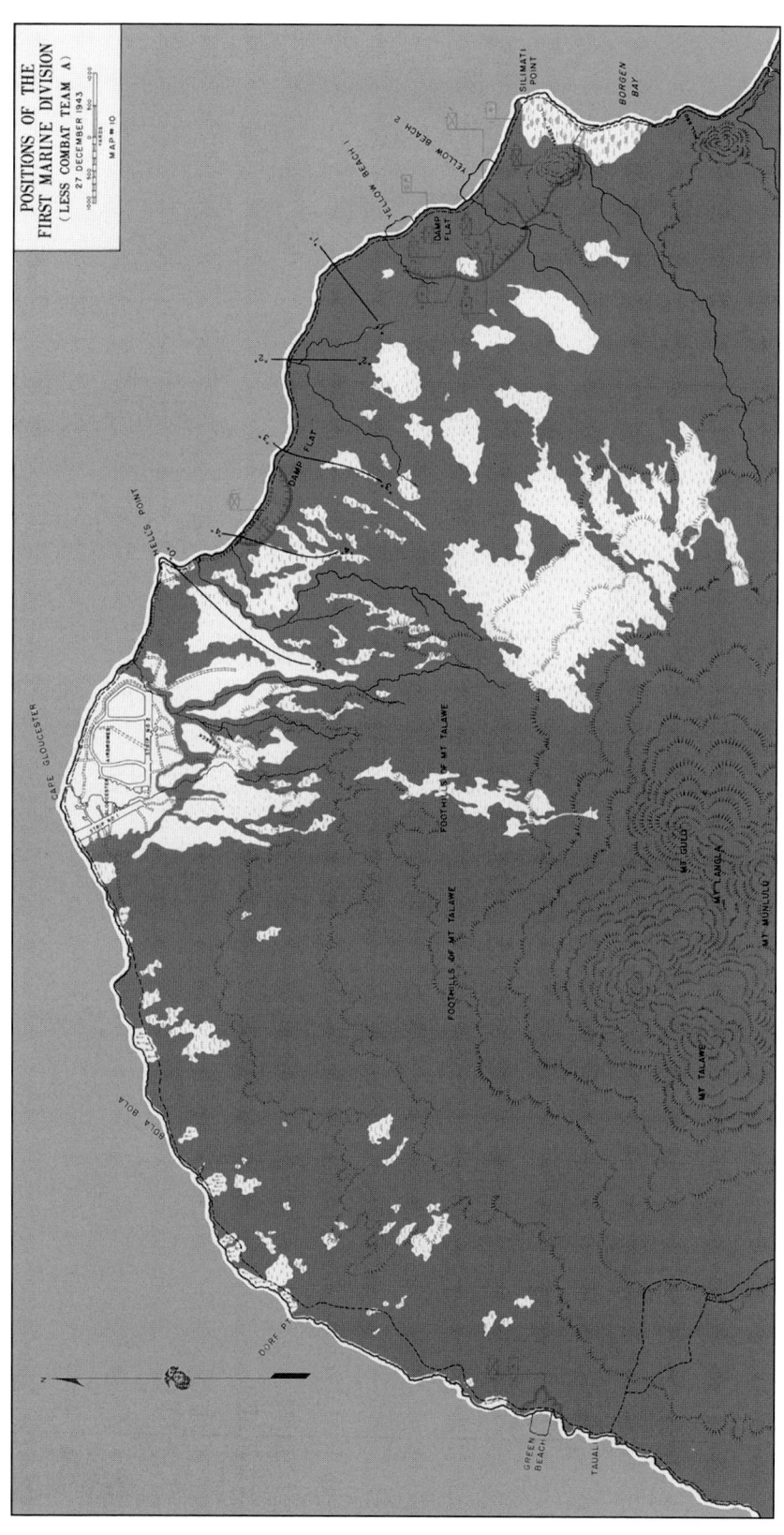

Map of Cape Gloucester area with Dampier Strait off western New Britain's west coast. Other pertinent sites include the two airstrips, Yellow Beaches 1 and 2, Hell's Point, the 'Damp Flats', Silimati Point, Target Hill, Hill 660, Borgen Bay, Natamo Point, Mount Talawe and Green Beach. (USMC)

A B-24 Liberator four-engine bomber flies above the Cape Gloucester aerodrome bombing Airstrip No.2 in October 1943, two months before the 26 December invasion, with Airstrip No.1, left of the stream, barely visible. MacArthur wanted Cape Gloucester's airfields seized by the 1st Marine Division to further isolate Rabaul and to control the Vitiaz Strait and the Dampier Strait to interdict IJA troop transfer from the bastion. (NARA)

A twin-engine B-25 Mitchell bomber races low from its bombing run along Cape Gloucester's Yellow landing beaches before the 26 December 1943 amphibious landing of the 1st Marine Division. Specifically, Natamo Point was blasted by the 5th USAAF bombers with Target Hill and Silimati Point (background). In May 1943, General Imamura, CG Eighth Area Army in Rabaul, sent understrength IJA 65th Brigade to the Cape area by barge and small boats from Rabaul along with an AT company with 37mm guns and an artillery unit with 75mm mountain guns. In September 1943, Major General Iwao Matsuda took command of the 65th Brigade along with various shipping companies and rear-echelon troops of the IJA 51st Division. On 5 October 1943, Lieutenant General Yasushi Sakai, CG 17th IJA Division, assumed command of the western New Britain defences, and assigned the division's main strength and a field artillery battalion to Matsuda to defend the two airstrips. (NARA)

Units of the 7th Marines, 1st Marine Division wade ashore from LCVPs and LSTs at Cape Gloucester at Yellow Beaches 1 and 2, which had narrow openings in the surrounding reef to the west of Silimati Point, on 26 December 1943. Target Hill, 450 feet high, south of Yellow Beach 2 near Silimati Point, and Hill 660, 2 miles farther south, both overlooked the landing beaches. The Cape Gloucester aerodrome was several thousand yards to the northwest of the two Yellow beaches through rough terrain. (NARA)

(**Above**) A White Motor Company M3 GMC TD with a 75mm AT howitzer, along with two 0.50-inch calibre mounted AA machine guns, exits into the surf at one of the Yellow beaches from an LST on 26 December 1943. The convoy of USN transports, cruisers and destroyers passed through the Vitiaz Strait and the Dampier Strait without incident. By 0600 hours, the naval bombardment began, lasting ninety minutes. There was no opposition as Rear Admiral Daniel Barbey's TF 76 landed 12,500 troops and 7,600 tons of equipment. Within thirty minutes of landing, Colonel Whaling's 1st Marines began a northwest advance, following the coast to the aerodrome, while to the east, Colonel Frisbie's 7th Marines occupied Target Hill by noon, but further progress was blocked by swamp and jungle. By the end of D-Day, the Marines held a 1,000-yard inland perimeter, encountering no sustained Japanese resistance. (*NARA*)

(**Opposite**) Marines at the Cape Gloucester beachhead haul a 37mm AT gun from the beach into the jungle just inland for a waiting jeep to tow, on 26 December 1943. In between the two Yellow beaches was an area of mud and standing water called 'Damp Flat'. Jungle canopy prevented aerial reconnaissance from identifying these swampy forests. Marine LVTs were often the only answer to the ubiquitous Cape Gloucester muddy terrain exacerbated by the rainy season. (*NARA*)

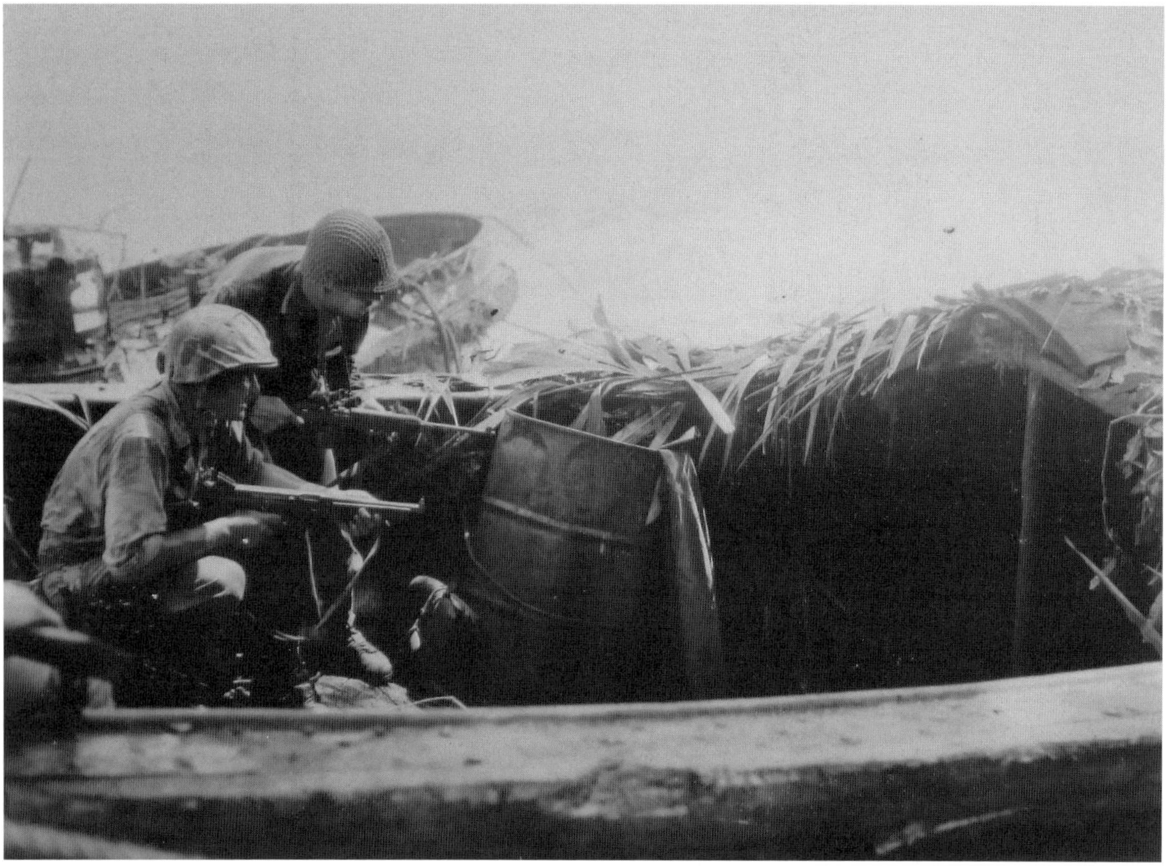

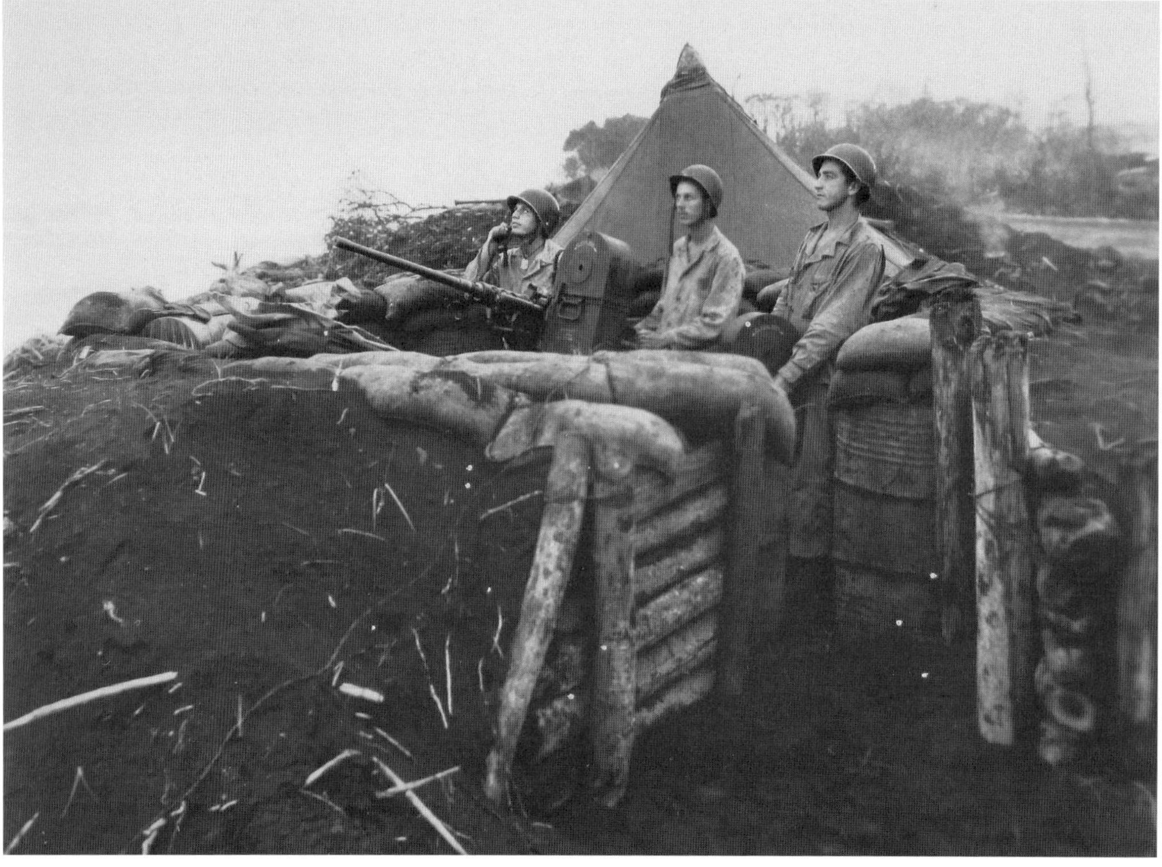

(**Opposite, above**) At the Cape Gloucester beachhead on 26 December 1943, two Marines inspect a Japanese boat for snipers. The numerous abandoned Japanese barges were excellent areas for concealment. Within thirty minutes of landing, elements of the 1st Marines encountered a roadblock consisting of four machine guns in a bunker supported by rifle pits. During the Marine attack on the enemy position, the CO of K Company and his XO were both killed, as an amphibious tractor was needed to ram the bunker, with Marine riflemen killing the enemy infantry. (NARA)

(**Opposite, below**) A Marine 0.50-inch calibre tripod-mounted AA machine gun in its log-reinforced emplacement at Cape Gloucester beachhead as a crew member (left) receives report of imminent Japanese air attack. At 1430 hours on 26 December 1943, the Japanese struck the beachhead with twenty-five Aichi D3A Type 99 Val dive-bombers and sixty fighters from Rabaul. The Val was the primary IJN dive-bomber, as either carrier-borne or land-based. Little damage was inflicted as the Japanese airstrike was intercepted by Allied fighters, which destroyed twenty-two enemy bombers and twenty-two fighters. However, serious damage was inflicted on three destroyers; the USS *Hitchins*, *Shaw* and *Brownson*, the latter sinking after two Val bombs struck, with over 100 dead American sailors. The last major Japanese air attack occurred on 31 December, with twelve enemy planes downed. From 15 to 31 December, the Japanese lost 163 planes at Arawe and Cape Gloucester to Allied fighters and ground AA batteries. (NARA)

(**Above**) Two Marines cross a jungle creek over a fallen tree log in their advance towards the airstrips. In addition to 'Suicide Creek', which bisected the initial Marine perimeter inland from the Yellow Beach 2 landing zone, swamps were abundant. As one Marine said, 'Damp Flat' (near Yellow Beach 1) was 'damp up to your neck'. Members of a Marine column could fall into waist-high sinkholes and would have to be pulled out, usually injuring legs. Marine infantry forward momentum stalled amid the mud and vines. (NARA)

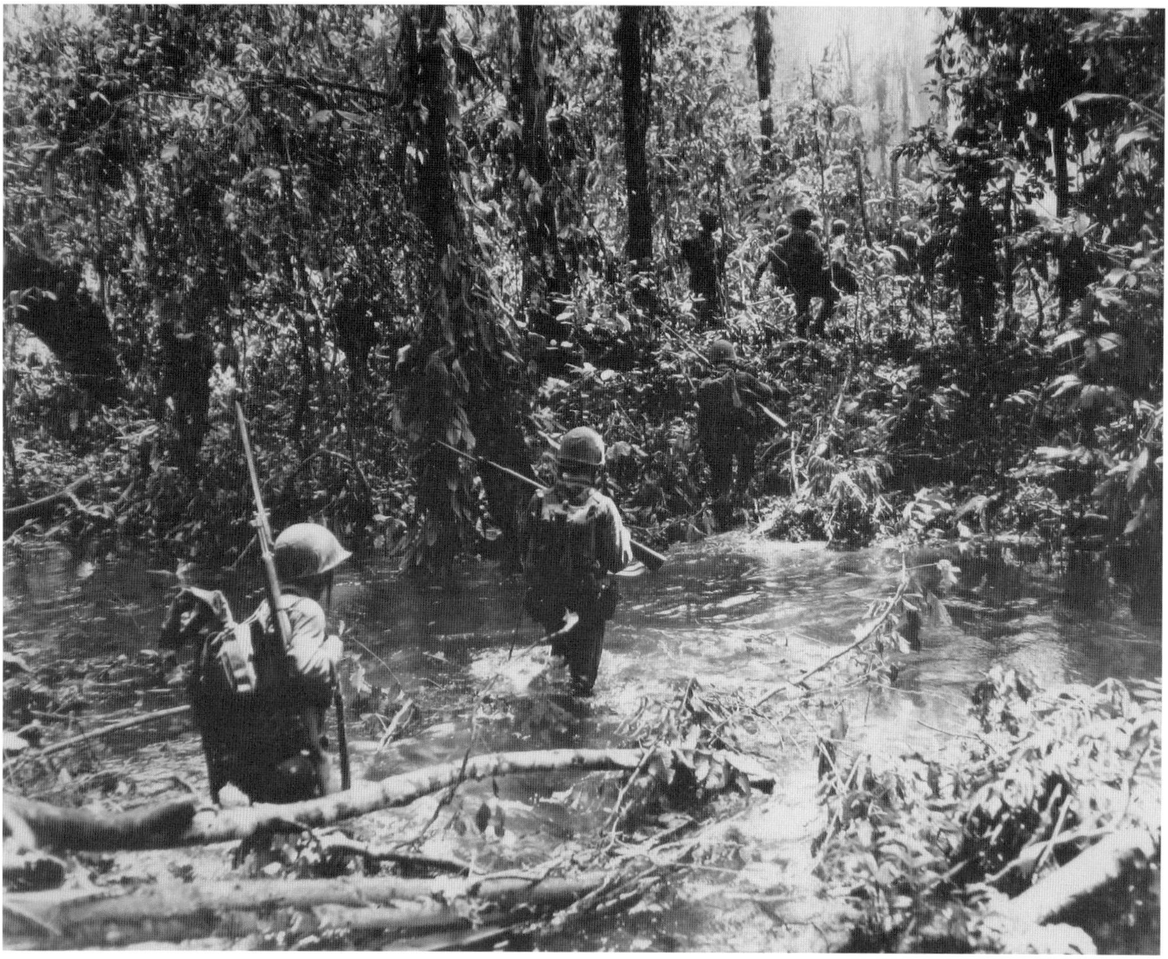
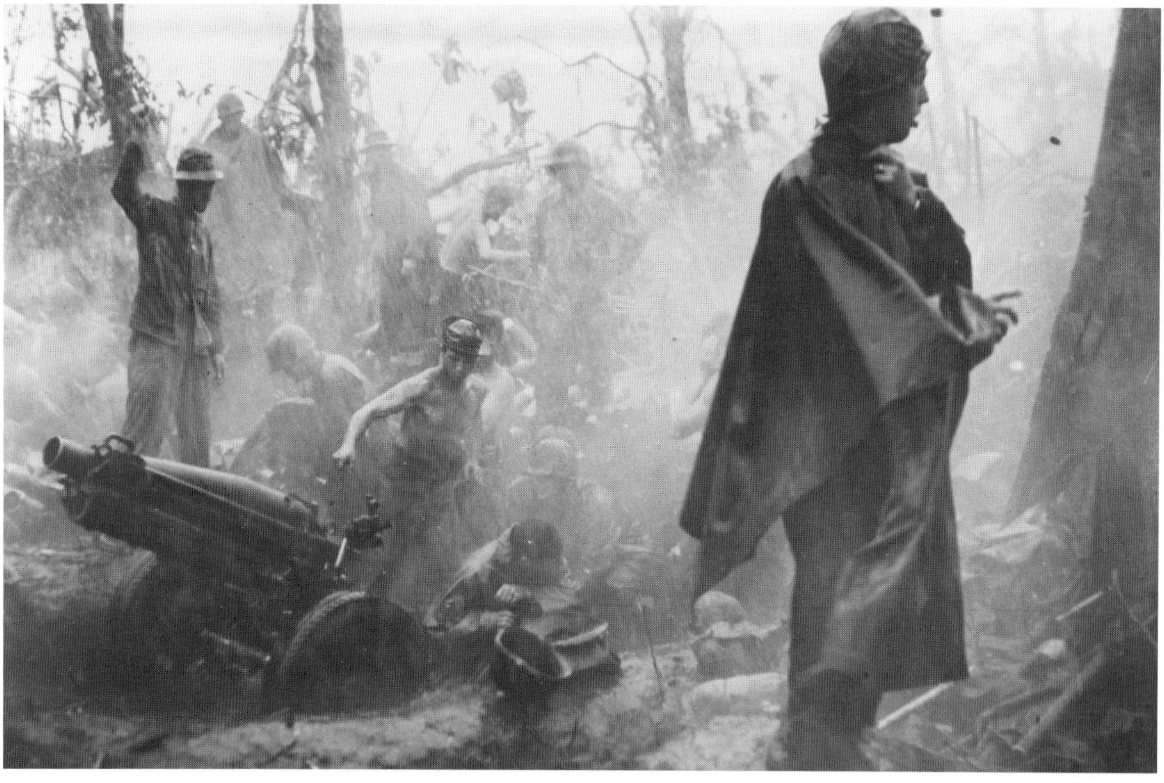

(**Opposite, above**) A Marine patrol crosses a jungle creek filled with knee-high water. The torrential rains started during the final week of December and continued for the next nineteen days, with as much as 16 inches falling in one day. All the streams flooded and the trails became seas of mud. A member of Major General Rupertus's staff commented that the weather on Cape Gloucester was worse than at Guadalcanal. Torrential rains, high winds and jungle terrain made only localized gains possible. (NARA)

(**Opposite, below**) 11th Marines gunners fire their M8 75mm pack howitzer in support of the airstrips drive on 27 December 1943, during a torrential downpour. The utility of this 1,300lb weapon was that it could be stripped down into component parts in seconds for animal packs (thus the term 'pack howitzer') or human transport, and had metal wheels and rubber tyres. The M8 fired HE ammunition in support of infantry to disrupt advancing enemy formations and concentration areas. On 27 December, a massive storm struck the Cape Gloucester area with a solid wall of water, lasting for hours and recurring at least once every day. Marines in front-line foxholes were soon up to their necks in water. (NARA)

(**Above**) A Marine M1 81mm infantry mortar crew in their sandbag-reinforced weapon pit fires a round, with additional mortar bombs handled like a 'bucket brigade' to rapidly load and lob. Each weapon was carried in three parts: the barrel, the base plate and the bipod. The standard ammunition was the M43A1 light HE round, which weighed 6.87lb and had a range of 200 to 3,290 yards. Heavier HE rounds were also produced. This weapon, with its 'plunging fire' on enemy positions, supported advancing Marine riflemen. The 81mm M1 mortar was the most powerful infantry weapon at the battalion level and was particularly important where the terrain did not always allow larger artillery pieces. (NARA)

(**Above**) An 11th Marines 105mm M2A1 howitzer crew fires at Japanese positions on 27 December 1943, in support of the 1st Marines' advance to the airstrips along the coastal road. These guns were especially useful against the Japanese defensive works at Hell's Point. The thick and tenacious mud caused by the torrential rains made it difficult to position these artillery pieces. This ordnance was a US division's standard field artillery piece, with a maximal range of 12,500 yards, firing HE, AP and canister rounds against enemy formations. (NARA)

(**Opposite, above**) The 1st and 3rd Battalions, 1st Marines advance in column through a large kunai grass patch with M4 medium tank support towards the airstrips on 28 December 1943, encountering a strongly defended position, Hell's Point, which flanked a crescent-shaped beach and 'Damp Flat' more than 1,000 yards to the southeast of the aerodrome, consisting of a dozen large bunkers manned by a score of Japanese infantrymen in each. Marine M4 medium tanks were brought up, firing their 75mm guns directly at the bunkers as Marine riflemen swarmed over them, killing the Japanese defenders with rifle fire and hand grenades. The 1st Battalion, 1st Marines reached Airstrip No. 2 at 1755 hours on 29 December and both strips were captured that day, with minimal casualties, to complete the invasion's major objective. (NARA)

(**Opposite, below**) Marine riflemen move past a wrecked bomber at Airstrip No. 2 on 29 December 1943. As the 1st Marines continued driving along the coast road to the airfield, the 5th Marines, under Colonel John Selden, made a wide left to cut off any enemy withdrawal and then attack an area of the No. 2 airstrip believed to contain prepared Japanese defensive positions, which were found abandoned. The 2nd Battalion, 5th Marines reached Airstrip No. 2's centre at 1925 hours on 29 December and then it was ordered farther west to the southern end of the north–south running Airstrip No. 1. On the morning of 30 December, the Japanese made three hours of futile *banzai* attacks staged from the thirty to forty bunkers only to be repulsed, with more than 150 dead Japanese and 13 Marines killed and 19 wounded. The site of this action came to be known as 'Nameless' or 'Razorback' Hill. (NARA)

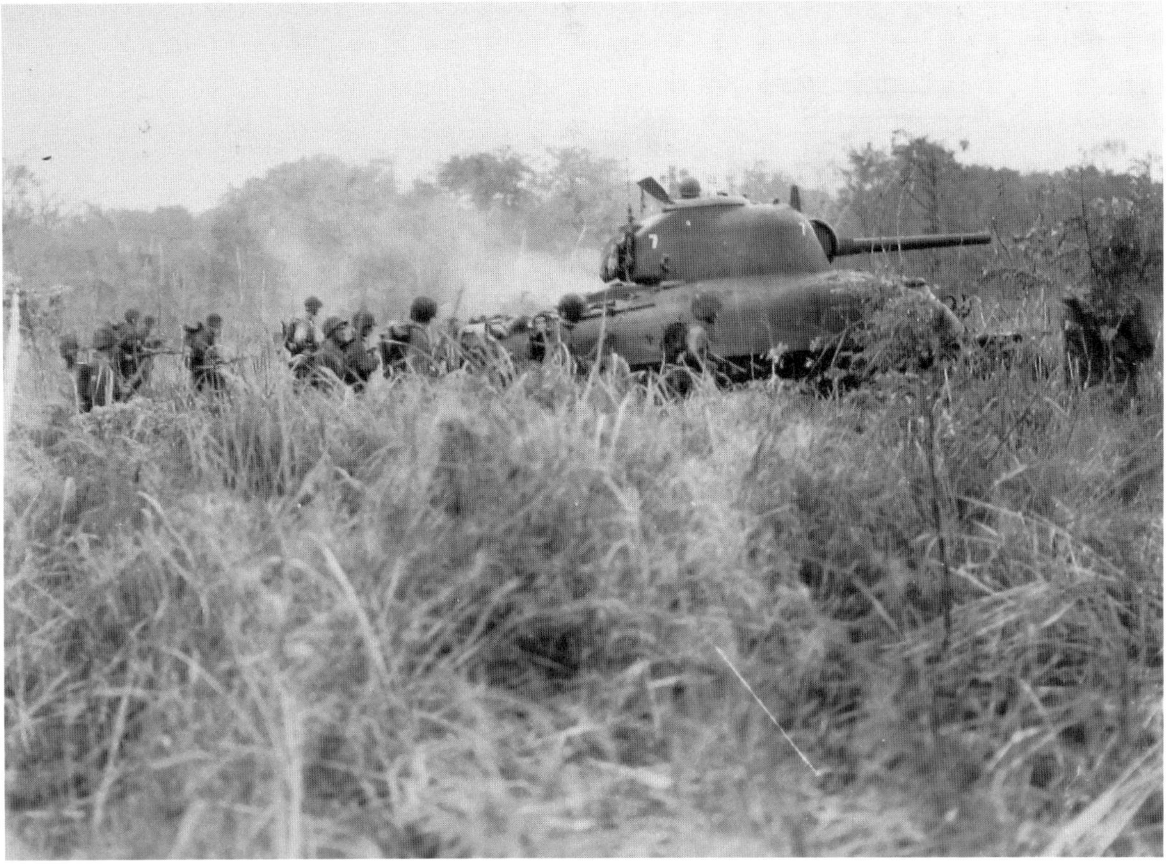

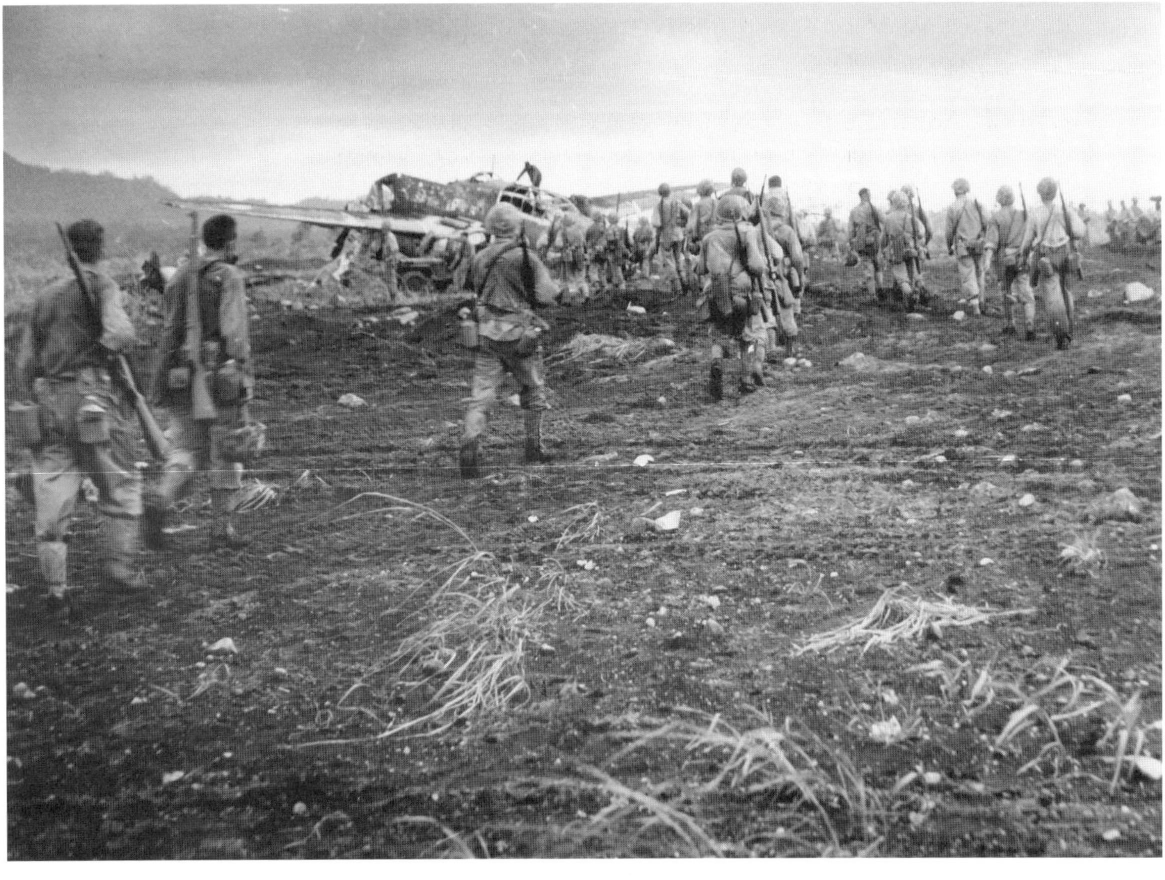

(**Above**) A Marine holds a folded American flag, about to be unfurled, standing next to Colonel William Whaling, CO 1st Marines, at an improvised flagpole in front of a wrecked IJN G4M1 Betty bomber, on 31 December 1943 at Airstrip No. 2, which had been seized two days earlier. This airfield, built by Australia before the war, was captured by Japanese SNLF troops on 17 December 1942. To the flagpole's right is Major General William Rupertus, CG 1st Marine Division, who radioed Krueger at Sixth Army HQ, 'First Marine Division presents to you an early New Year gift, the complete aerodrome of Cape Gloucester,' delighting Krueger, with MacArthur sending a congratulatory message. The aerodrome's capture cost the Marines 250 casualties, with an estimated 1,000 Japanese troops killed. (NARA)

(**Opposite, above**) Two Marines stand in a large Japanese tank trap. At this juncture of the campaign, with the airfields captured, the Japanese goal was to delay the Marine advance in order to extricate IJA troops from western New Britain eastwards, along jungle trails towards Rabaul. Marine patrols were dispatched in an attempt to thwart the Japanese retreat by cutting across the jungle trails and villages and eventually seizing the Talasea airstrip on the eastern coast of the Willaumez Peninsula. The Marines did not move farther east to another small enemy airfield at Cape Hoskins. (NARA)

(**Opposite, below**) A Marine infantry column moves along a washed-out trail from the torrential rains of Cape Gloucester's northwest monsoon. The 17th Marines (Engineer Regiment) were vital along with the 3rd Battalion USN 'Seabees', who cleared jungle for Marine riflemen, bulldozed stream banks for the tanks to get to enemy positions and built 'corduroy' causeways to traverse the flooded trails. (NARA)

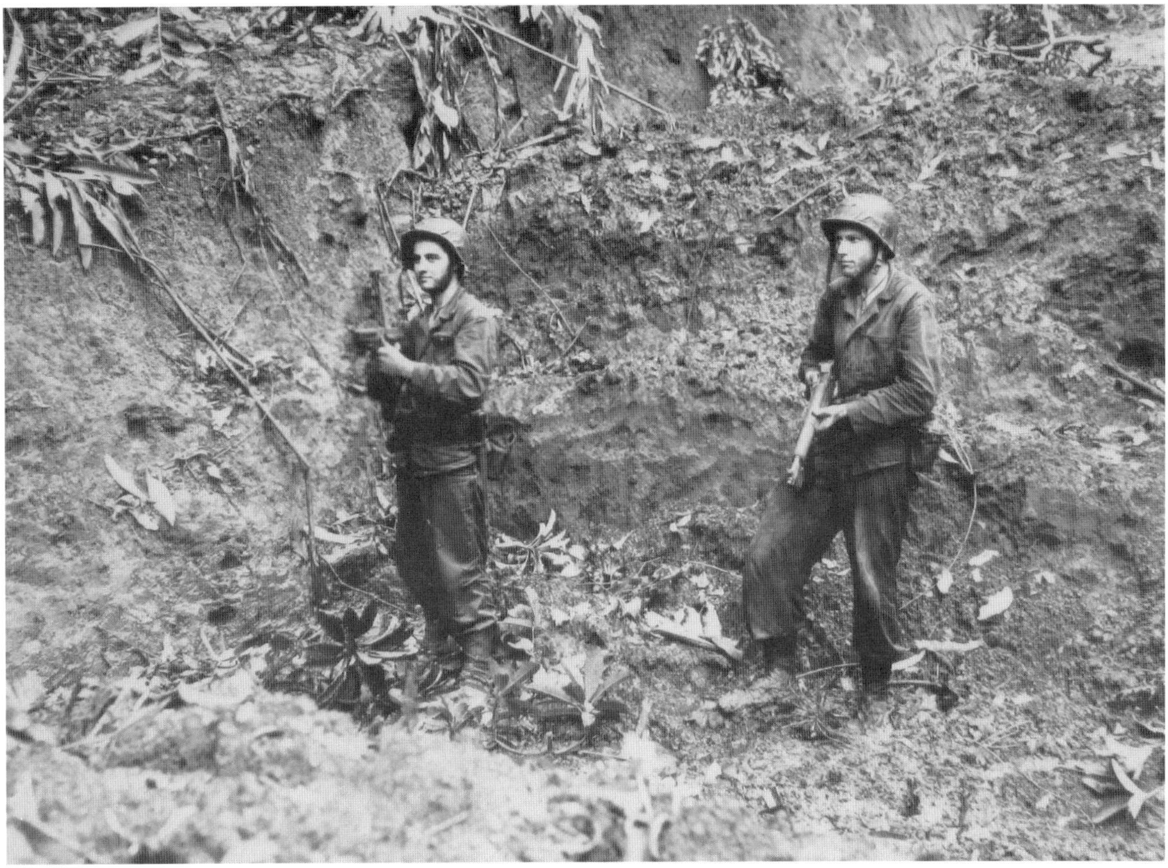

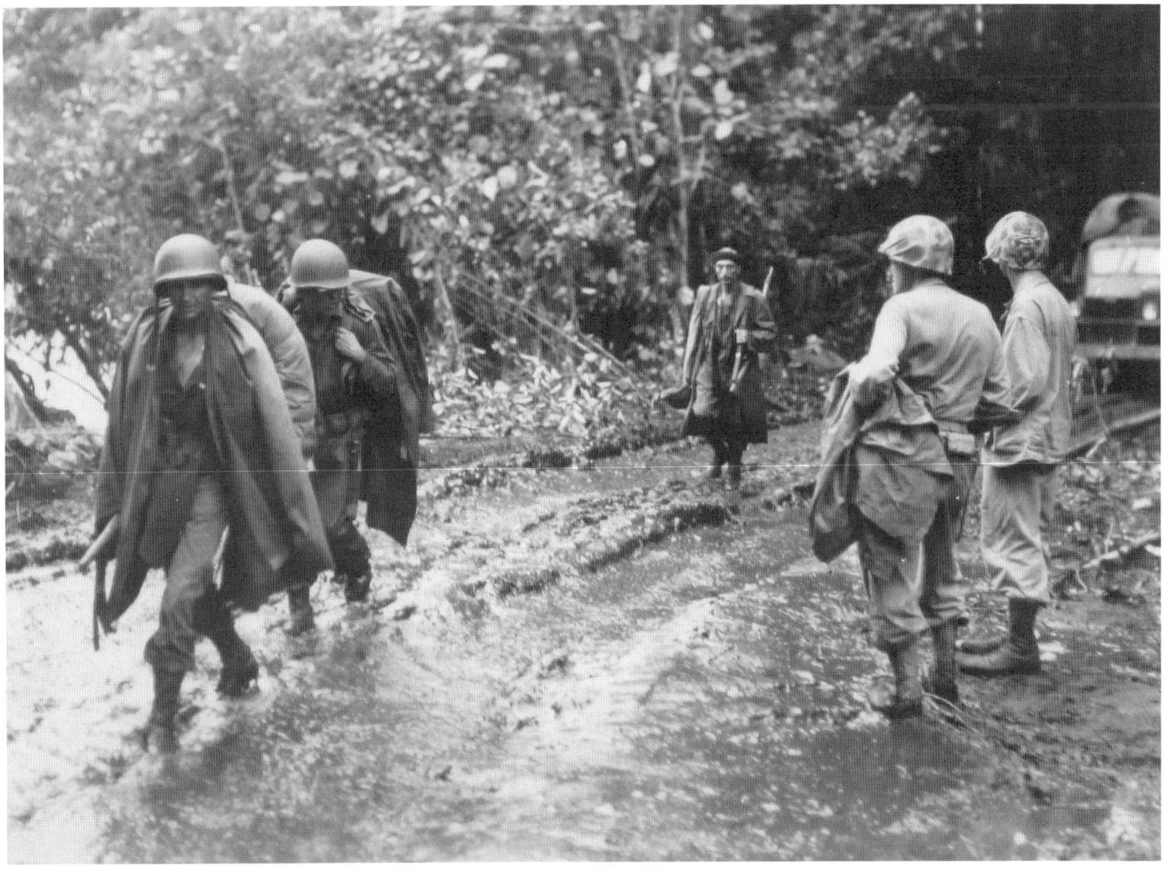

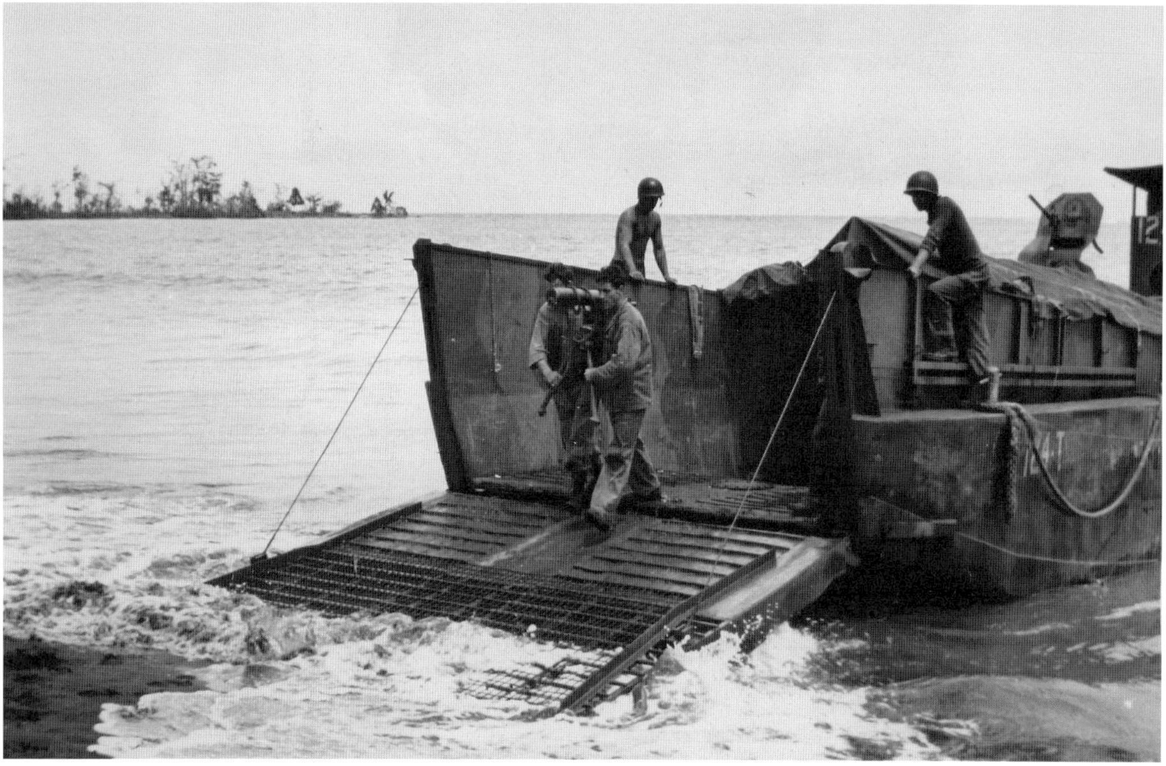

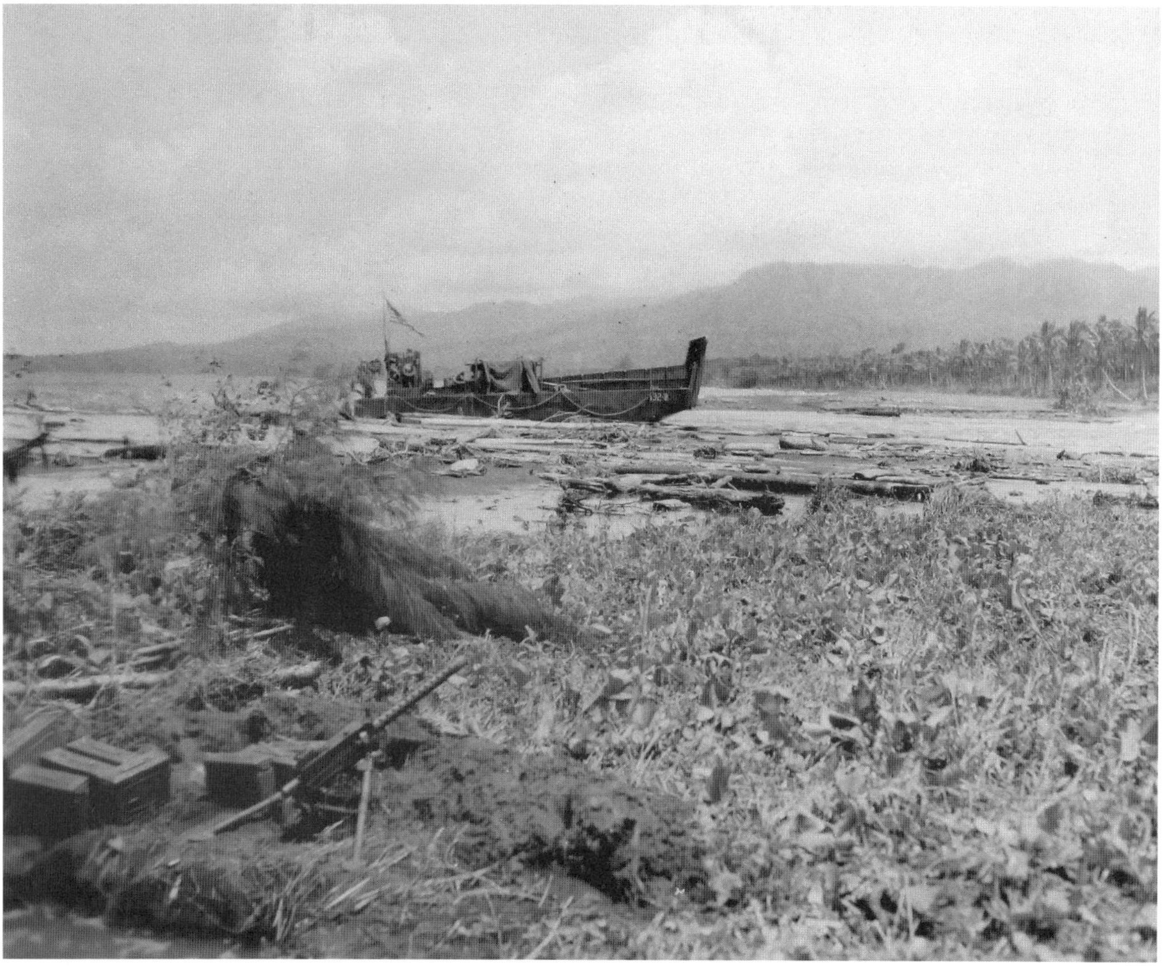

(**Opposite, above**) Marines unload a 0.30-inch calibre medium machine gun from a tank lighter at Natamo Point facing the middle of Borgen Bay, on 27 January 1944. Landing craft were indispensable for moving men, supplies, ordnance and equipment. Colonel John Selden's 5th Marines were tasked with dealing with the Japanese rearguard, led by IJA Colonel Sato along Borgen Bay's coastal road and in the immediate interior. On 20 January, a company of the 1st Battalion, 5th Marines ran into strong Japanese defences, with at least a hundred IJA infantry manning fifteen machine guns and a 75mm emplaced cannon at the base of Borgen Bay. (*NARA*)

(**Opposite, below**) A USN tank lighter or LCM, with its American flag unfurled, cruises into the mouth of the Natamo River. The Japanese were dug in on the riverbank and their machine gunners and riflemen halted the Marine advance for five days, inflicting casualties on 5th Marines. The USN tank lighter provided the necessary cover and gunfire to extricate the wounded Marines. When the Marines finally crossed the river on 29 January 1944, the Japanese abandoned their defences and pulled back past Natamo village, which the Marines reached on 2 February. In their advance, the Marines used LCMs to leapfrog ahead by as many as 10 miles during each operation. On 24 February, the 5th Marines reached the large native village of Iboki, at the head of a major north–south trail near the Aria River, 50 miles west of the Willaumez Peninsula. (*NARA*)

(**Above**) A heavily armed White Motor Company M3 GMC Marine half-track TD with a 75mm gun, gun shield, and crew with personal weapons is shown. The armoured vehicle also had heavy machine guns for AA defence and use against Japanese bunkers and pillboxes. This armoured vehicle and crew went in to rescue Marines trapped in a crossfire from Japanese machine-gun positions at the mouth of the Natamo River in late January 1944, with three of the crew dying. (*NARA*)

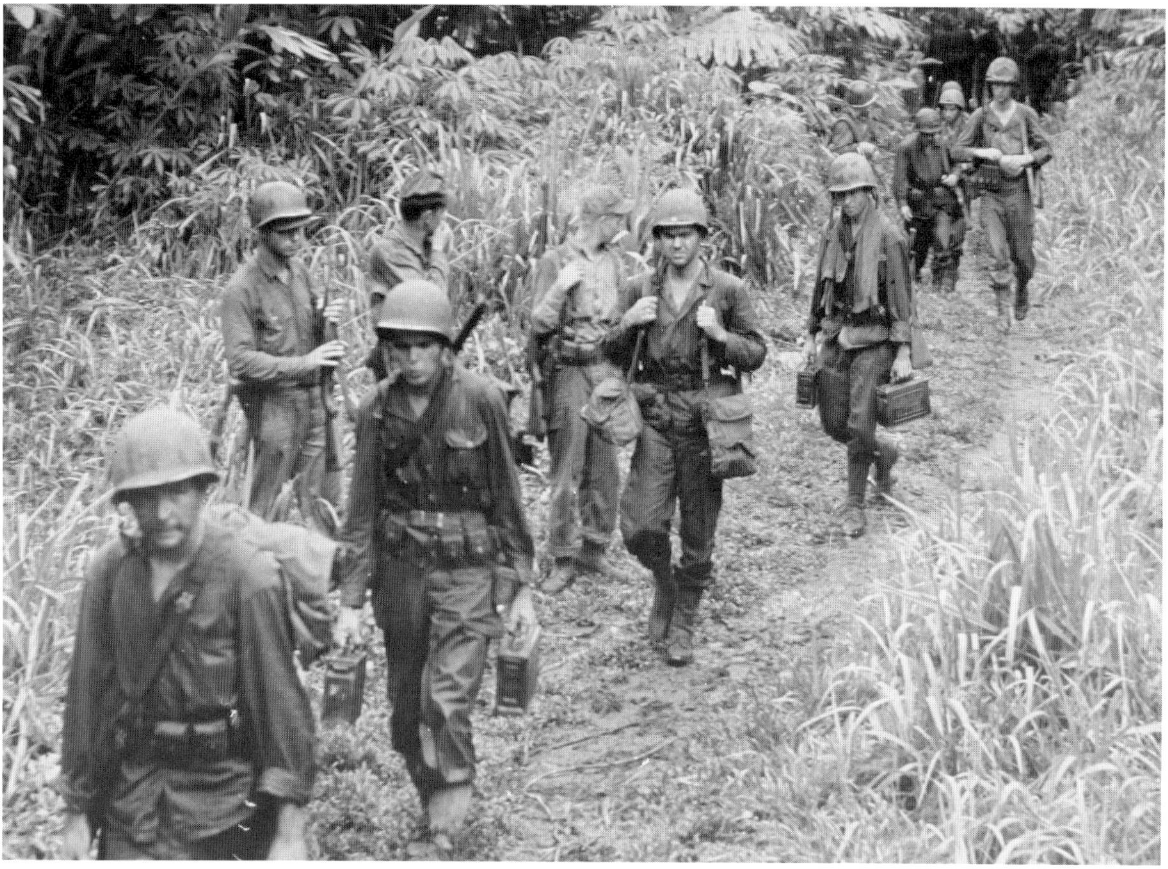

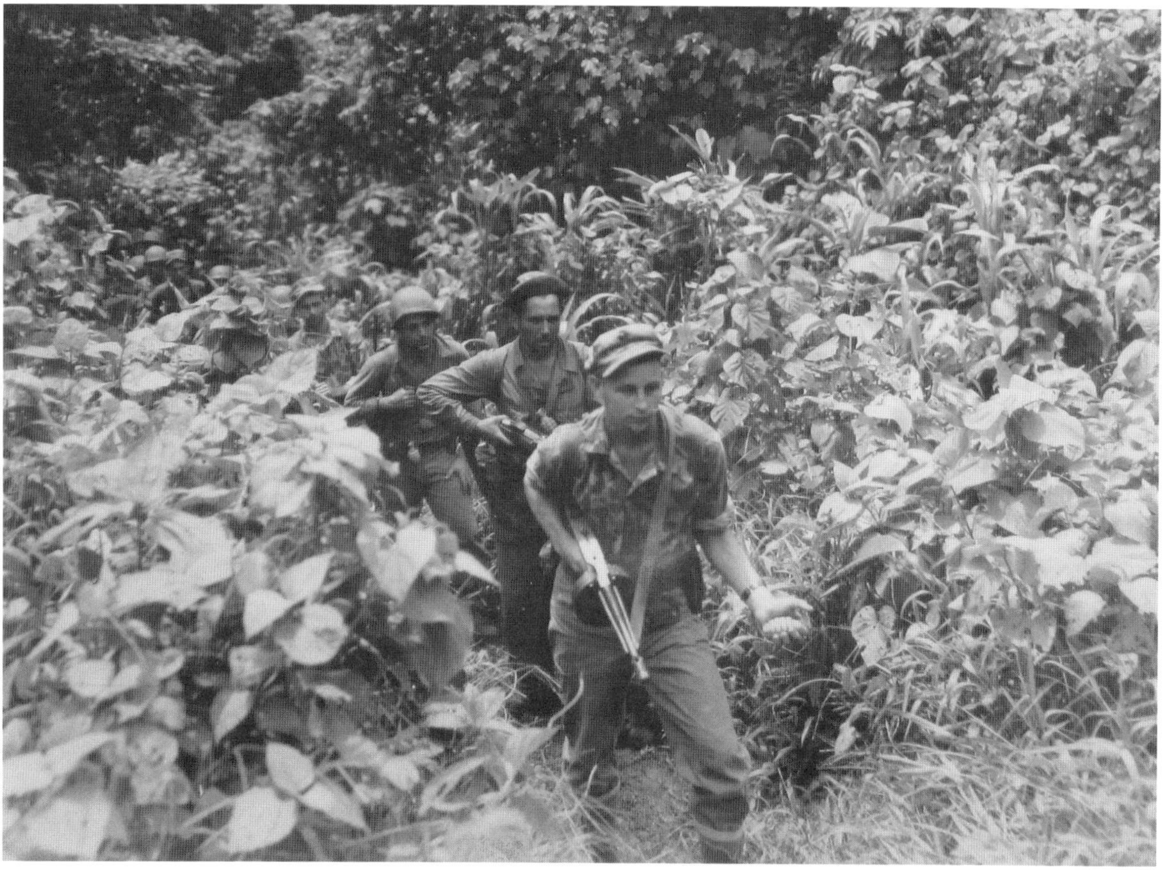

(**Opposite, above**) Marines move up a trail in pursuit of eastward-retreating Japanese Matsuda Force along the northern tip of New Britain. A combat team of the 5th Marines landed along the western coast of the Willaumez Peninsula on 6 March 1944 and advanced eastwards through jungle and dense scrub towards the Talasea landing strip on the peninsula's opposite coast, which they captured. Retreating Japanese defenders prevented the Marines from cutting off the withdrawing enemy force heading east for Rabaul. (NARA)

(**Opposite, below**) A Marine patrol pursues the withdrawing Japanese through jungle vegetation. By 9 April 1944, the bulk of the Matsuda Force and whatever it could carry retreated east past Cape Hoskins. On 22 April, the 2nd Battalion, 5th Marines ambushed a Japanese patrol, killing twenty of the enemy, comprising the final Marine action fought on New Britain. In seizing western New Britain as part of the isolation of Rabaul, the 1st Marine Division suffered 310 killed in action and 1,083 wounded, with 4,300 Japanese killed. Both Admiral Nimitz and General Vandegrift, the new commandant of the Marine Corps, did not want the 1st Marine Division idle on New Britain and they departed in two echelons on 6 April and 4 May, being replaced by the Army's 40th Infantry Division, under Major General Rapp Brush, on 10 April. (NARA)

(**Above**) The strain and fatigue of twenty-three days on the line at Cape Gloucester is clearly visible in the faces and postures of the men of the 7th Marines. The entire 1st Marine Division left MacArthur's SWPA command and went to a new training base on Pavuvu in the Russell Islands, in the southern Solomons, for extensive reinforcements, refitting, and preparation for the Peleliu invasion in the Palau Islands, slated for mid-September1944, to protect the flank of MacArthur's October 1944 invasion of Mindanao, which did not occur, as Leyte became the Philippine target instead. (NARA)

Stretcher-bearers take marine dead to a landing craft to be transported to a cemetery for burial on drier ground for deceased Marines and airmen. An LCM is in the background. *(NARA)*

Chapter Five

US 1st Cavalry Division's Invasions of Los Negros and Manus in the Admiralty Islands (February to March 1944)

In mid-February 1944, MacArthur and Halsey wanted to seize the larger two Admiralty Islands of Los Negros and Manus and their airfields, 200 miles northeast of mainland New Guinea and 270 miles west of Kavieng, to further isolate Rabaul, 360 miles away to the east. The smaller Lorengau Drome at the northern end of Manus was improved by the Japanese from a civil landing strip in April 1942. In October 1943, the Japanese built the larger Momote Drome at Momote Plantation on eastern Los Negros, with a 5,000ft runway complete with dispersals and revetments. Towards the end of 1943, the Japanese used the two airfields for staging aircraft flying between Rabaul, Wewak and Hollandia.

To the north of the two islands is Seeadler Harbour, an excellent anchorage for Second World War fleets, being 6 miles wide, 20 miles long and 120 feet deep, which the Japanese did not extensively use with possession of Rabaul's Simpson Harbour. Guarding Seeadler Harbour to the north is a line of islets: Koruniat, Ndrilo, Hauwei, Pityilu and others that parallel Manus's north coast. To the south of the Admiralties is the Bismarck Sea. Manus, the largest in the group (49 miles from east to west and 16 miles across) and of volcanic origin, is separated from Los Negros by a narrow strait, Loniu Passage. Irregularly shaped Los Negros is cut by several inlets, with Papitalai Harbour, an extension of Seeadler Harbour, separated from Hyane Harbour by a low, 50-yard-wide native skidway.

The Japanese garrison on the Admiralties consisted of the 51st Transport Regiment, commanded by Colonel Yoshio Ezaki, which was augmented by units of the 14th Naval Base Force, and in January 1944 by the

2nd Battalion, IJA Independent Mixed Regiment and 1st Battalion, IJA 229th Infantry Regiment, all from Kavieng on New Ireland. Ezaki placed his main strength on Los Negros to defend Seeadler Harbour and Momote Drome against an attack from the north, as he believed that an Allied attack from the east at Hyane Harbour was not practical with its narrow and defensible entrance.

The Allied Air Forces bombed the Admiralties and Kavieng during February's first two weeks. By 6 February, Momote and Lorengau airfields were unserviceable, cratered and overgrown with grass, with no planes present. During a 23 February B-25 low-level reconnaissance over Los Negros and Manus, the medium bombers were not fired on and no Japanese ground troops or vehicles were seen under Colonel Ezaki's orders.

On 25 February 1944, MacArthur ordered a reconnaissance-in-force, with 1,000 men of the US 1st Cavalry Division and other units transported from Papua's Oro Bay (see Map 3) to Los Negros by two APDs (high-speed transport destroyers), one destroyer division and the USN cruisers *Phoenix* and *Nashville* for bombardment. The amphibious force was to arrive no later than 29 February, with the cavalrymen seizing Momote Drome, preparing the airfield for transport arrival, and holding their positions for reinforcements.

The reconnaissance force's CO was Brigadier General William C. Chase, commanding the 1st Cavalry Brigade, comprising its HQ troops; the 2nd Squadron, 5th Cavalry; two 75mm howitzers of B Battery, 99th FA Battalion; the 673rd AA Battery with 0.50-inch calibre machine guns; and an ANGAU. A 'Brewer' Support Force, under Colonel Hugh Hoffman, would land on D-Day +2 with the remainder of the 5th Cavalry; C Battery, the 99th FA Battalion (90mm guns); 168th AA Battalion; and A Battery, 211th Coast Artillery AA Battalion (multiple 0.50-inch calibre multiple mount machine guns); and other support, engineer, medical detachment and 'Seabees'.

Hyane Harbour's shoreline was covered by mangroves, but on the south, just 150 yards east of Momote Drome was a 1,200-yard sandy beach with three jetties, offering passage for troops and vehicles of the 2nd Squadron, 5th Cavalry. H Hour was 0815 on 29 February, with USN cruisers and destroyers taking their support and firing stations at 0740 hours. Japanese 20mm machine guns fired on the landing craft as they passed through Hyane Harbour's entrance as heavier enemy guns targeted the USS *Phoenix* (on which MacArthur was aboard) and accompanying destroyers, but they were silenced by naval gunfire. The first wave of landing craft, carrying G Troop, 2nd Squadron, 5th Cavalry, met little resistance passing through the entrance and turned south towards the beach, touching down at 0817 without any American casualties. Several Japanese were killed making off towards nearby Momote Drome. However, American landing craft received enemy fire on the way in and out of Hyane Harbour's entrance, damaging four of the twelve LCP(R) of the third landing wave.

By 0950, 2nd Squadron troopers overran dilapidated Momote Drome, with the entire Reconnaissance Force ashore by 1250 hours, with 0.50-inch calibre AA machine guns and two 75mm howitzers manhandled ashore. Vice Admiral Thomas Kinkaid and MacArthur came ashore at 1600 hours for MacArthur to award a DSC to Lieutenant Marvin Henshaw, the first man ashore leading his platoon across the beach. Returning to the USS *Phoenix*, MacArthur radioed orders for more troops, equipment and supplies to be urgently sent to Los Negros. The destroyers, USS *Bush* and *Stockton*, remained to support the cavalrymen as the invasion flotilla returned to New Guinea. The cavalrymen could not deploy their 75mm howitzers due to the narrow beachhead; they lacked barbed wire; and digging foxholes through coral rock near the airstrip was difficult.

Only the 1st Battalion, IJA 229th Infantry Regiment was responsible for the defence of the now-captured airfield and the penetrated Hyane Harbour. Another regimental battalion defended Lorengau Airfield on Manus, while the 2nd Battalion, IJA 1st IMR was at Salami Plantation to the north of Hyane Harbour. General Imamura on Rabaul ordered Ezaki to attack with his entire strength but the IJA colonel only directed the 1st Battalion, IJA 229th Infantry Regiment to attack on the night of 29 February, and by daylight of 1 March, most of this force withdrew. Seven cavalrymen died, with fifteen wounded, compared to sixty-six enemy corpses within the perimeter. The next night's Japanese infiltration of the cavalrymen's perimeter cost eighty Japanese dead.

After the 2 March landing of 'Brewer' Support Force with 1,500 combat troops, 500 'Seabees', and the 2nd Engineer Special Brigade, Momote Airfield was entirely in American possession, as from 29 February to 2 March, the 2nd Squadron, 5th Cavalry's perimeter abutted only the eastern edge of Momote Airfield.

The final IJA attack on the night of 3/4 March met the cavalrymen's improved defences; nonetheless, some areas of the cavalry's perimeter were pierced by effective Japanese use of mortars and artillery, but over 160 Japanese were killed without any prisoners. Sixty-one Americans were killed with 244 wounded, including nine 'Seabees' killed and forty-four wounded.

The 12th Cavalry, Chase's other 1st Cavalry Brigade regiment, landed at Los Negros's Hyane Harbour three days sooner than planned, on 6 March, and the division's 2nd Cavalry Brigade now slated to land on 9 March instead of on the 16th. The 12th Cavalry's RCT, commanded by Colonel John Stadler, comprised over 2,000 men including the 12th Cavalry, the 271st FA Battalion (105mm howitzers) and three light tanks of the 603rd Tank Company as well as engineers, medical and signal troops. Krueger wanted Seeadler Harbour operational as Hyane Harbour and the original beachhead were too congested to receive the 2nd Cavalry Brigade. By the end of 6 March, the 1st Cavalry Brigade squadrons held the Salami beachhead, after their tanks and 75mm howitzers blasted Japanese bunkers there, to enable the 9 March 2nd Cavalry Brigade landing.

Major General Innis Swift, 1st Cavalry Division CG, proceeded to Los Negros to take command ashore on 5 March. Swift instructed the 2nd Cavalry Brigade, after it arrived at Salami Plantation, to be prepared to move to Manus at Lugos Mission, west of Lorengau, and attack eastwards against that airfield and secure the eastern half of the island.

Allied naval gunfire and aerial attacks completely neutralized Japanese guns guarding the entrance to Seeadler Harbour from 5 to 7 March. From 6 to 8 March, the 5th Cavalry extended its control beyond the Momote Drome. The 2nd Squadron took Porlaka on 6 March, and crossed Lemondrol Creek in assault boats and amphibious tractors to seize Papitalai village on 7 March. The 12th Cavalry, with its tanks, patrolled to the northwest tip of Los Negros at Mokerang to cover the 2nd Brigade landing at Salami. On 9 March, destroyers shelled Lorengau on Manus and minesweepers cleared Seeadler Harbour for the six LSTs and one cargo ship bringing Brigadier General Verne D. Mudge's 2nd Cavalry Brigade to Salami Plantation. Los Negros was firmly in Allied hands. The next target was the seizure of Lorengau Airfield on Manus by Mudge's 2nd Cavalry Brigade.

Reconnaissance showed Lorengau Aerodrome and Lorengau village, east of it, was fortified, while Lugos Mission was practically undefended. Beaches Yellow 1 and 2, on the east and west side of the Liei River, were chosen as landing sites to the west of Lugos Mission on Manus's northern coast. Squadrons from the 7th and 8th Cavalry were to make the landings on 15 March. Elements from this force would move east along No. 3 Road against Lorengau Airfield while other units moved inland to No. 1 Road, and then east towards Lorengau village.

Hauwei Island, bordering Seeadler Harbour to the north, the Butjo Luo group of islets at the southern end of Seeadler Harbour, and Pityilu Island, at the northwestern end of Seeadler Harbour, were all occupied by US FA units to provide supportive gunfire for the 2nd Cavalry Brigade's landing at Lugos Mission at 0400 hours on 15 March. Other support included USN destroyer 5-inch gunfire and B-25 strafing and bombing sorties from Nadzab. Landing without casualties, the 8th Cavalry's two-squadron advance against Lorengau Airfield and Lorengau village along No. 3 and No. 1 Roads, respectively, began. The 1st Squadron fought its way along the coast on No. 3 Road. Even with the aid of Hauwei's 105mm howitzers of the 271st FA Battalion, B Troop's attack was halted by Japanese pillboxes. Continued tank and artillery gunfire along with RAAF P-40 Kittyhawk attacks with 500lb bombs neutralized Japanese pillboxes, the airstrip's western defences, allowing the 1st Squadron to move along the coast road. By 1700 hours, the 1st Squadron was overlooking Lorengau Airfield; however, only the centre of the airfield was reached on 16 March. There were light casualties on both sides. The major obstacle for the 2nd Squadron was the terrain along No. 1 Road inland.

Mudge relieved the 1st Squadron, 8th Cavalry with the 7th Cavalry. A coordinated attack was made on 17 March as the 7th Cavalry and the 2nd Squadron, 8th Cavalry took the remainder of the airstrip and pushed over the Lorengau River to Lorengau village. Supporting tank gunfire, artillery and flamethrowers wiped out the Japanese pillboxes.

Most of the Japanese defences at Lorengau village faced seaward. The Lorengau River was 60ft wide and 10–20ft deep, making the 2nd Brigade's best approach route to the village over an alluvial sandbar at the mouth of the waterway. On the morning of 18 March, the 2nd Squadron, 8th Cavalry attacked and the enemy retreated inland over No. 2 Road towards Rossum in Manus's interior, which the 2nd Cavalry Brigade cleared on 25 March. Approximately 100 Japanese were killed defending Lorengau village while the 2nd Squadron, 8th Cavalry captured it at a cost of seven wounded.

The capture of Momote and Lorengau airfields were the main strategic objectives achieved in the Admiralties campaign, which cost the 1st Cavalry Division 326 troopers killed, 1,189 wounded, and 4 missing. Over 3,200 Japanese corpses were buried, with 75 prisoners taken. Momote Drome was first used by No. 76 Squadron RAAF on 9 March as nine P-40 Kittyhawks arrived from Kiriwina, staging via Finschhafen. The runway was 7,000ft long by 18 May 1944. Lorengau Drome proved unsuitable. Seeadler Harbour was transformed into one of the largest naval bases in the Pacific, with repair facilities for all types of warships and transports. This naval base served the Third, Fifth and Seventh Fleets in later operations and Momote Drome supported MacArthurs's drive along the Dutch New Guinea coast.

Emirau Island

In late 1943, Halsey met with MacArthur to oppose the SWPA CG's plan to seize Kavieng on New Ireland's northern tip. Halsey preferred seizing Emirau Island in the St Matthias group, 90 miles northwest of Kavieng (see Map 2), as they were not occupied by the Japanese, whereas Kavieng was a major, strongly defended Japanese air and naval base. The JCS and Nimitz agreed with Halsey, and an air and naval base was to be established at Emirau to further blockade the Bismarck Archipelago, while continued operations to neutralize Rabaul and Kavieng proceeded.

Halsey selected a new regiment, the 4th Marines, created from recently disbanded Marine Raider battalions, to seize Emirau Island. The landing force sailed from Guadalcanal on 18 March 1944 and made an uncontested voyage past the Solomons and New Ireland to Emirau. On 20 March, while four old USN battleships bombarded Kavieng, the Marines landed unopposed. Within a month, 18,000 men and 44,000 tons of supplies were delivered to Emirau. The first airstrip and naval facilities were operational in May, from which Allied planes and PT boats patrolled Kavieng and the rest of New Ireland. When Allied bomber strips were ready, long-range bombers from Emirau could reach Truk. The occupation of Emirau Island by SPA forces completed Rabaul's encirclement and Kavieng's neutralization by air.

(**Opposite, above**) Momote Drome is bombed by 5th USAAF units on 20 February 1944, nine days before the 5th Cavalry's amphibious assault. Destroyed aircraft and vehicles are at the runway's end as other bombs explode in a clearing towards the shore. The 5th USAAF was actively striking the Admiralty Islands repeatedly in January, with major aerial assaults mounted on 6 and 13 February. American pilots reported that there were few Japanese on either Los Negros Island or Manus Island, as strict concealment orders were issued as the enemy commander suspected an imminent invasion. However, a pre-invasion American reconnaissance team found Los Negros having a large Japanese garrison. (NARA)

(**Opposite, below**) General MacArthur (centre), Vice Admiral Thomas Kinkaid, CO US Seventh Fleet and Commander Allied Naval Forces SWPA since November 1943 (left), and Colonel Lloyd Lehrbas (right) view the Admiralty Islands' naval bombardment from the cruiser USS *Phoenix* on 28 February 1944, the day before the amphibious assault. Lehrbas was MacArthur's personal press aide from March 1942. Kinkaid was promoted to admiral on 3 April 1945. (NARA)

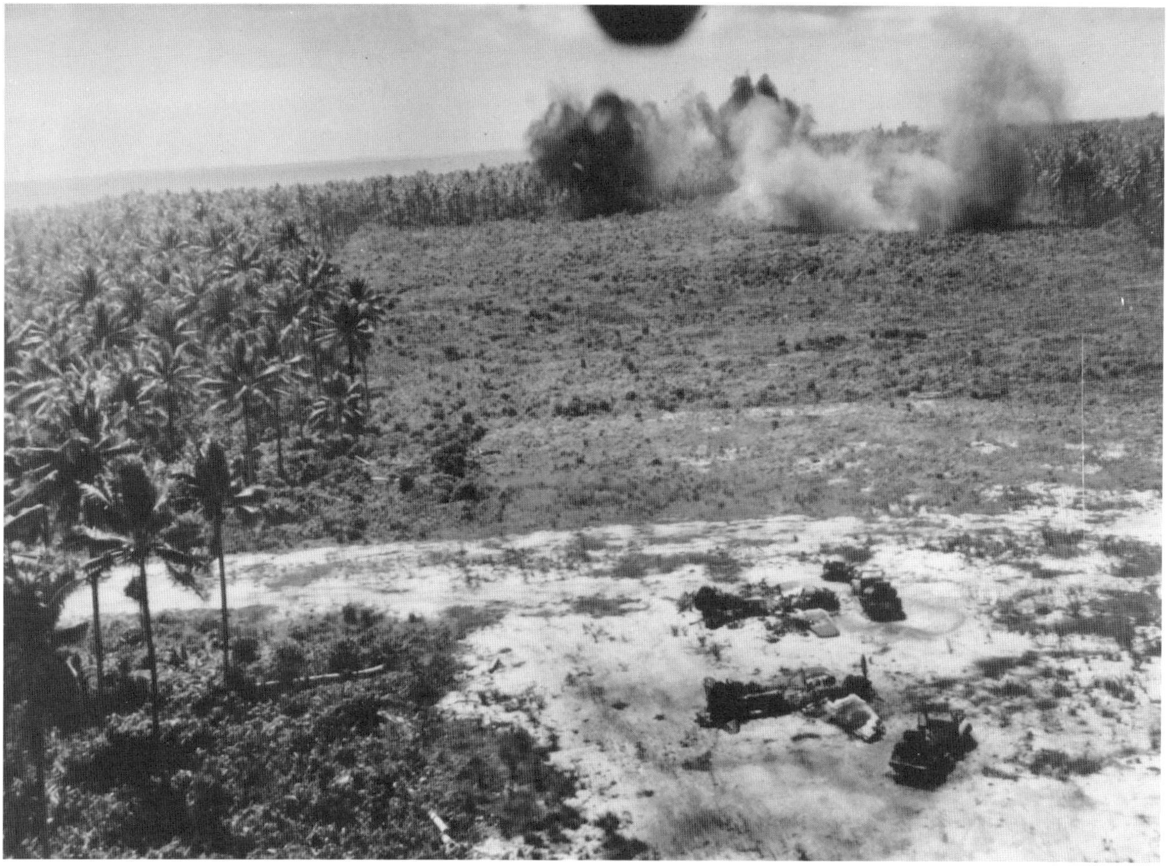

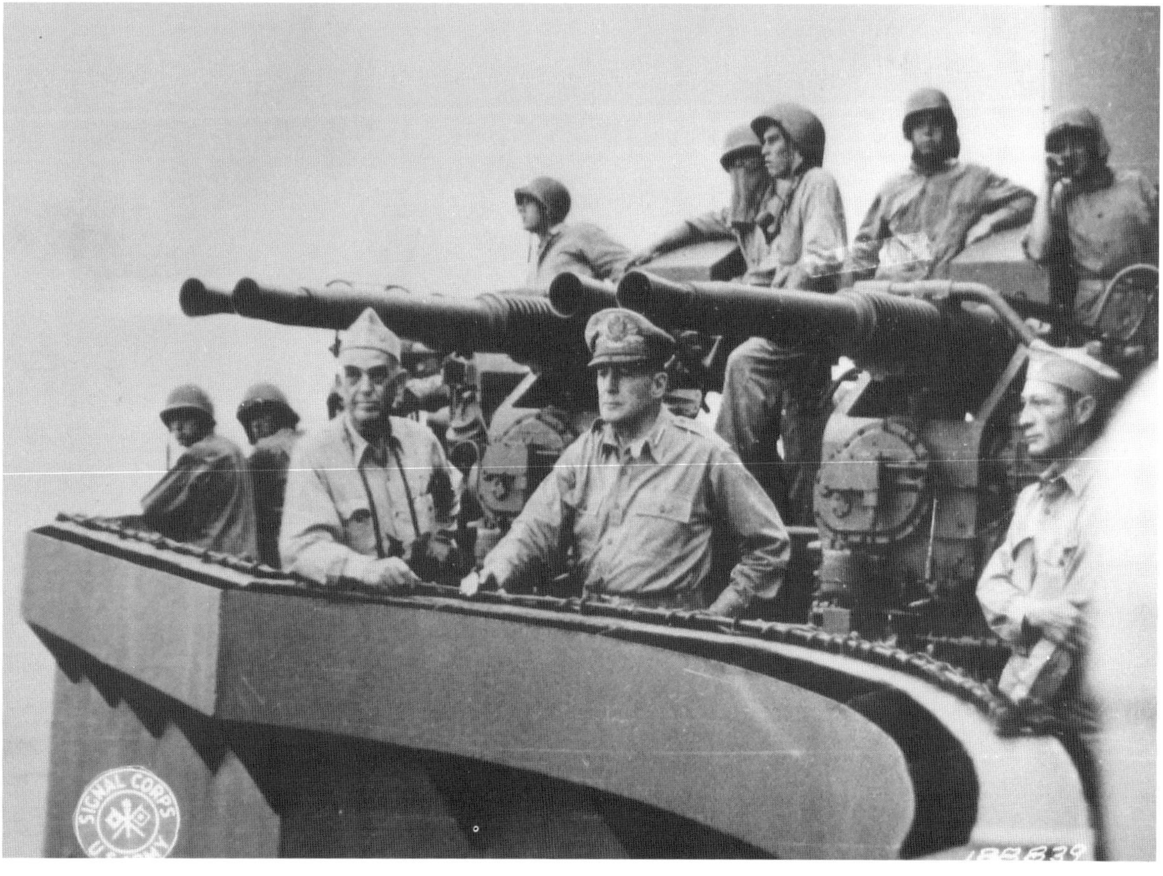
SIGNAL CORPS
U.S. ARMY

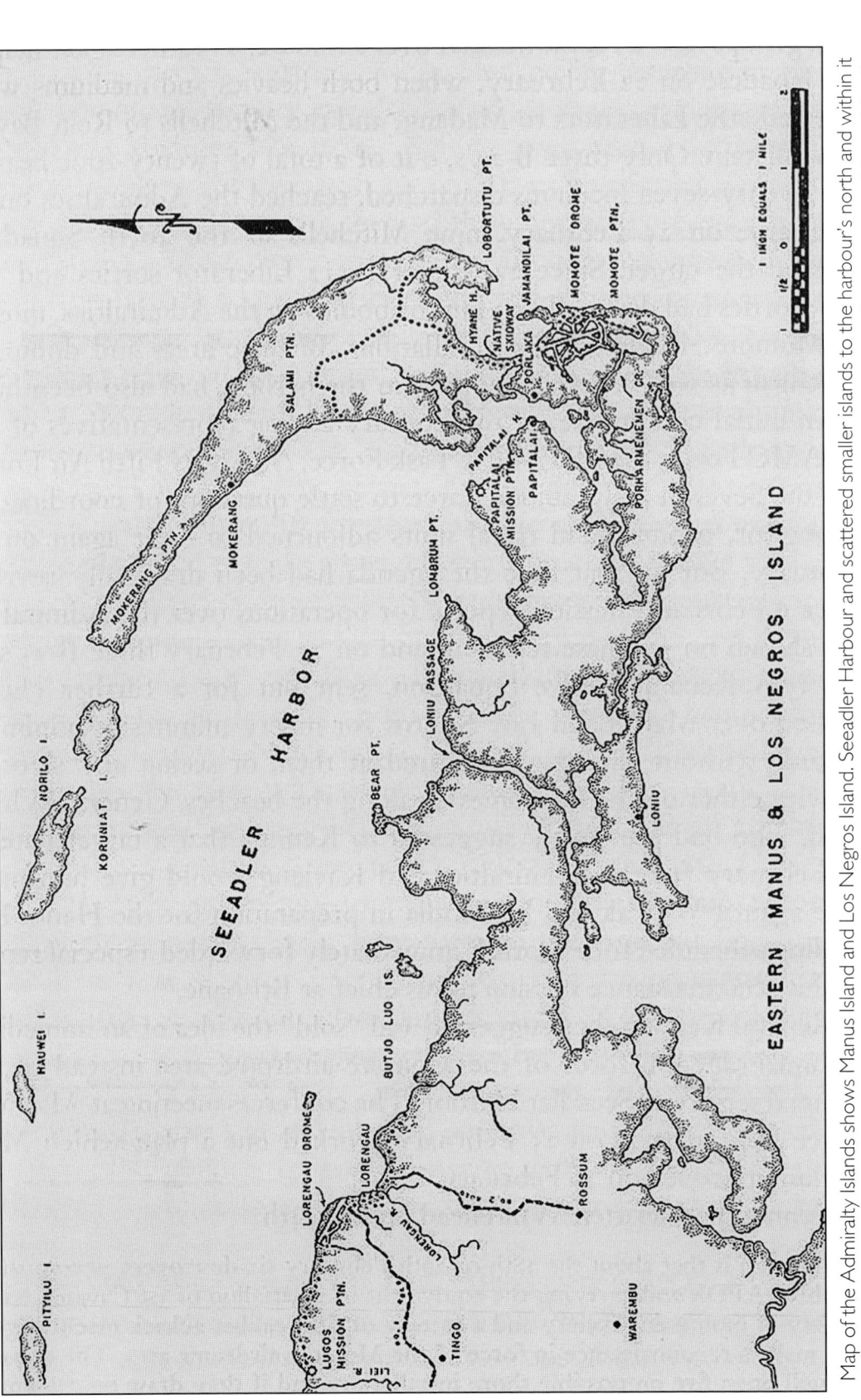

Map of the Admiralty Islands shows Manus Island and Los Negros Island. Seeadler Harbour and scattered smaller islands to the harbour's north and within it are shown. Momote Drome was situated on Los Negros's east coast of the island near Hyane Harbour's entrance. Lorengau Drome was on Manus Island's northern coast, west of Lorengau village. (USN)

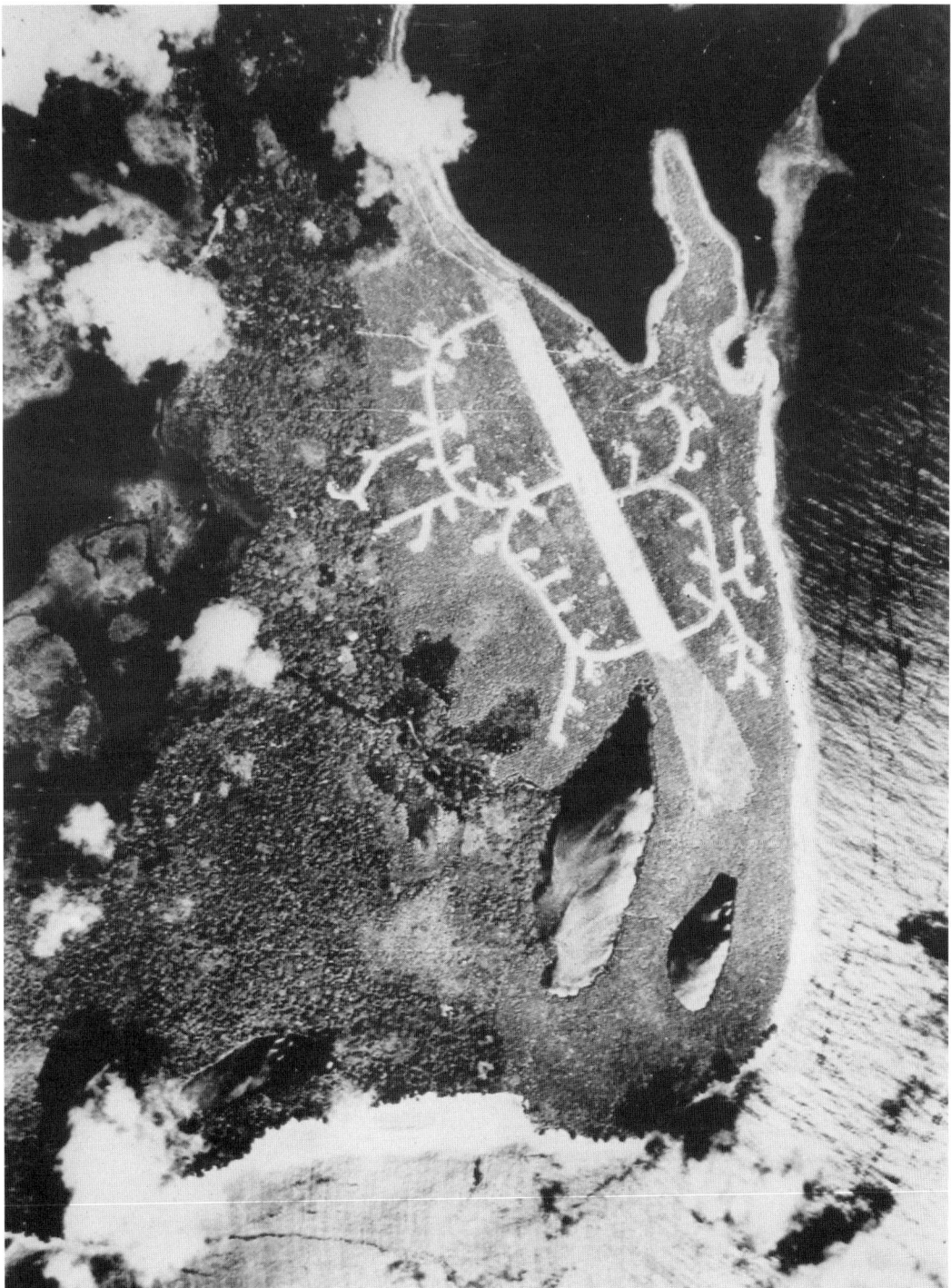

Aerial photograph of Los Negros's Momote Drome on the island's east coast at Hyane Harbour's southern end, with a major runway, taxiways and revetments. The 2nd Squadron, 5th Cavalry's landing beach was just to the right of the upper runway area as the airfield's seizure was the primary objective of the 29 February 1944 Cavalry's reconnaissance force amphibious assault. (NARA)

(**Above**) The first wave of G Troop, 2nd Squadron, 5th Cavalry lands on Los Negros near Hyane Harbour's southern end from LCP(R) assault craft on 29 February 1944. The initial 150 cavalrymen of G Troop, 2nd Squadron ashore, commanded by Lieutenant Colonel William Lobit, reached Momote Airfield by 0950 hours on D-Day. Few Japanese were encountered, as they retreated past the airfield. After the fourth wave landed, a 300-yard defensive perimeter inland was established. By 1300 hours, the entire 2nd Squadron, 5th Cavalry Reconnaissance Force along with two 75mm pack howitzers was ashore. American casualties for the landing were low, with two men killed and three wounded. (NARA)

(**Opposite, above**) By 1600 hours on 29 February 1944, MacArthur (background with cap) and Kinkaid came ashore in the rain and tramped through the mud to inspect the troops and confer with Brigadier General William C. Chase (middle), CO 1st Cavalry Brigade, 1st Cavalry Division, accompanied by Colonel Lloyd Lehrbas (right), MacArthur's aide. Some 5th Cavalry troopers bring supplies forward in a cart to Momote Airfield, which had been captured within hours of the landing. (NARA)

(**Opposite, below**) A US Signal Corpsman uses a field telephone under a poncho to avoid the rain (foreground) amid several downed trees from the pre-invasion naval bombardment of Los Negros. He aids a mortar crew (background) adjusting their target sighting in defence of the 5th Cavalry Regiment's perimeter near Momote Airfield at dusk on 29 February 1944. Brigadier General Chase, CO 1st Cavalry Brigade, asked Krueger's HQ for an airdrop of small arms and mortar ammunition, which was accomplished the next day. MacArthur, upon his return to USS *Phoenix* after his D-Day inspection tour, ordered Krueger to send reinforcements from Finschhafen, New Guinea. (NARA)

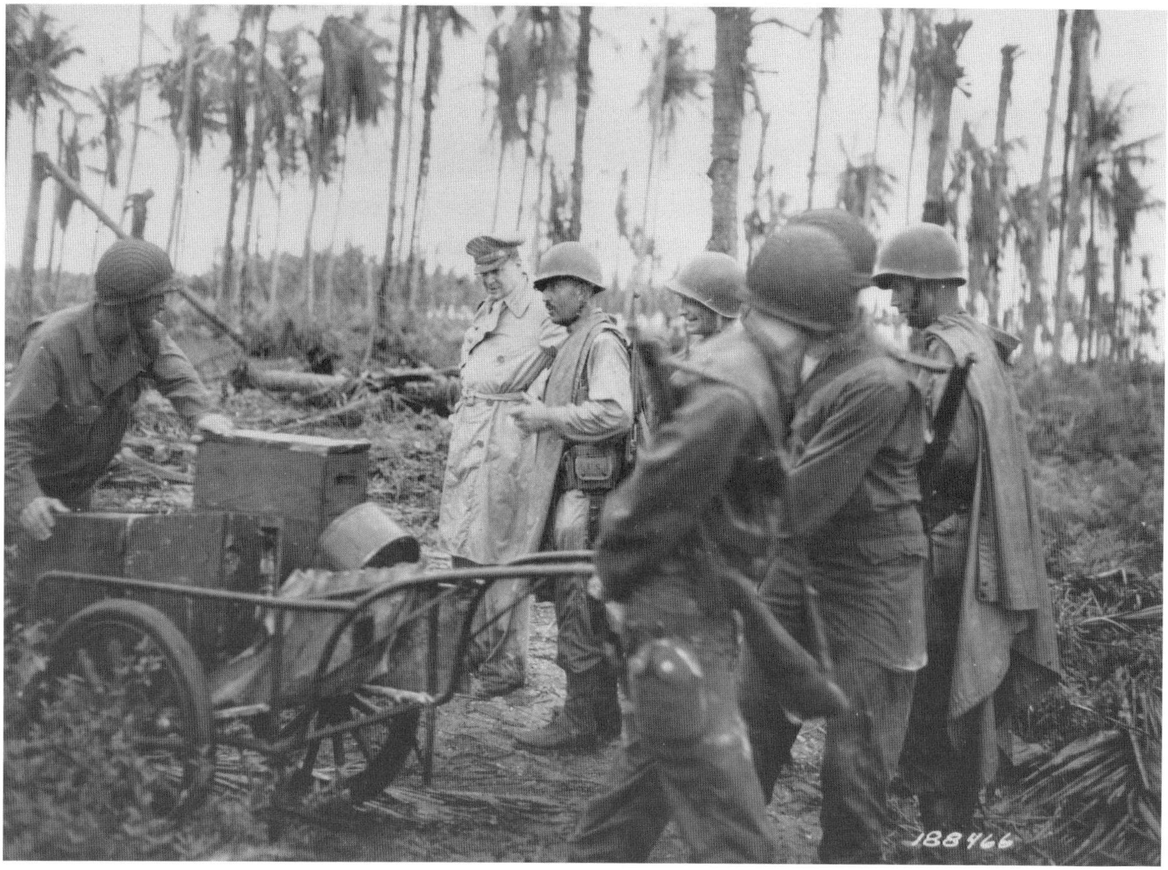
188466

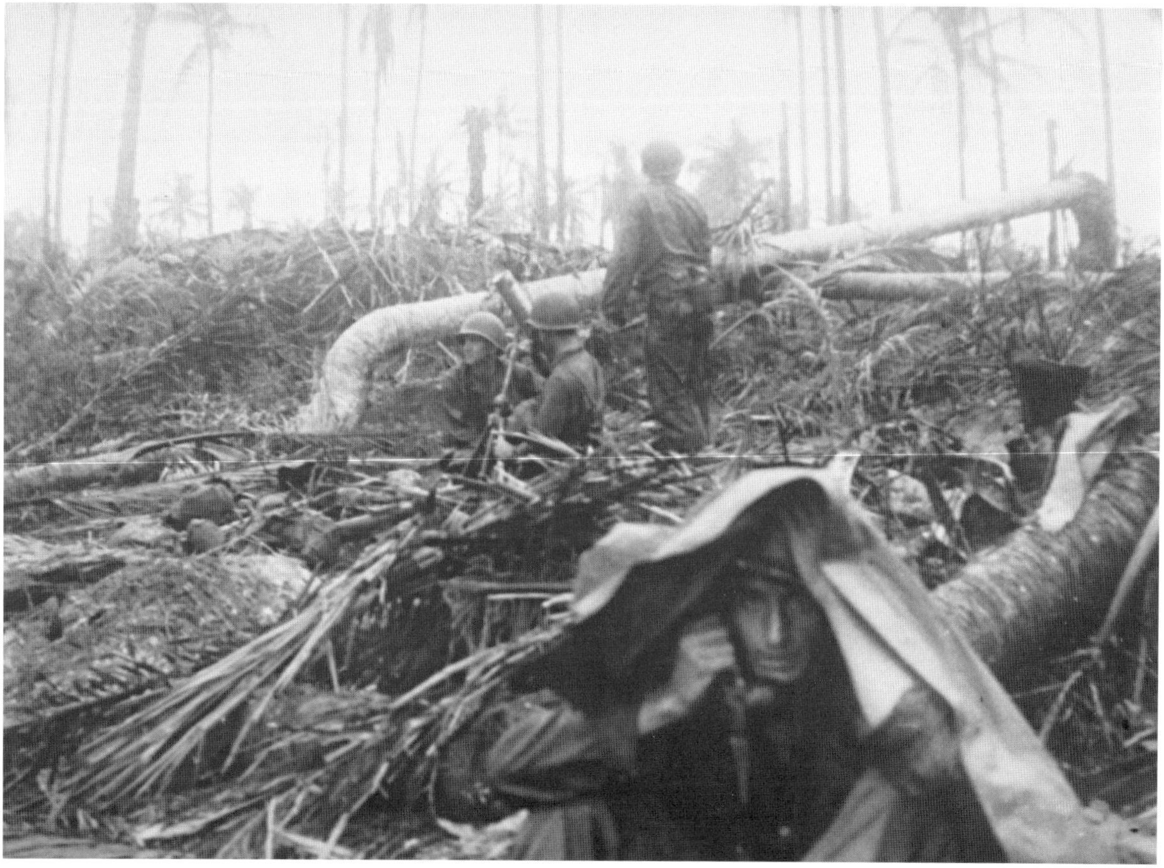

(**Above**) Cavalrymen arduously dig foxholes with picks in the hard coral to Momote Airfield's east, late on 29 February 1944. Their supporting arms were only 0.50-inch calibre machine guns, mortars, and the two 75mm pack howitzers that landed that day. The USN covering force left two destroyers, which provided crucial 5-inch naval gunfire until reinforcements arrived. At dusk, elements of the 1st Battalion, IJA 229th Infantry Regiment, commanded by Captain Baba, commenced a series of failed, disjointed attacks against the 5th Cavalry's perimeter, leaving sixty-six dead Japanese with seven dead and fifteen wounded cavalrymen. (NARA)

(**Opposite, above**) On 2 March 1944, Chase, in anticipation of the reinforcements from Finschhafen, expanded the perimeter to control the entire airfield again. A quadruple 0.50-inch calibre AA machine gun, mounted on a 4-wheel trailer and manned by the 211th Coast Artillery AA Battalion with extra ammunition containers, was delivered with the reinforcements and was dug into a coral gun pit near the airfield, with 'Seabees' using bulldozers and graders (left background) and an abandoned Japanese aircraft revetment (right background). (NARA)

(**Below**) A 75mm pack howitzer from Battery B 99th FA Battalion, attached to the 5th Cavalry, fires rounds at the Japanese from Momote Airfield. At dusk on 3 March 1944, the IJA 2nd Battalion, 1st IMB delivered the main attack against G and F Troops, 2nd Squadron, 5th Cavalry. Many Japanese succumbed to the American perimeter minefield while others received heavy small-arms fire by the cavalry troopers. Chase called for fire support from his offshore destroyers, which fired on Ezaki's troops. These 75mm guns and the 105mm howitzers of the newly arrived 82nd FA Battalion fired 8,500 rounds before the Japanese attacks ended on 5 March. *(NARA)*

(**Above**) A B-17 Flying Fortress takes off from the Momote airstrip on 29 March 1944. A total of five airstrips were built in the Admiralty Islands by January 1945. At Momote, the 40th Naval Construction Battalion, which had defended the airstrip at Momote on 3–4 March, was joined by other 'Seabees' of the 17th, 46th, 78th and 104th Naval Construction Battalions. The 'Seabees' worked on the Momote airstrip, dock and road construction. A damaged B-25 was the first airplane to land on the strip, on 6 March. Nine RAAF 76th Fighter Squadron P-40 Kittyhawks landed on the 4,000ft strip on 9 March. By 18 May, Momote Drome was extended 7,000 feet and surfaced with coral, completely equipped with taxiways, revetments and storage areas, but the captured Lorengau aerodrome on Manus Island was not suitable for the second planned Allied aerodrome in the Admiralties. (NARA)

(**Opposite, above**) A 61st FA Battalion artilleryman fires one of forty rounds at the enemy defences on 23 March 1944 on Pityilu Island using a Japanese 120mm, Type 3, 1914 naval gun that was originally captured on Hauwei Island. Pityilu and Hauwei are the two westernmost islands comprising the northern barrier of Seeadler Harbour, with the former thought to have been lightly defended. Although the landings of Troops A, B and C 1st Squadron, 7th Cavalry on 30 March 1944 were unopposed, the cavalrymen encountered pockets of resistance from dug-in enemy machine-gun positions and bunkers needing elimination by the gunfire. (NARA)

(**Opposite, below**) A 5th Cavalry's bazooka team on 7 March 1944, immediately after knocking out four Japanese pillboxes in the Papitalai area on Los Negros. A reconnaissance platoon from Troop B, 5th Cavalry moved across Lemondrol Creek, separating Porlaka to the east and Papitalai to the west, on the same day. Fifty Japanese soldiers at Papitalai staged a heated skirmish before withdrawing. (NARA)

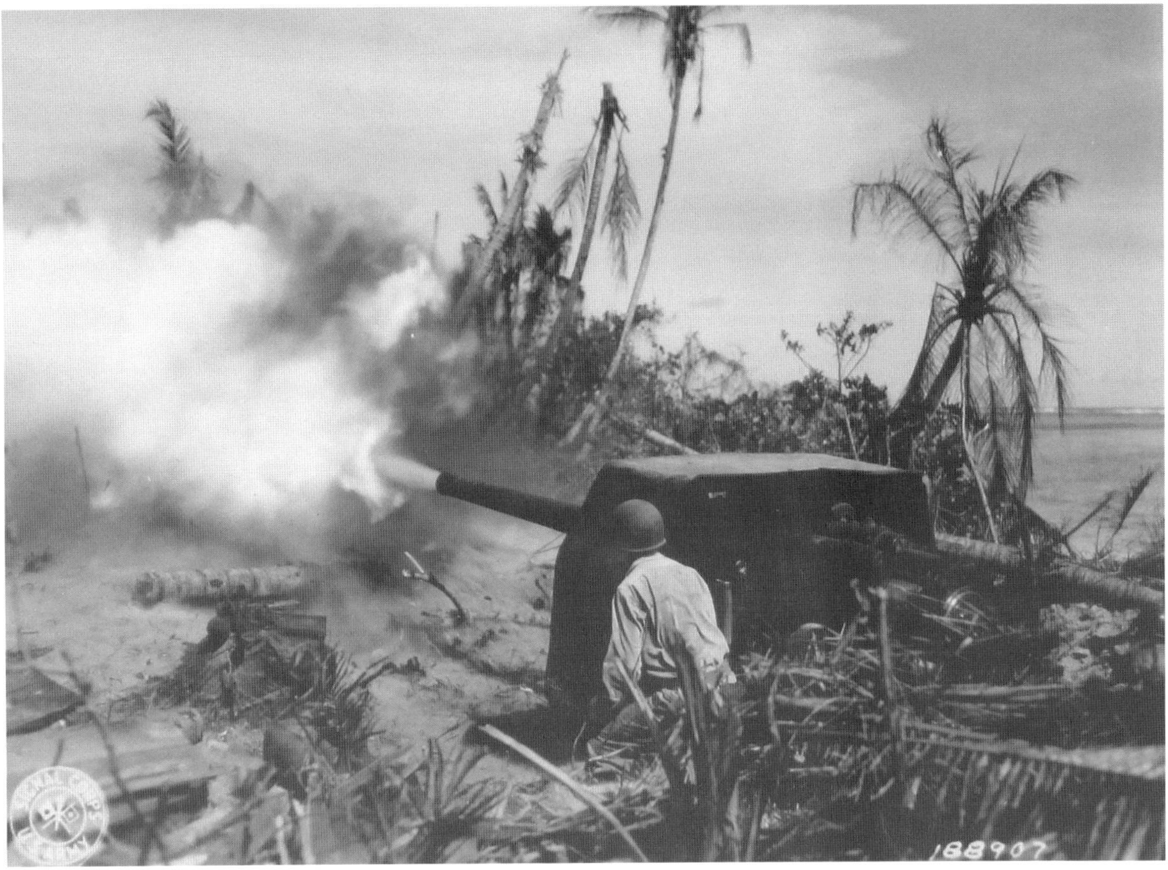
188907

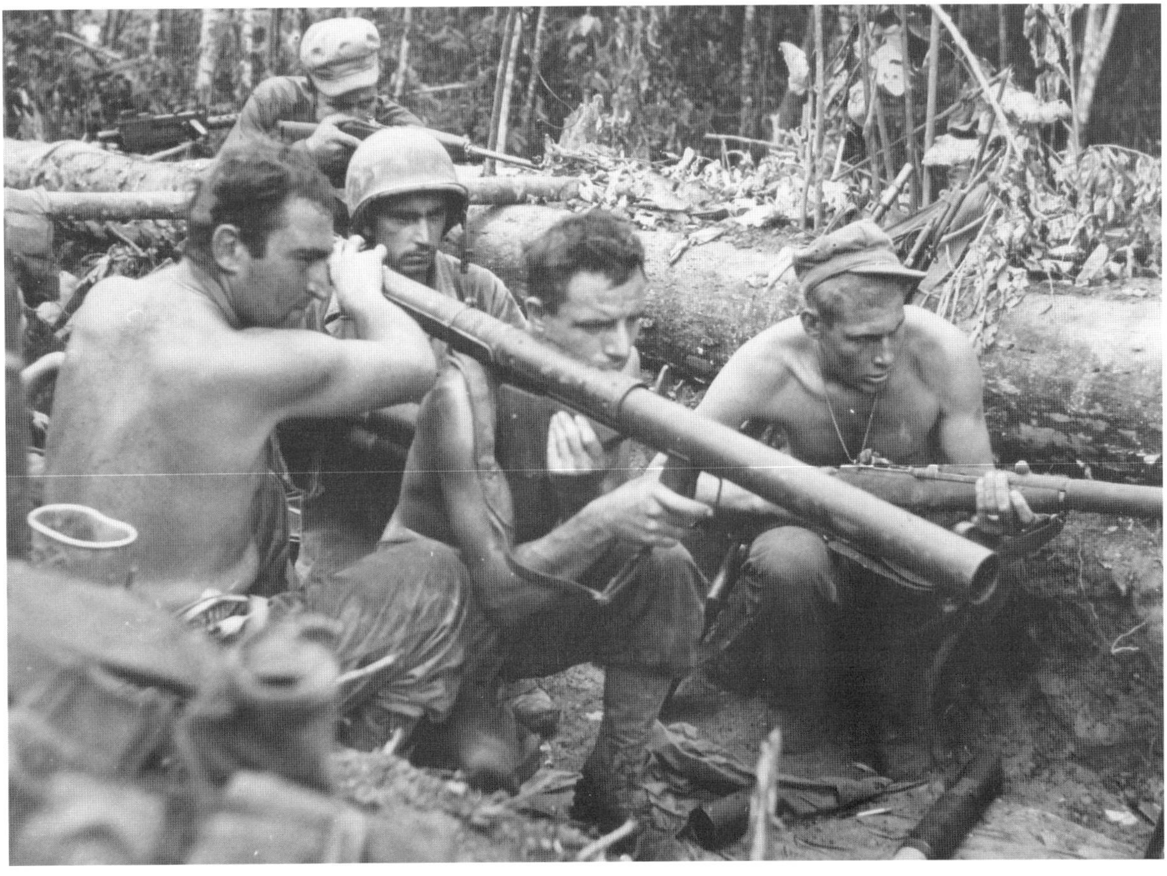

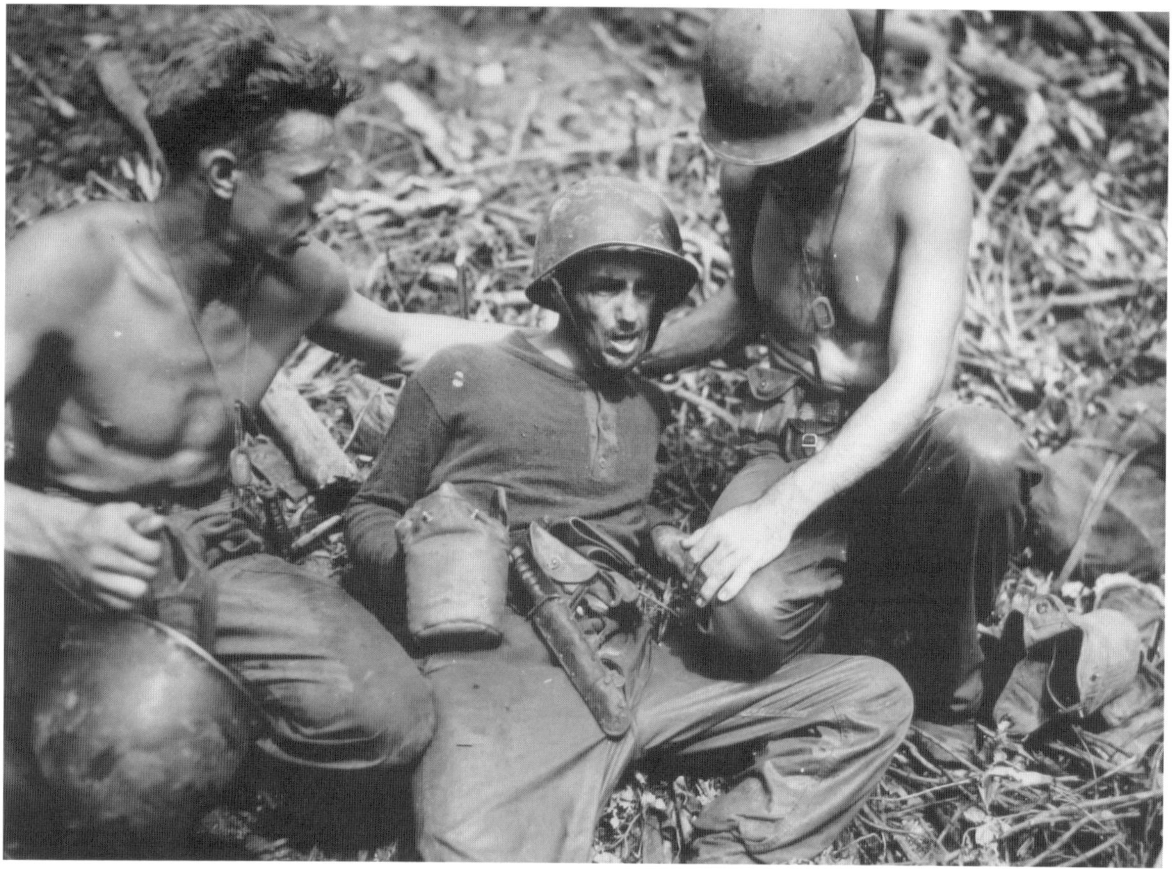

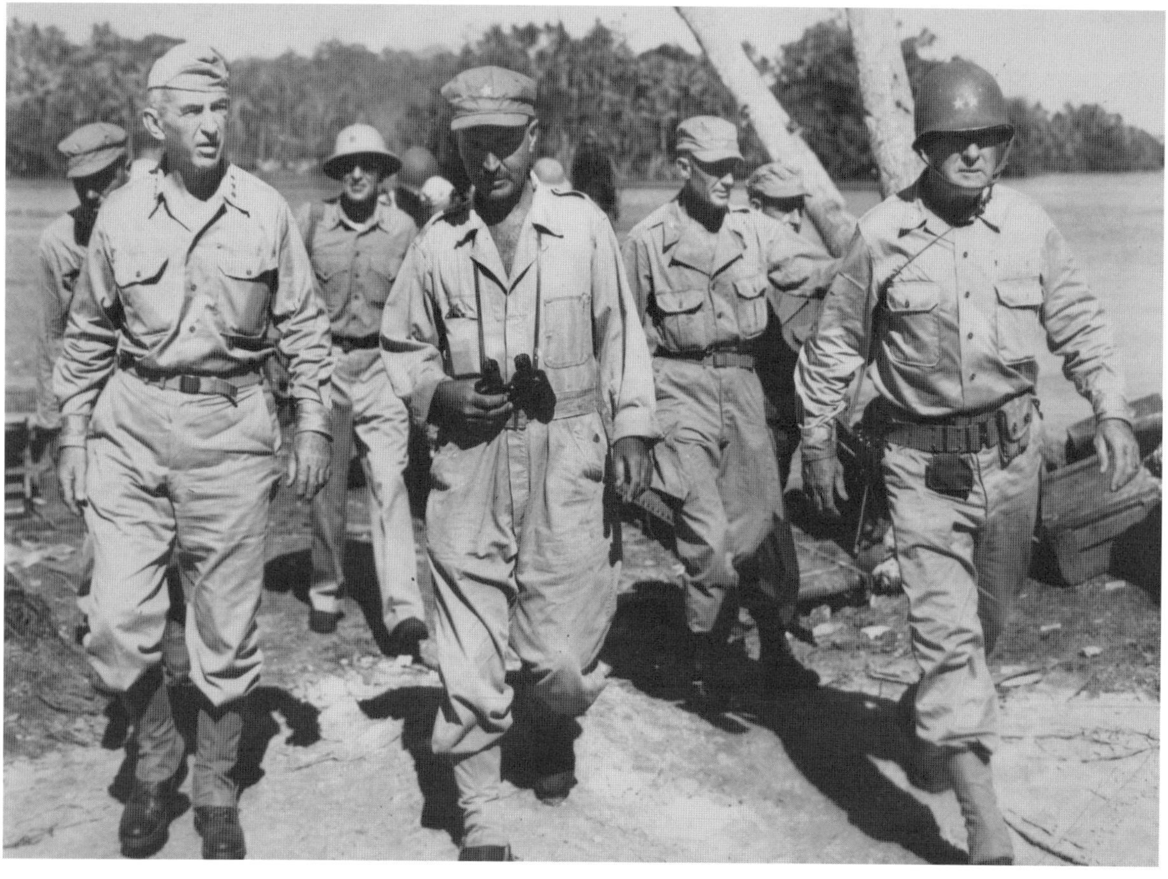

(**Opposite, above**) A cavalryman is tended to by two others after returning from the Papitalai Mission front lines. The 2nd Squadron, 12th Cavalry was to take Papitalai Mission, the promontory northwest of Papitalai, with the assault starting from Salami Beach on the western shore of the Mokerang Peninsula on 7 March 1944. Troop G, 2nd Squadron, 12th Cavalry crossed Seeadler Harbour in five amphibious tractors, with the 271st FA Battalion providing artillery fire support. (NARA)

(**Above**) Wounded and dead cavalrymen are tended to behind the front lines near Papitalai on Los Negros Island. Losses among the 1st Squadron, 5th Cavalry for taking Papitalai on 7 March 1944 were three officers wounded, one officer and one enlisted man killed in action as the cavalrymen were expanding the beachhead from Porlaka across Lemondrol Creek to Papitalai. Control of Los Negros's western shores was essential for the safe landing of the 1st Cavalry Division's 2nd Brigade, due to arrive at Salami on the Mokerang Peninsula's western shore on 9 March. (NARA)

(**Opposite, below**) US Sixth Army CG, Lieutenant General Walter Krueger (left) on an inspection tour with Brigadier General William C. Chase, CG of the 1st Cavalry Brigade (centre), and Major General Innis Swift, CG of the 1st Cavalry Division (right), as the trio leave the jetty at the Salami Plantation on 18 March 1944. (NARA)

(**Above**) A sailor aboard a USN LST fires his 0.50-inch calibre machine gun against Japanese positions on Manus Island, separated from Los Negros by Loniu Passage. After Momote Drome's capture, the next 1st Cavalry Division objective was Manus's Lorengau Aerodrome, to be seized by the newly landed 2nd Brigade, commanded by Brigadier General Verne D. Mudge, which arrived at Salami Beach on Los Negros's Mokerang Peninsula on 9 March 1944. Troops A and C, 8th Cavalry were to land on the undefended beaches near Lugos Mission on 15 March 1944 in LCMs and LCTs, 2 to 3 miles west of Lorengau Drome, the latter and Lorengau village suspected of being defended by 2,000 Japanese troops. The 8th Cavalry's fourth wave was carried up to the beach on the LST. (NARA)

(**Opposite, above**) A 61st FA Battalion 105mm howitzer crew fires from Hauwei Island at Japanese positions south across Seeadler Harbour onto the northern coast of Manus Island on 15 March 1944 to divert the enemy's attention from the 8th Cavalry's landing beaches around Lugos Mission. Hauwei was taken by the 2nd Squadron, 7th Cavalry on 12 March after naval aerial and artillery bombardment. At 1500 hours on 13 March, the 61st FA Battalion disembarked from LCMs onto Hauwei. (NARA)

(**Opposite, below**) Troopers from the 8th Cavalry, 2nd Cavalry Brigade manhandle a 37mm AT gun at Lorengau village to use against Japanese bunkers and pillboxes 100 yards away on 18 March 1944. Previously, the cavalrymen moved east down a coast road from the landing beaches at Lugos Mission to Lorengau Drome, a 3,000ft-long strip used by the Japanese as an auxiliary field. (NARA)

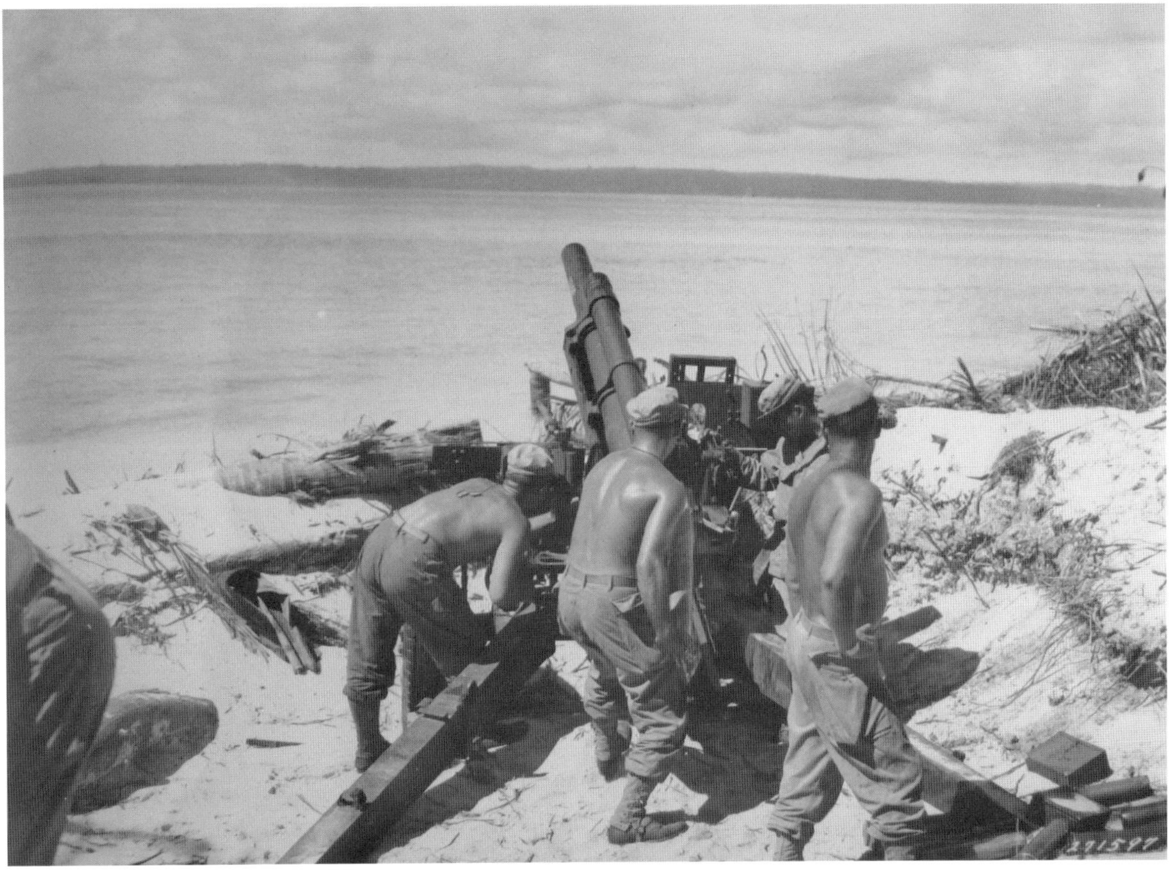
271597

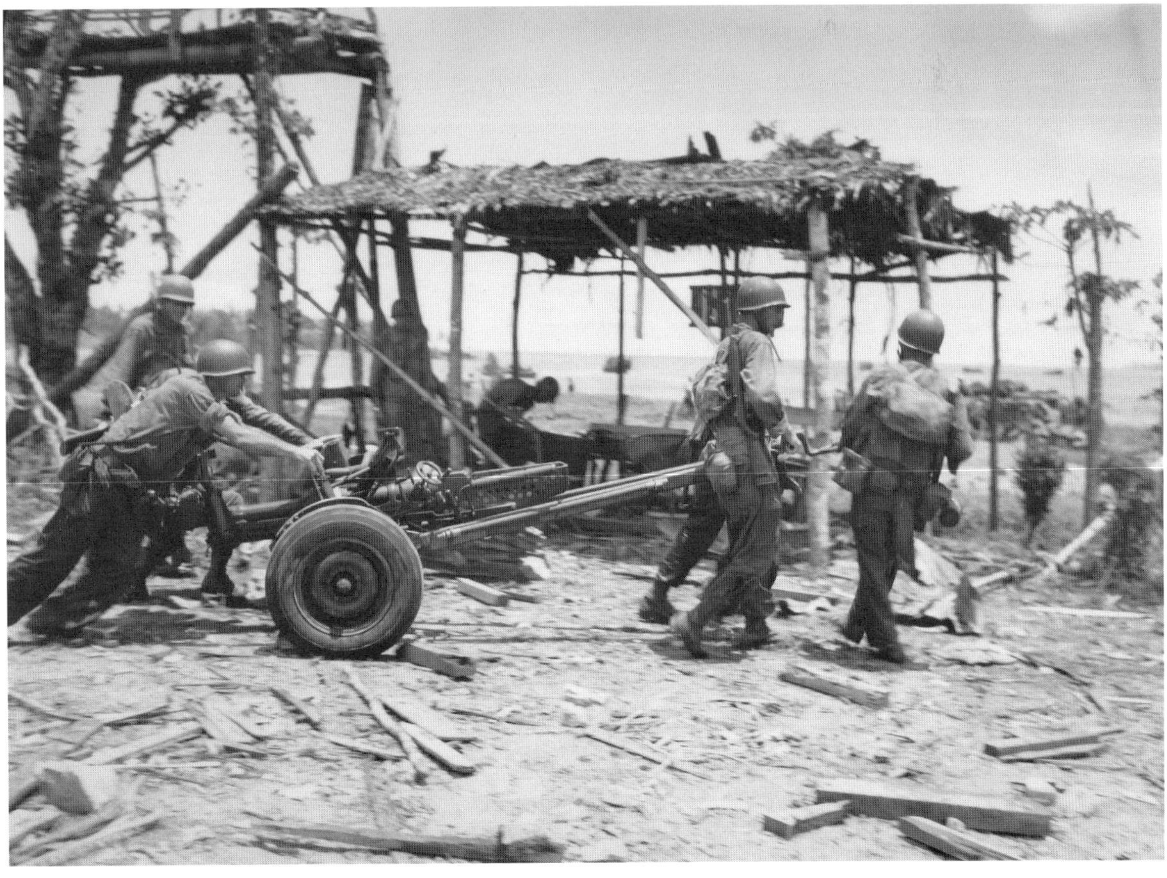

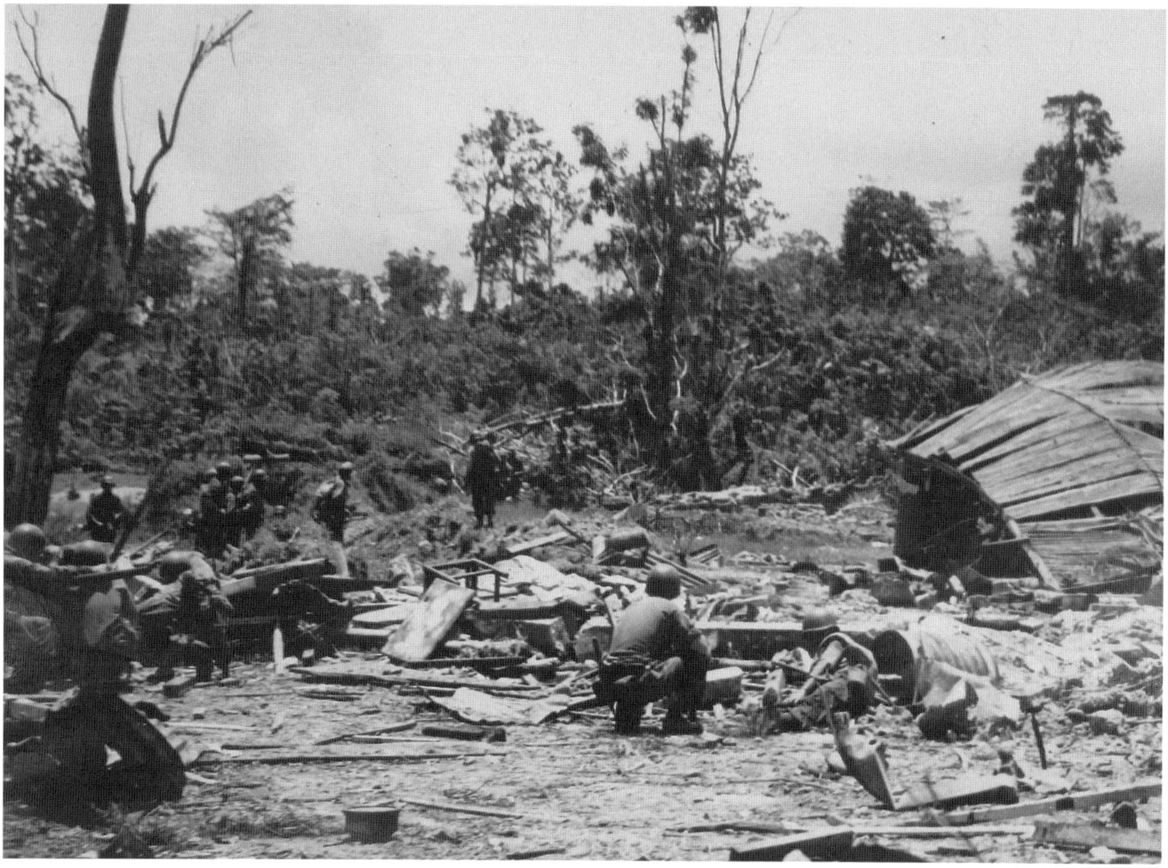

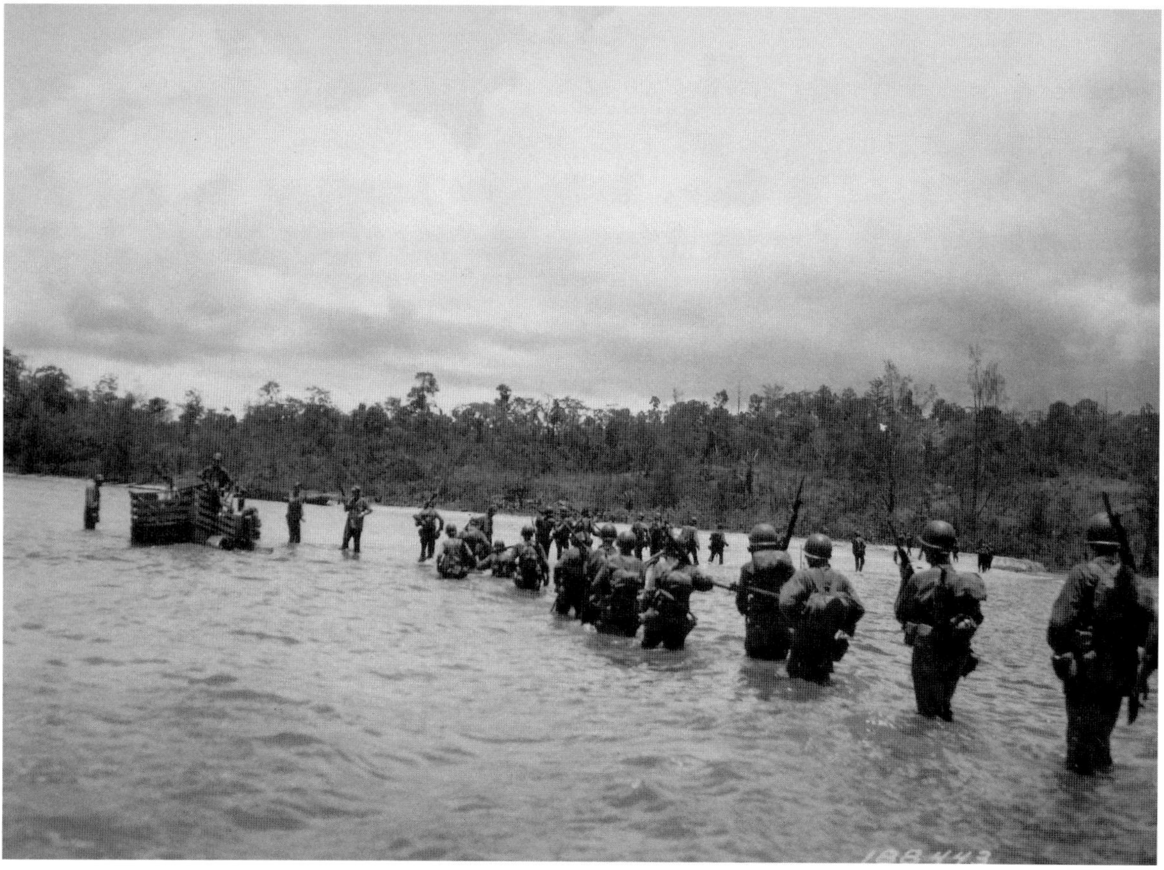
188443

(**Opposite, above**) Troop G, 8th Cavalry, 2nd Cavalry Brigade exits dense jungle bordering No. 1 Road and cautiously advances through a clearing near thick vegetation on the west side of the Lorengau River on 17 March 1944. On 16 March, the Japanese mounted their heaviest resistance on Manus in defence of Lorengau Drome, using bunkers along the southern edge of the airfield with snipers north of the airstrip in the coconut grove. No attack could be made along the open airstrip until the snipers were removed. Once Troop C, 8th Cavalry attacked onto the airfield, heavy Japanese fire came from some untouched bunkers, stopping the cavalrymen's attack. The unsuccessful attack cost the 1st Squadron, 8th Cavalry nine killed and nineteen wounded. Brigadier General Mudge ordered the 1st Squadron, 7th Cavalry, in reserve at Lugos Mission, to relieve the exhausted men of Troop C, 8th Cavalry holding the high ground south of the airstrip after their inland No. 1 Road trek. (NARA)

(**Opposite, below**) Members of the 2nd Squadron, 8th Cavalry, 2nd Brigade are seen moving along a sandbar at the mouth of the Lorengau River, which allowed for an easy crossing on 18 March 1944. Well-defended Lorengau village was sheltered in a valley surrounded by jungle-covered hills rising to 440 feet. The enemy anticipated a seaborne attack on Lorengau village and sited their defences covering the shoreline. After the 2nd Brigade's capture of the Lorengau Drome to the west, the only approach to the village was over the sandbar at the mouth of the Lorengau River, a slow-moving stream 20 yards wide and 10–20 feet deep, except at the sandbar. Once across the river's sandbar, the cavalrymen attacked the village at 1000 hours under cover of mortar and artillery fire. The weakness of the Japanese resistance at Lorengau village indicated that the earlier estimates of enemy resistance on Manus Island were too high. Instead of a Japanese force of 2,000 troops, the 2nd Brigade encountered only 500 enemy soldiers. (NARA)

(**Above**) On 20 March 1944, Marine amphibious tractors bring the 4th Marines over coral reefs to the shores of undefended Emirau Island in the St Matthias group, across the Ysabel Channel from New Hanover and situated halfway between Kavieng and the Admiralty Islands (see Map 2). With units of the 3rd New Zealand Division seizing the Green Islands, 103 miles from Rabaul, on 15 February 1944, along with an airstrip completed on Nissan Island, the capture of Emirau would be the last link in the ring around Rabaul for that Japanese bastion's aerial isolation and neutralization. (NARA)

Marine Vought F4U Corsair fighters positioned in their revetments adjacent to a crushed coral runway on Emirau Island on 27 May 1944. The first airstrip, only 76 miles from Kavieng on New Ireland, was operational early in May after construction by 'Seabees' in fewer than sixty days. When bomber strips were ready, long-range aircraft could reach Truk, the Imperial Japanese Fleet base, in the eastern Caroline Islands. (NARA)

Chapter Six

The Aerial Neutralization Campaign against Rabaul

When the Japanese seized Rabaul on 22 January 1942, there were two Australian airstrips: Lakunai, situated between Simpson and Matupi harbours, and Vunakanau, 9 miles inland and southwest of Keravia Bay. Pre-war, Lakunai was surfaced with sand and volcanic ash for RAAF and civilian aircraft, while Vunakanau had a single unpaved runway. The IJN resurfaced Vunakanau with all-weather concrete material by autumn 1943, despite repeated Allied bombings at Vunakanau beginning in late January 1942. The Japanese expanded Lakunai with revetments and taxiways, and in mid-February 1942, the first six A6M2 Zeros from an IJN carrier landed there. At Vunakanau, the IJN built two parallel 5,000ft runways with taxiways and revetments on both sides for sixty-four bombers and eighty-one fighters. The first IJN G4M1 Betty bombers arrived in mid-February 1942.

Rapopo, built by the Japanese at Lesson Point on the eastern end of Blanche Bay near Cape Gazelle and St George's Channel, 14 miles southeast of Rabaul, had a single runway, largely completed by early January 1943. Afterwards, taxiways and revetments were constructed and it served as an IJAAF base for bombers and transports. Rapopo was also used as an IJN fighter base with A6M Zeros to defend Rabaul. Tobera Airfield, situated 11 miles inland between Vunakanau and Rapopo, was completed by the Japanese in August 1943, and having the shortest single concrete-surfaced runway of all Rabaul's airfields, was primarily used for fighters. Several taxiway loops with revetments were added. Keravat airfield, to Vunakanau's west and 13 miles southwest of Rabaul, had drainage problems and served only as an emergency strip.

During 1943, AA defence priority was shared between IJA and IJN units. IJA detachments were in the vicinity of Rapopo and supply dumps/installations near Simpson Harbour. IJN units guarded Simpson Harbour and its shipping, as well as Tobera, Lakunai and Vunakanau airfields. Surrounding Rabaul, the Japanese built strong coast defences with heavily fortified ground defences, including 260 AA guns ranging from 13mm machine guns to 127mm cannons. The Southeast Area Fleet built an extensive and efficient early warning radar system with 90-mile coverage. Other radar locations were on western New Britain and Kavieng, and at Buka, just north of Bougainville. The Eleventh Air Fleet at Rabaul mustered 300 planes and 10,000 men, including 1,500 air crewmen. Land-based naval units in quiet Pacific sectors were scavenged for additional planes and pilots.

The Japanese had other supporting positions for Rabaul. Gasmata, to Rabaul's west along southern New Britain, was developed from an existing Australian runway captured in February 1942. Poor dispersal facilities made Gasmata nonoperational once repeated Allied air attacks commenced. In September 1943, to replace Gasmata, the Japanese began developing a satellite strip at Cape Hoskins on New Britain's northern coast, east of the Willaumez Peninsula, for Rabaul's defence and to protect convoys in the Bismarck Sea. The two airstrips at Cape Gloucester were potentially dangerous to Allied fields on New Guinea. Talasea, on the east coast of the Willaumez Peninsula, was another emergency landing strip.

By the summer of 1943, the transfer of Fourth Air Army's sixty IJAAF fighters and forty bombers from Rabaul to Wewak to assume responsibility for New Guinea reduced the desired strength of the air garrison at Rabaul. Previously, the Fourth Air Army, headquartered at Rabaul, covered both the Solomon Islands and New Guinea. The destructive attacks by 5th USAAF at Wewak's airfields in August and September 1943 severely weakened the IJAAF's Fourth Air Army in New Guinea. Rabaul was reinforced with air groups from Carrier Divisions stationed at the IJN fleet base at Truk.

In early October 1943, Japanese aircraft at Rabaul numbered no more than 230 medium bombers and fighters. Rabaul's air garrison could mount a defence until destroyed, retreat or receive further air reinforcements. As Imperial HQ decided to defend the SPA and SWPA to the last, Tokyo sealed Rabaul's fate for aerial destruction.

The Allied Air Forces responded to their mostly ineffective high-altitude horizontal bombing of Rabaul from October 1942. RAAF engineers developed P-38 fighter and RAAF Beaufighter, Beaufort and Boston bases at Kiriwina Island and Goodenough Island, southwest of Rabaul. Then, B-25 strafer bombers – which could carry a ton of either 100lb demolition or 20lb parafrag bombs (invented by Kenney in the late 1920s) – assembled at Dobodura (and later from RAAF-built B-25 strips on Kiriwina Island as a staging base), along with two heavy Bombardment Groups and four Fighter Squadrons at Port Moresby's Jackson (7 Mile Drome), Wards (5 Mile Drome), Schwimmer (14 Mile Drome), and Durand (17 Mile Drome) airfields. An opening 5th USAAF attack of the major Rabaul aerial offensive was set for 12 October 1943, after a 1 October aerial reconnaissance showed an IJN heavy cruiser, one light cruiser, ten destroyers, five submarines, and twenty-six merchant ships in Simpson Harbour. Intensified Allied air raids with novel tactics signalled a renewal of the Allied aerial effort to neutralize Japanese power there.

On 12 October 1943, 113 B-25 strafers, 87 B-24 heavy bombers with over 100 P-38 fighters (from Dobodura and Kiriwina) as escorts, and 12 RAAF Beaufighters attacked during daylight. The 3rd Bombardment Group, using three squadrons of B-25 strafers and achieving surprise flying at treetop level with a P-38 escort, attacked Rapopo, strafing the airfield and dropping bundles of parafrag bombs. The few enemy fighters that made it airborne were savagely attacked by the P-38s. Four squadrons of the 345th Bombardment Group and two of the 38th Bombardment Group attacked Vunakanau, with similar tactics employed against little opposition. One squadron of RAAF Beaufighters, out of Kiriwina, targeted Tobera and Rapopo as soon as the B-25s cleared the area. The 5th USAAF revised their earlier exorbitant claims to sixty Japanese planes destroyed on the ground and another five in the air. Ground personnel took heavy casualties, with fuel dumps and airfield buildings destroyed.

Following the medium bomber attacks on the Japanese airfields, B-24s of the 90th and 43rd Bombardment Groups from Port Moresby, escorted by P-38s of the 89th and 38th Fighter Squadrons from Kiriwina, attacked shipping in Simpson Harbour from 20,000 feet, with six 1,000lb bombs per Liberator. 5th USAAF daylight bombing accuracy improved considerably from its earlier attacks on Salamaua, Lae and Wewak. The 5th USAAF's initial higher estimates of Japanese losses at Simpson Harbour were revised to include seven warships damaged, six cargo ships sunk and numerous barges destroyed. The 90th Bombardment Group's B-24s engaged an estimated forty Japanese fighters from an untouched Lakunai Airfield and in a running fight for over forty minutes, 5th USAAF gunners claimed at least ten Zeroes with two B-24s shot down. The 43rd Bombardment Group's B-24s followed the 90th Bombardment Group over the target without much opposition and after dropping their bombs headed for Port Moresby or Kiriwina, if needed.

The 5th USAAF made additional October raids against Rabaul, often interrupted for many days by bad weather. Kenney learned from his New Guinea attacks on Wewak, Hollandia and other Japanese air bases that it was imperative for his air assaults to be incessant in order that the runways and revetments could not be repaired for Japanese air reinforcements to be flown into Rabaul.

The Japanese retaliated by sending bomber and fighter contingents from Rabaul. These included fifteen Aichi D3A Val dive-bombers and thirty-nine A6M3 Reisen Zeros as fighter cover, against Allied shipping in Oro Bay off New Guinea on 15–17 October to limit supplies to the 5th USAAF airfields at Dobodura and against Finschhafen on 17–19 October, thinking that the Allied attacks of 12 October were a prelude to a New Britain invasion. The Japanese were attacked by P-38 Lightnings and P-40 Warhawks, with five Zeroes shot down and fourteen enemy dive-bombers failing to return to Rabaul. Ten Allied planes were lost but no Allied ships were sunk.

Another 5th USAAF mass raid sortied for Rabaul on 18 October, with eight squadrons of B-24s and two groups of B-25 strafers to hit Vunakanau, Lakunai and Tobera, but again, a weather front caused the airstrike's heavy bombers to abort. The B-25s flying just above the waves avoided the bad weather, with the 38th Bombardment Group achieving surprise at Tobera, where they claimed sixteen planes destroyed with their 100lb bombs. The 345th Bombardment Group's B-25s made two runs over Rapopo, claiming twenty-five enemy planes on the ground and about a dozen Japanese fighters that took off to intercept them.

Aerial reconnaissance photographs from 19 October showed that the Japanese rebuilt their fighter strength at Rabaul to 211 planes. With the weather clearing on 23 October, Allied air planners launched a fighter sweep with three P-38 squadrons prior to a heavy B-24 bomber attack on Lakunai and Vunakanau that day. However, both airfields were obscured by clouds but the B-24s found their secondary target at Rapopo and bombed the runways and dispersal areas. The P-38 escort shot down thirteen enemy planes, with one of their own lost. The bombers shot four enemy fighters and claimed twenty planes destroyed on the ground.

On 24 October, only medium bombers of the 3rd and 345th Bombardment Groups were launched. The 3rd Bombardment Group spotted only four planes at Tobera, but claimed twenty-one destroyed on the ground at Rapopo. The 345th Bombardment Group claimed twenty-seven planes destroyed at Vunakanau in addition to the eight fighters shot down. Two B-25s were lost. As a fighter escort, the P-38s accounted for thirty-seven Japanese planes lost without losing any of their own.

Another 5th USAAF strike was launched on 25 October, but most of the B-24s and P-38 escort fighters were turned back by increasingly bad weather. Nonetheless, some B-24s continued on flying by instruments and reached Rabaul with eight P-38s of the 432nd Fighter Squadron. The B-24s were met by fierce AA fire from IJN warships over Simpson Harbour and several types of Japanese fighters attacked the bombers as they started their run. Lakunai was bombed but some of the B-24s were shot down. On 29 October, full-scale assaults on Rabaul were resumed, with forty-six B-24s hitting Vunakanau aerodrome with fragmentation and 500lb bombs. Several Japanese planes were hit on the ground, with many enemy fighters shot down in the air.

On the morning of 2 November 1943, the day after Halsey's Bougainville invasion and the ensuing 1/2 November nocturnal IJN and USN cruiser battle at Empress Augusta Bay, Allied reconnaissance planes found seven IJN destroyers, one tender, and twenty merchant vessels in Simpson Harbour, and over 250 Japanese planes on the airfields. By 1100 hours, eighty 5th USAAF B-25s and a similar number of fighters headed for Rabaul. Two fighter squadrons, the 39th and 80th, made a fighter sweep of the harbour while the strafers of the 345th Bombardment Group attacked enemy AA land batteries. Five squadrons of B-25s from the 3rd and 38th Bombardment Groups were to hit shipping. The 39th Fighter Squadron met little opposition as it led the attacking planes over Simpson Harbour and Lakunai, but the 80th Fighter Squadron met intense AA and Japanese fighter interception. The strafers of the 345th Bombardment Group also met stiff AA opposition and fighter interception, with eight B-25s in the lead position hit, three of which failed to return to base, although seventeen Japanese fighters were shot down. Sixteen Japanese aircraft were destroyed on Lakunai aerodrome, and the leading planes of the shipping strike neutralized the enemy shore AA batteries, enabling the striking B-25 squadrons to come in from the east over Crater Peninsula, circle north of the North Daughter volcano, pass over the town of Rabaul, and then make runs of Simpson Harbour – a route normally protected by heavy Japanese AA fire. The 3rd Bombardment Group's forty-one attacking B-25s used 1,000lb bombs on targets in Simpson Harbour, as IJN cruisers and destroyers used their AA fire against the B-25s that had broken formation due to Japanese fighters to bomb or strafe in two-plane individual attacks. Although some of the B-25s were shot down, these low-level bombing attacks were quite accurate. Of the forty-one enemy ships attacked, Allied HQ claimed three IJN destroyers, eight large merchant vessels, and four coastal vessels sunk, with damage to twenty-two other vessels. The B-25s also shot down twenty-six enemy fighters while destroying sixteen on the ground at Lakunai. The 5th USAAF paid a steep price, with forty-five pilots and crew members listed as killed or missing. Eight bombers and nine P-38s were lost.

By the end of November 1943, the western New Britain landings at Arawe, and landings at Cape Gloucester in December, diverted the

5th USAAF's attention from Rabaul raids. During these Army and Marine campaigns, dozens of Japanese fighters from Rabaul and Gasmata were lost in a useless attempt to prevent MacArthur and Krueger's landings, which the Japanese bastion could ill afford.

USN Carrier Aircraft Strikes against Rabaul, 5 November to 9 December 1943

While Kenney's 5th USAAF was attacking Rabaul on 2 November 1943, Halsey had successfully landed the 3rd Marine Division at Cape Torokina on Empress Augusta Bay in his Bougainville invasion on 1 November. During the night of 1/2 November, USN Task Force 39, under Rear Admiral Stanton Merrill, comprising four light cruisers with two destroyer divisions, inflicted a significant defeat on an IJN Eighth Fleet surface force from Rabaul. That IJN force had two heavy cruisers (*Myōkō* and *Haguro*), two light cruisers and two destroyers sent to counter the invasion by attacking the USN transports as well as a dawn (2 November) attack by 100 IJN carrier planes that had arrived at Rabaul from Truk the day before. The IJN lost a light cruiser and a destroyer, with two destroyers heavily damaged. The USN suffered damage to seven ships but none was sunk.

The IJN Second Fleet had several heavy cruisers at Truk posing a threat, especially since Nimitz was involved with the Gilbert Islands invasion and could not spare any heavy cruisers to protect Halsey's shipping at Empress Augusta Bay. Koga decided to reinforce Rabaul with seven of Truk's heavy cruisers (*Takao*, *Maya*, *Atago*, *Suzuya*, *Mogami*, *Chikuma* and *Chokai*), one light cruiser (*Noshiro*), and four destroyers and tankers, under Vice Admiral Takeo Kurita. At noon on 4 November, American reconnaissance discovered the vanguard of Kurita's surface force from Truk off the Admiralties and heading towards the western entrance of St George's Channel, with an anticipated arrival at Simpson Harbour early on 5 November. At 1638 hours on 4 November, Halsey ordered a fast carrier Task Force under Rear Admiral Frederick Sherman, built around the veteran USS *Saratoga*, with the best-trained air group in the Pacific, and the *Independence*-class light carrier USS *Princeton*, complemented by two *Atlanta*-class cruisers and nine destroyers, 'to launch all planes at 0900 hrs on 5 November in an all-out strike on shipping in Rabaul'. All ninety-seven of TF 38's attacking planes, including fifty-two F6F Hellcat fighters, twenty-three Avenger torpedo bombers and twenty-two Dauntless SBD dive-bombers, were dispatched with a CAP provided by AirSols shore-based USN and Marine F4U Corsairs flying from Munda Airfield. Halsey requested 5th USAAF units to flatten Rabaul town and cover the aerodromes, so Kenney sent twenty-seven B-24s and sixty-seven P-38s to attack Rabaul's waterfront, an hour after the carrier planes attacked the IJN shipping, comprising Kurita's heavy cruiser and destroyer force from Truk joining the defeated IJN surface ships after the failed 1/2 November attack at Empress Augusta Bay. Some IJN warships were refuelling in Simpson Harbour for another massive heavy cruiser night attack on the USN ships defending Empress Augusta Bay, only 200 nautical miles from Rabaul. Seventy Japanese A6M Zeros fighters, recently deployed from the IJN's *Zuihō* and *Zuikaku* carrier groups, were alerted by radar and in the air awaiting the USN carrier aircraft strike approaching Rabaul from its launch 230 miles to the southeast to reach Simpson Harbour at about 1200 hours.

Simpson Harbour was attacked from the north as USN aircraft flew through St George's Channel until they were north of Crater Peninsula, giving the American pilots a southerly escape route through the harbour's opening into Blanche Bay. As the USN planes split up to commence their solitary attacks, every Japanese AA gun ashore and afloat opened up, while the Zeros remained outside the flak. The IJN Second Fleet heavy cruisers from Truk were moored in Simpson Harbour, with three light cruisers, eleven destroyers, and dozens of freighters as other targets. The heavy cruiser *Maya* was hit while refuelling, with the bomb exploding in her engine room. It took five months to repair her. *Takao* took two hits, which opened a large hole at the waterline. *Atago* and *Chikuma* suffered multiple near misses. *Mogami* was sent back to Kure to repair bomb damage. Light cruisers *Agano* and *Noshiro* were hit, the latter by a torpedo, and three destroyers were lightly damaged. All these ships except *Maya* retired under their own power, but the carrier strike ended Simpson Harbour for Japan's heavy ships. The USN lost five fighters and five bombers. F6F Hellcats shot down three Japanese aircraft and a twin-engine bomber that was taking off from Tobera Airfield. The Bougainville beachhead was spared a second major IJN heavy cruiser surface assault by Halsey's combativeness and his pilots' courage over Simpson Harbour.

On 11 November 1943, five USN carriers struck Rabaul, which now included the new heavy carriers USS *Essex* and USS *Bunker Hill* along with the light carrier USS *Independence*. One Japanese destroyer, *Suzunami*, was sunk; one light cruiser (*Agano*) and one destroyer (*Naganami*) were damaged. Vice Admiral Kusaka sent fourteen Nakajima B5N2 Kate Type 96 torpedo bombers, twenty-seven Aichi D3A Type 99 Val dive-bombers and sixty-seven Mitsubishi A6M Zero fighters followed by a flight of Mitsubishi G4M Betty bombers against the three USN carriers, one of the largest anti-carrier strikes since the start of the war. All fourteen Kate torpedo bombers failed to return to Rabaul. Other IJN air losses over the USN carrier Task Force included seventeen Val dive-bombers, two Zero fighters and several Bettys. Koga withdrew the remnants of his carrier planes from Rabaul as his carrier air groups were decimated, losing 85 per cent of their Vals, 90 per cent of their Kates and 50 per cent of their Zeros.

On 19 February 1944, Japanese fighters from Rabaul took off for the last time to challenge American air raids. When Allied bombers returned on 20 February, not a single operational Japanese fighter remained at Rabaul's heavily cratered airfields. The defence of Rabaul now depended exclusively on ground forces after all operational Japanese aircraft were removed to safer bases.

Several hundred Japanese troops of the Maizuru 2nd SNLF, part of Major General Tomitarō Horii's 5,300-man South Seas Detachment, along with the IJA 144th Infantry Regiment, walk ashore at Rabaul to overpower Australian (Lark Force) defensive installations on 23 January 1942 during Operation R. Rabaul was a vital objective for the Japanese southern expansion, as Simpson Harbour would become a major IJN fleet anchorage and the town of an IJA garrison. Ample flat terrain south of the volcanic craters was suitable for the development of newer airfields. (*Author's collection*)

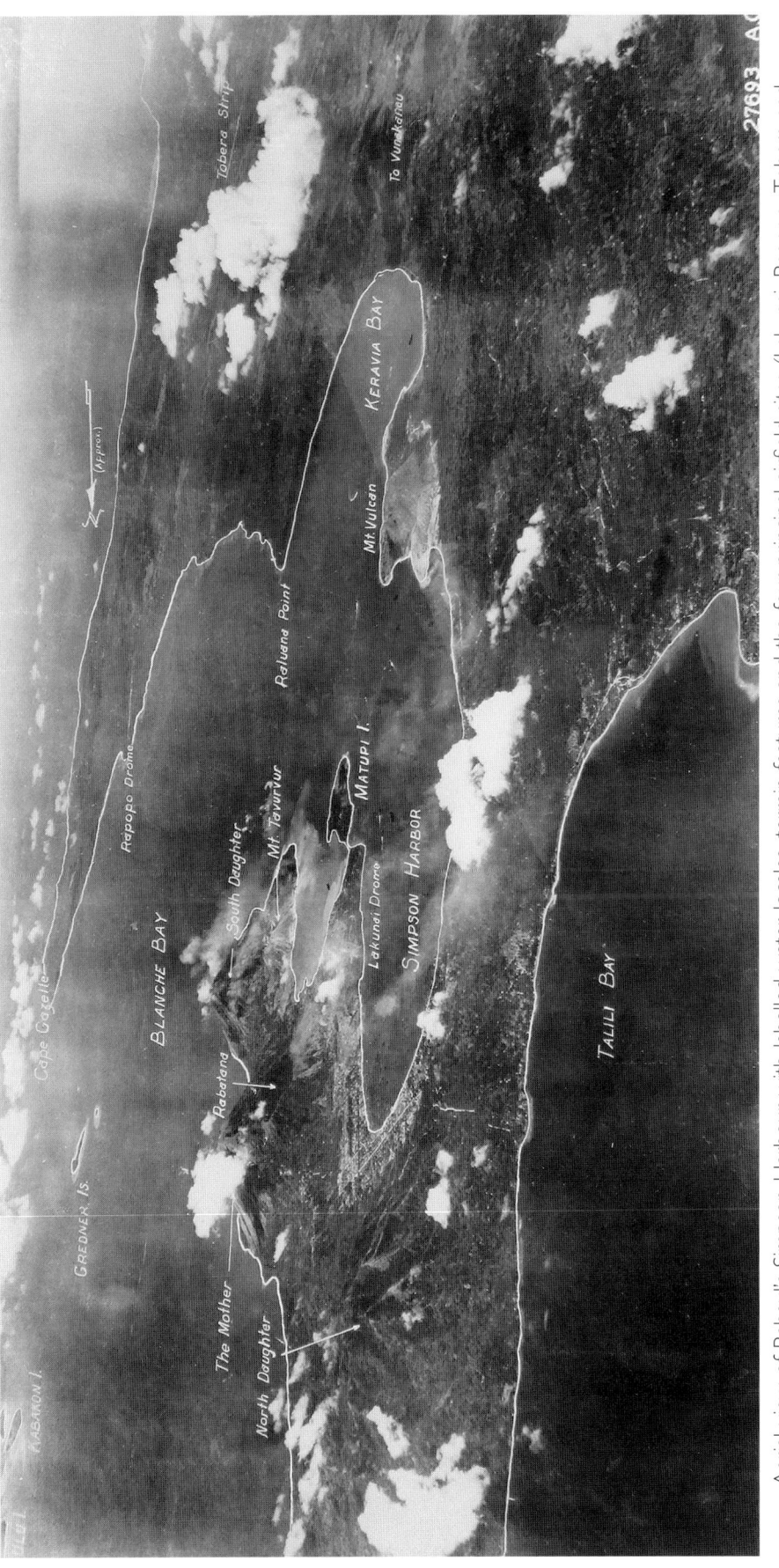

Aerial view of Rabaul's Simpson Harbour with labelled water locales, terrain features and the four principal airfield sites (Lakunai; Rapopo, Tobera and Vunakanau). Rabaul's principal volcanoes — North Daughter, The Mother, South Daughter and Mount Tavurvur — the latter bordering Matupi Bay near Matupi Island with Mount Vulcan farther south, ring Simpson Harbour. Also shown are Blanche, Talili and Keravia Bays. (NARA)

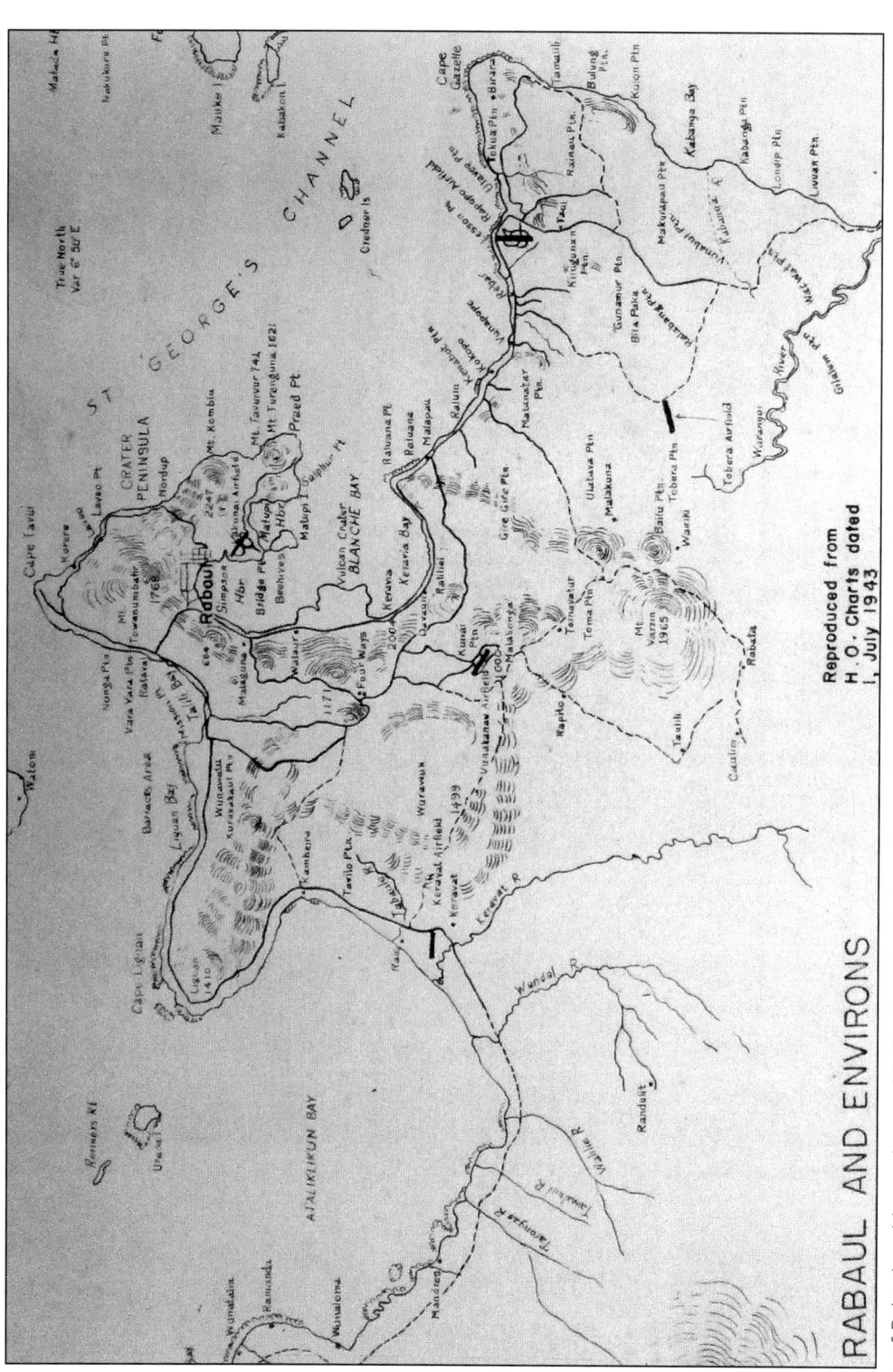

RABAUL AND ENVIRONS

Map of Rabaul and its environs with the town located on the northern edge of Simpson Harbour, which became New Guinea's capital under first German then Australian rule. Tobera Drome is located to Rapopo Drome's southwest, the latter at the southeastern end of Blanche Bay. Vunakanau Drome is southwest of Keravia Bay while Keravat Drome is farther west, bordering Ataliklikun Bay. Lakunai Airfield is situated between Simpson and Matupi harbours. (NARA)

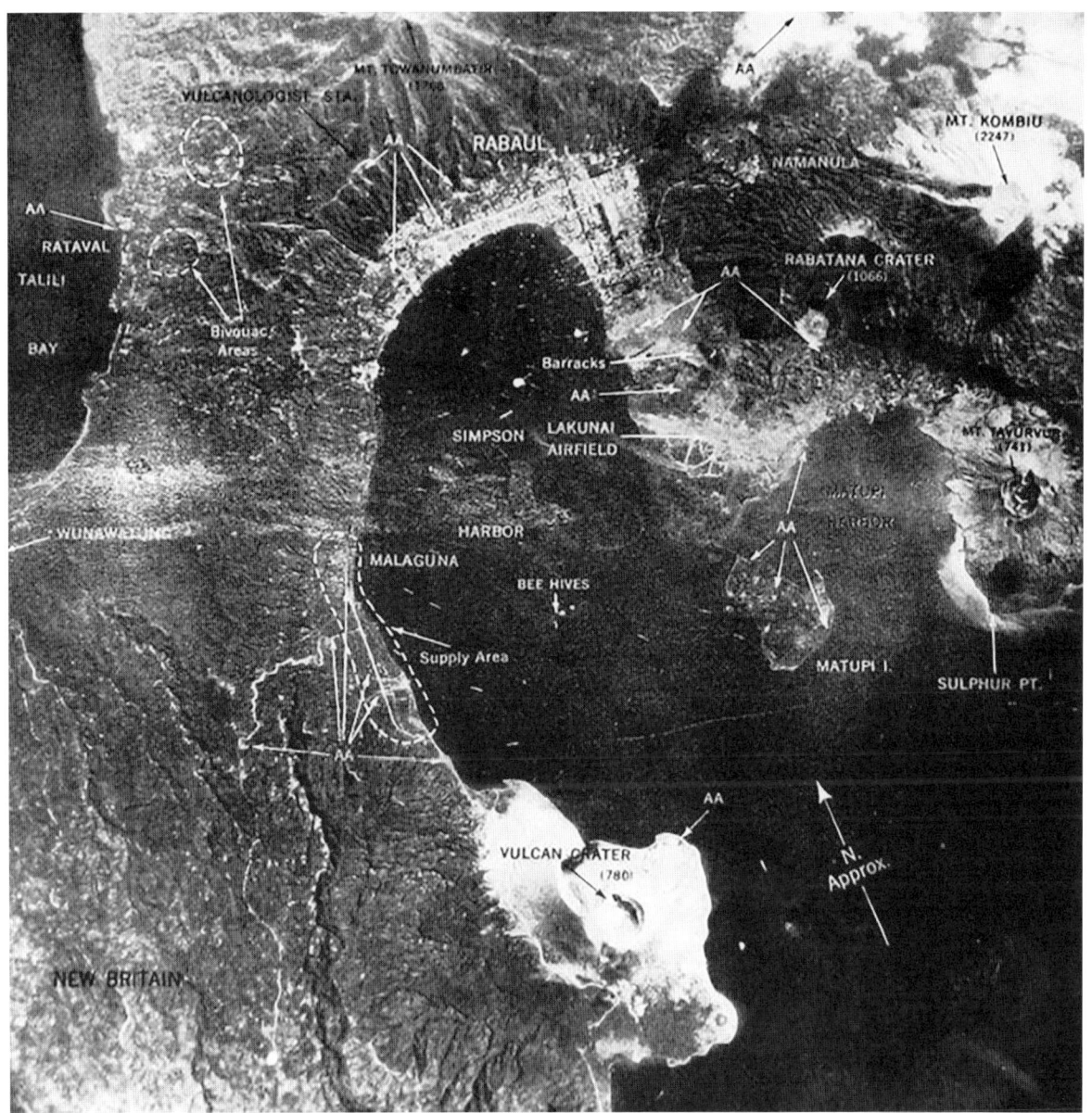

An aerial photograph shows Simpson and Matupi harbours with Talili Bay to the west, near Rataval. AA batteries located around the Simpson Harbour's perimeter, as well as bivouac, supply and barracks areas, are indicated. An AA position was also located at Sulphur Point (far right). The Beehives, also called Dawapia Rocks or Two Stones, is a pair of volcanic rock outcroppings in the centre of Simpson Harbour, west of Matupi Island. Rabaul town and waterfront are at Simpson Harbour's north. (*Author's collection*)

(**Above**) IJN Nakajima B5N2 Type 97 Kate, a three-seat, carrier-borne or land-based horizontal or torpedo bomber flies over Rabaul and Simpson Harbour on 20 January 1942, having participated in the carrier raids prior to the South Seas Detachment's invasion. IJN reconnaissance planes appeared over Rabaul as early as June 1941, with the first aircraft sighted a twin-engine IJN Mitsubishi G3M Type 96 Nell land-based bomber from Truk, 700 miles to the north. Rabaul was first raided on 4 January 1942, followed by an airstrike at Vunakanau Airfield two days later, destroying an RAAF Wirraway fighter, damaging a Hudson reconnaissance/bomber and cratering the runway. Pre-invasion air strikes resumed on 16 January to neutralize Australian airfields while avoiding collateral damage to Rabaul. On 17 January, Vice Admiral Chūichi Nagumo, C-in-C First Air Fleet's four IJN aircraft carriers, rendezvoused with Major General Tomitarō Horii's South Seas Detachment north of Rabaul as the amphibious invasion started on 22 January, after more days of IJN aerial attacks. (Author's collection)

(**Opposite, above**) A flight of IJN Mitsubishi G4M1 Betty land-based, twin-engine horizontal or torpedo bombers of the 751 Air Group (Kōkūtai) over its base at Vunakanau Airfield in November 1942. The G4M1 possessed remarkable range at the expense of adequate crew protection, self-sealing fuel tanks and an ability to absorb battle damage. On 16 January 1942, Mitsubishi G4M1 bombers destroyed an Australian fuel and bomb dump and other installations at RAAF's Vunakanau Airfield. (Author's collection)

(**Opposite, below**) IJN A6M2 and A6M3 Reisen Zeros from IJN carrier *Zuikaku* prepare for an 11 January 1943 mission against Guadalcanal. Two types of Zeroes flew from Rabaul, the older A6M2 (called 'Zeke' by the Allies) and the mid-war version A6M3 (called 'Hap' or 'Hamp'). The A6M2 had a range of 1,600 miles while the A6M3 had a shorter range, but was capable to fly from IJN Combined Fleet base at Truk to Rabaul to provide for airfield defence. IJN aviators at Rabaul preferred the older A6M2 due to its greater manoeuvrability. During the start of the Allied air offensive against Rabaul, the IJN fighter force was frequently reinforced with carrier-based aircraft. (Author's collection)

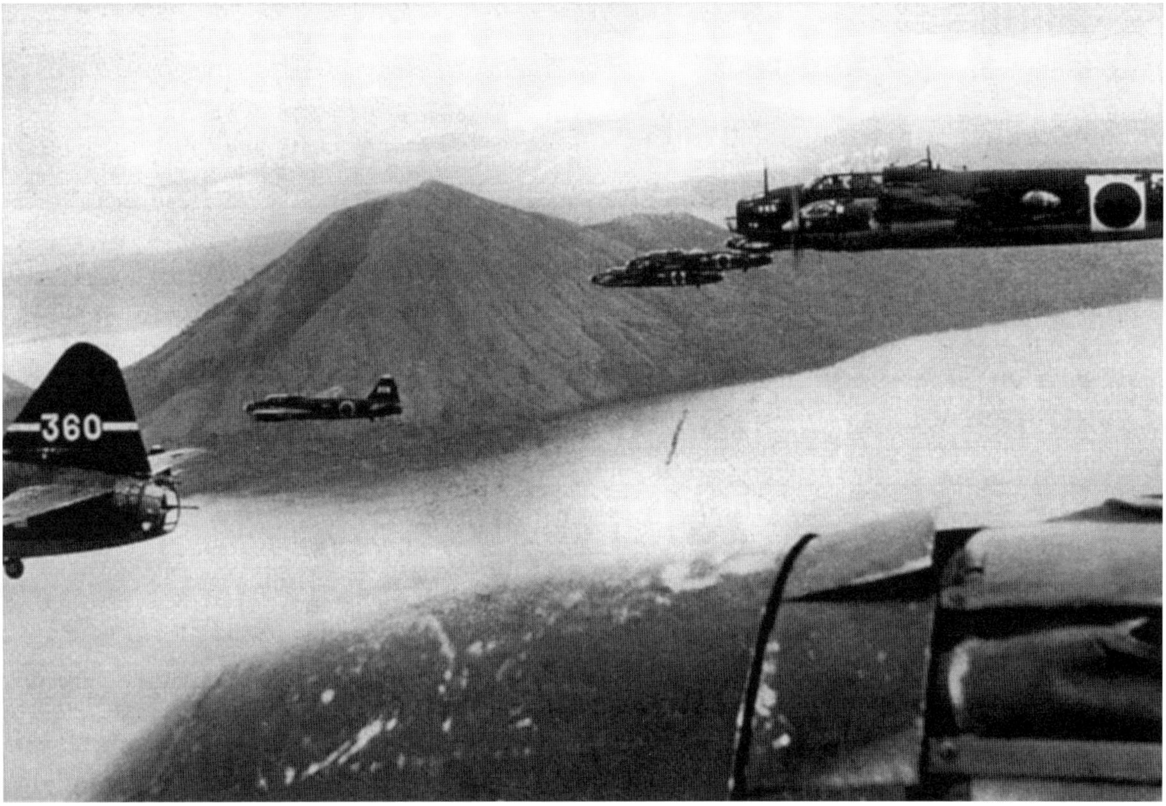
360

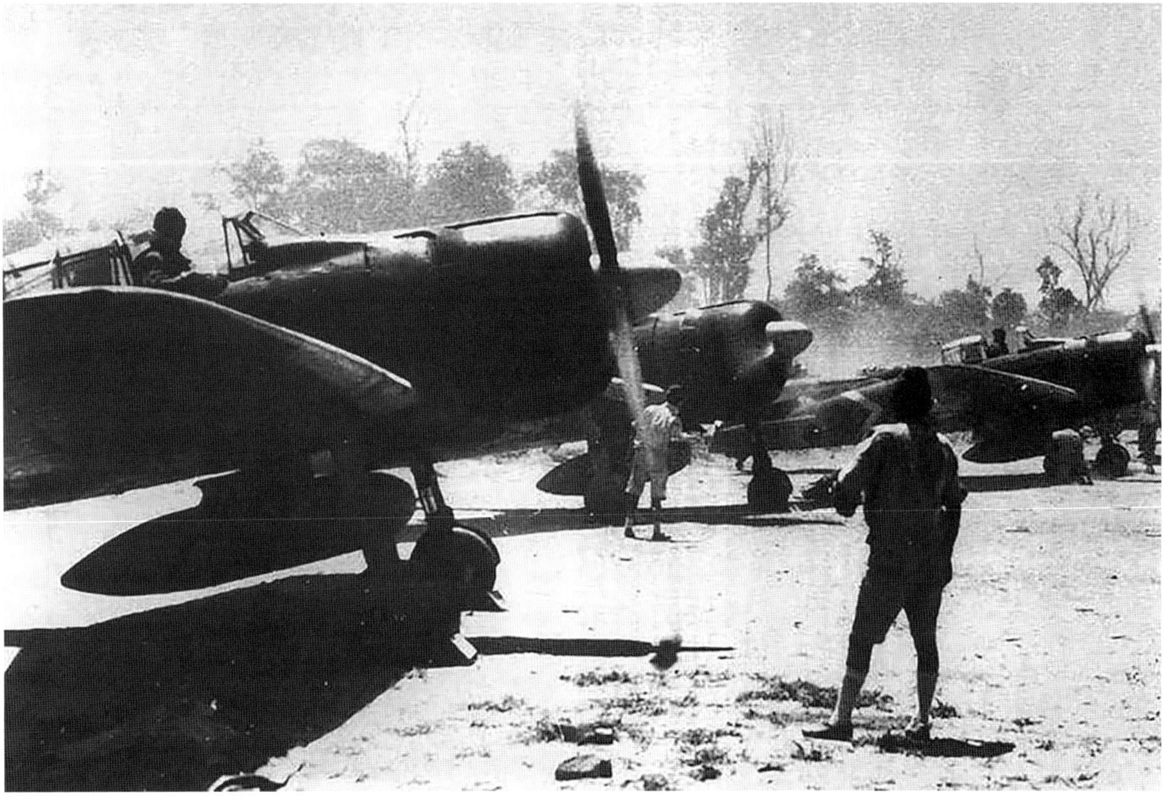

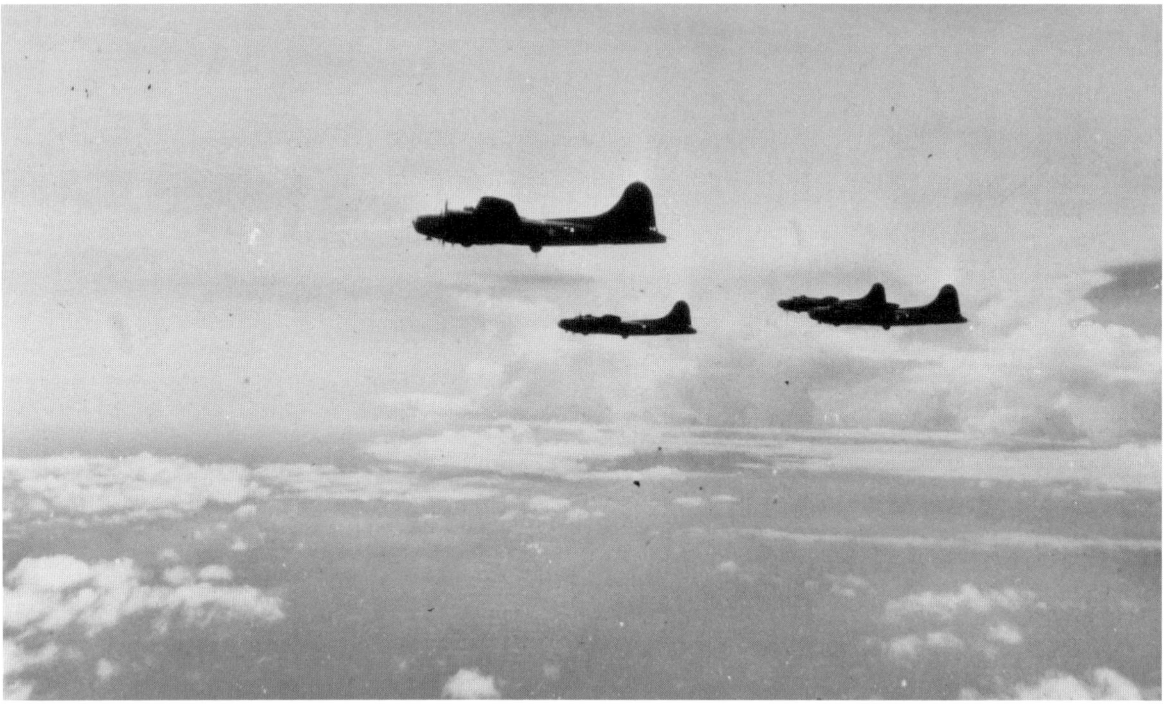

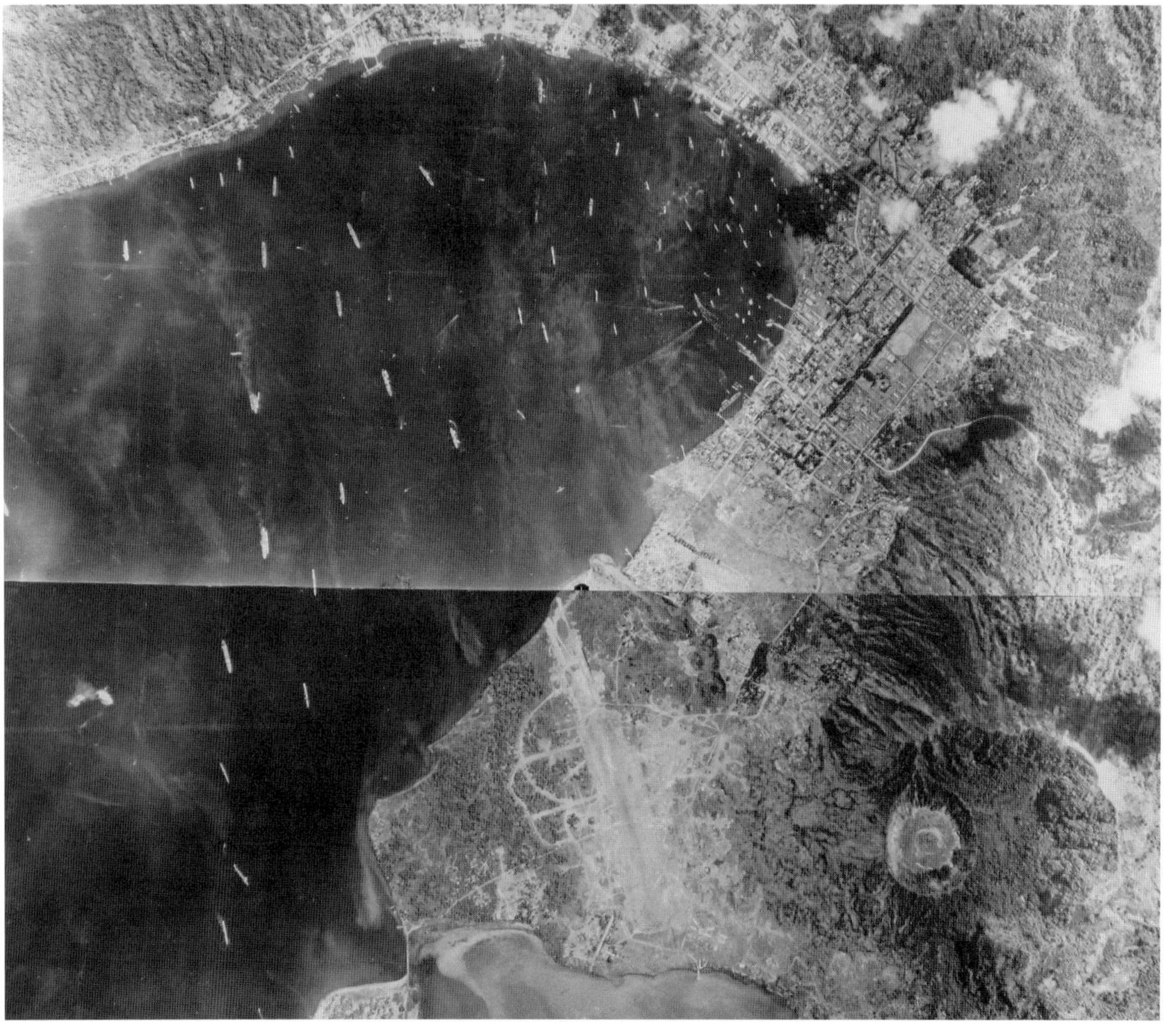

(**Opposite, above**) Four of the six Boeing B-17 Flying Fortresses of the 43rd Bombardment Group/ 64th Bombardment Squadron, 5th USAAF fly in formation from Jackson Field (7 Mile Drome) near Port Moresby, along with six Consolidated B-24 Liberators for their 5 January 1943 raid on Simpson Harbour, which at December 1942's end had twenty-one IJN warships and 300,000 tons of merchant shipping. Allied intelligence suspected an IJN convoy departing Rabaul on 6 January to reinforce Lae. Brigadier General Kenneth Walker, CG V Bomber Command, was ordered to mount a 5 January heavy bomber attack to break up the convoy at its source at dawn since there would be no Allied fighter escort. One of the B-17 bombers, *San Antonio Rose*, was shot down by Japanese fighters during the mission, with nine crew members killed in action, one of whom was Walker, with two taken prisoner. Another B-17 ditched in the sea with all but two crewmen rescued on 6 January by a PBY Catalina flying boat. All six B-24s were damaged but managed to return to base. The raid reportedly damaged ten IJN ships and sunk the 5,833-ton *Keifuku Maru*. Walker received a posthumous Congressional Medal of Honor on 25 March 1943. (*NARA*)

(**Opposite, below**) A composite 5th USAAF photograph by a B-24 Liberator heavy bomber of either the 43rd or 90th Bombardment Group during the 12 October 1943 raid, with Simpson Harbour replete with Japanese shipping and the waterfront and town of Rabaul (top and right), Lakunai Drome (centre), with Rabatana Crater to its right. (*NARA*)

(**Above**) Vunakanau Airfield attacked by 5th USAAF B-25 Mitchell medium bombers with parafrag bombs on 12 October 1943, the opening of the 12 October to 4 November 1943 aerial offensive. Twin-engine Mitsubishi G4M1 Betty bombers in their revetments near taxiways were targeted. Allied reconnaissance flights on 9 October estimated 270 Japanese aircraft at Rabaul's airfields. An overstated claim by Kenney's HQ listed 177 Japanese planes destroyed with 150 destroyed on the ground and 27 fighters in aerial combat. Probably only sixty Japanese planes were destroyed on the ground. Japanese ground personnel at Vunakanau took heavy casualties with their huts and tents nearby (foreground). (*NARA*)

(**Above**) A bombardier's view of Simpson Harbour on 2 November 1943, with numerous IJN targets for 5th USAAF's raid focusing on enemy shipping. In addition to merchant vessels, the IJN dispatched two heavy and two light cruisers escorted by two destroyers from Truk to reinforce Rabaul's naval force, but these warships were repulsed during the 1/2 November overnight surface engagement at the Battle of Empress Augusta Bay, which was intended to contest the US 3rd Marine Division's transports that landed at Bougainville's Cape Torokina on 1 November. The surviving IJN warships from Truk were in Simpson Harbour on 2 November. Also, 150 aircraft launched from IJN Combined Fleet carriers *Shōkaku*, *Zuikaku* and *Zuihō*, which sailed from Truk, arrived at Rabaul on 1 November for an Empress Augusta Bay air battle. Allied intelligence missed both forms of IJN reinforcements reaching Rabaul for the 2 November 5th USAAF raid. (NARA)

(**Opposite, above**) At Simpson Harbour on 2 November 1943, seventy-five B-25s of the 5th USAAF's 3rd Bombardment Group sunk four Japanese transports, with the *Hakone Maru* ablaze (middle). In the foreground is the 10,000-ton *Nachi*-class cruiser, *Haguro*, which was damaged in the 1/2 November Empress August Bay naval battle during the overnight hours. The American squadrons of B-25s were relatively unmolested by 100 Japanese fighters occupied with fifty-seven P-38 strafing attacks on Lakunai Airfield. However, the B-25s flew into heavy AA gunfire from Simpson Harbour's shore and warships' batteries. IJN cruisers, like the *Haguro*, opened up with their main 8-inch batteries against the low-flying B-25 strafers armed with a mix of parafrag, 1,000lb HE, and 100lb WP bombs. (NARA)

(**Opposite, below**) As Japanese merchant ships and parts of the Rabaul waterfront burn during the 2 November 1943 5th USAAF raid, a B-25 low-flying strafer (foreground) attempts its egress from Simpson Harbour, flying over a damaged Japanese freighter as near misses bracketed the ship. Four transports, including two 5,000-ton vessels, were sunk. Two heavy cruisers and one destroyer were damaged by near-miss 'mining effects'. The air assault over Simpson Harbour lasted nine minutes, with the Americans losing nine B-25s and twelve P-38s. Eighteen Japanese aircraft were destroyed. (NARA)

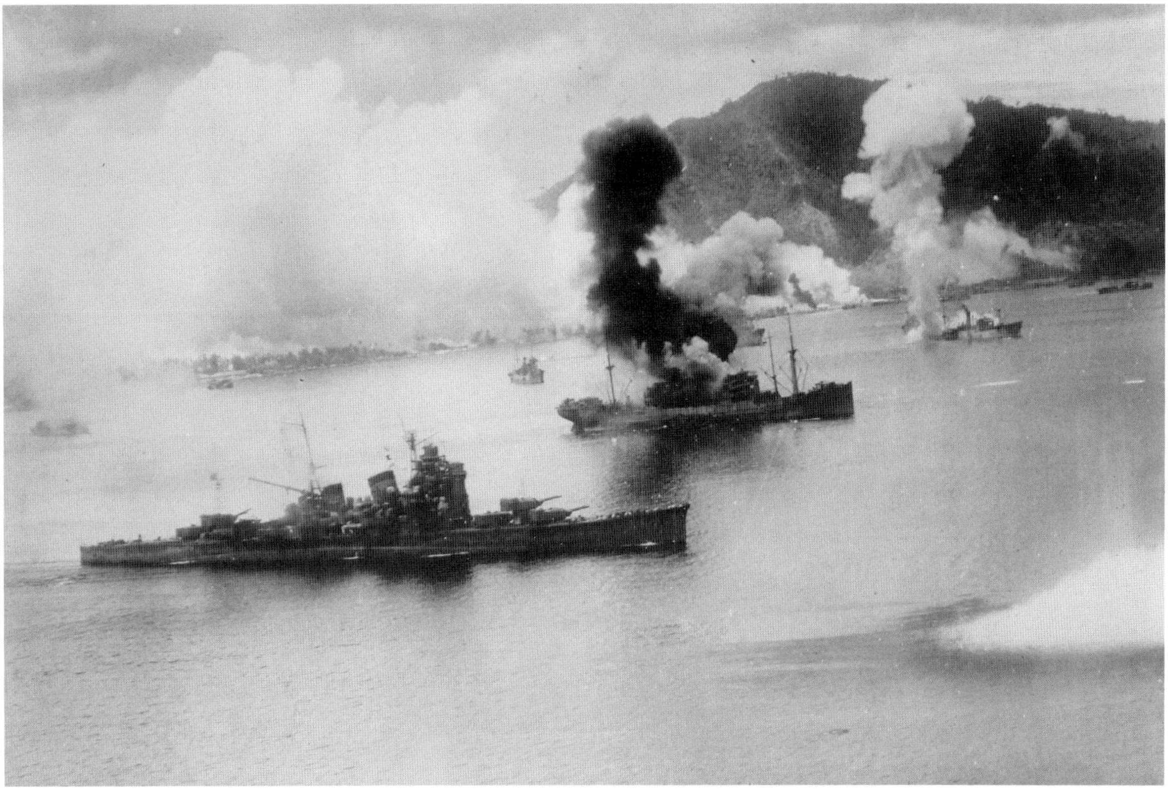

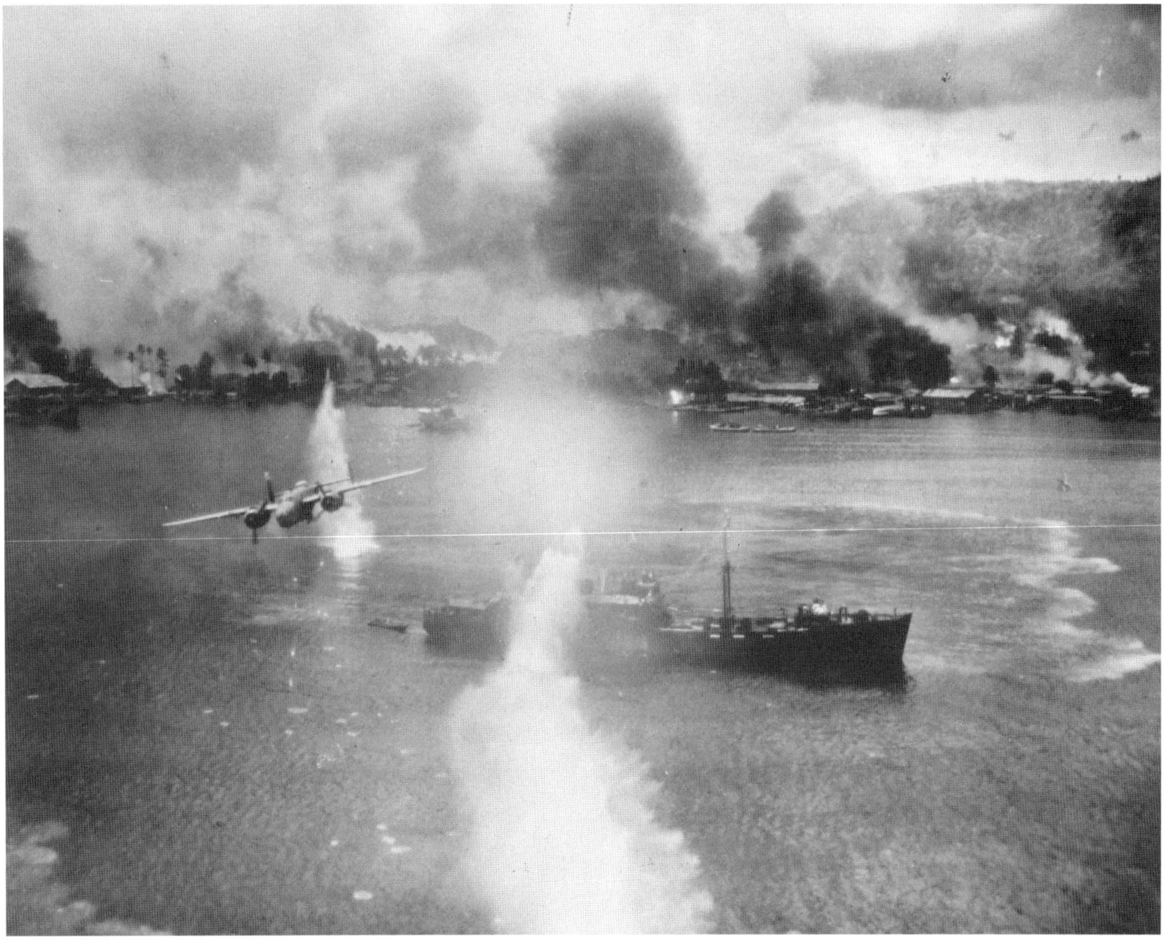

(**Above**) On 2 November 1943, the 5th USAAF struck Simpson Harbour and Rabaul's waterfront with over seventy B-25s. Planes armed with parafrag bombs struck docks, harbour warehouses and barges. Other B-25 strafers attacked Japanese merchant shipping in the harbour with their nose machine guns and other ordnance (above). Other B-25s hit ships in the harbour with 1,000lb demolition bombs in addition to the strafing runs. Closer to the waterfront, the smoke is seen rising from Japanese targets hit during the raid. Some flak from the Japanese AA gun cordon is visible (upper left). (NARA)

(**Opposite, above**) Rabaul's waterfront, the town's warehouses and other structures burn from the low-level attacks of B-25s from the 345th Bombardment Group's 498th Bombardment Squadron dropping parafrag and HE bombs during the 2 November 1943 aerial attack. The barges lined up at the docks (foreground) were hit by the machine guns of the B-25 strafers. (NARA)

(**Opposite, below**) Lakunai Airfield and Japanese shipping in adjacent Simpson Harbour are bombed by 5th USAAF B-24 Liberators on 2 November 1943, when the Japanese were focused on Operation RO, in anticipation of Halsey's Bougainville invasion at Empress Augusta Bay slated for 1 November 1943. Admiral Koga's Operation RO was to deliver a massive IJN aircraft reinforcement to Vice Admiral Kusaka's Rabaul-based Eleventh Air Fleet of only 200 aircraft. Koga sent Truk's entire carrier plane strength of Vice Admiral Jisaburō Ozawa's Third Carrier Fleet, comprising 173 aircraft (82 fighters, 45 dive-bombers, 40 torpedo bombers and 6 reconnaissance) on 6 carriers. Operation RO, scheduled for 28 October, was delayed until 1 November, when the aircraft were delivered to Rabaul to commence raiding the Allied supply routes and crush Halsey's Bougainville offensive. It was a repetition of Yamamoto's ill-fated air offensive, Operation I-GO, of April 1943. (NARA)

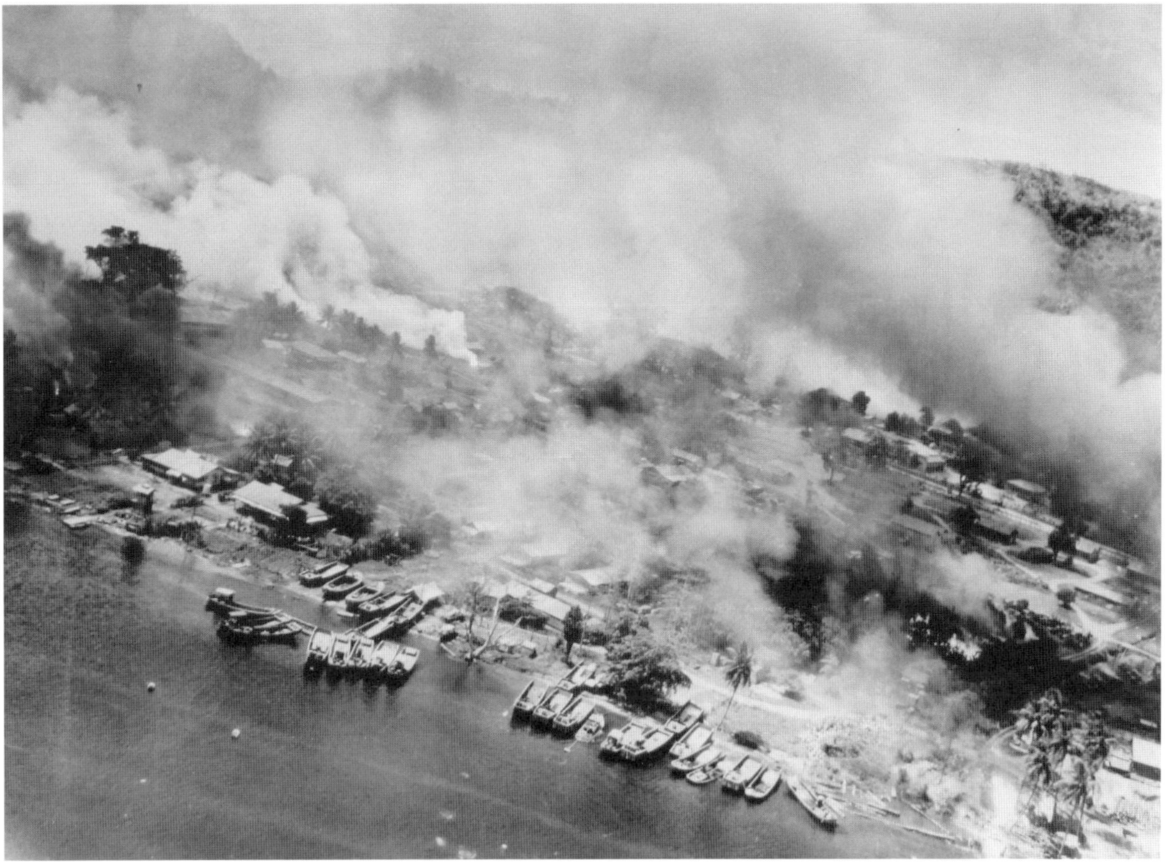

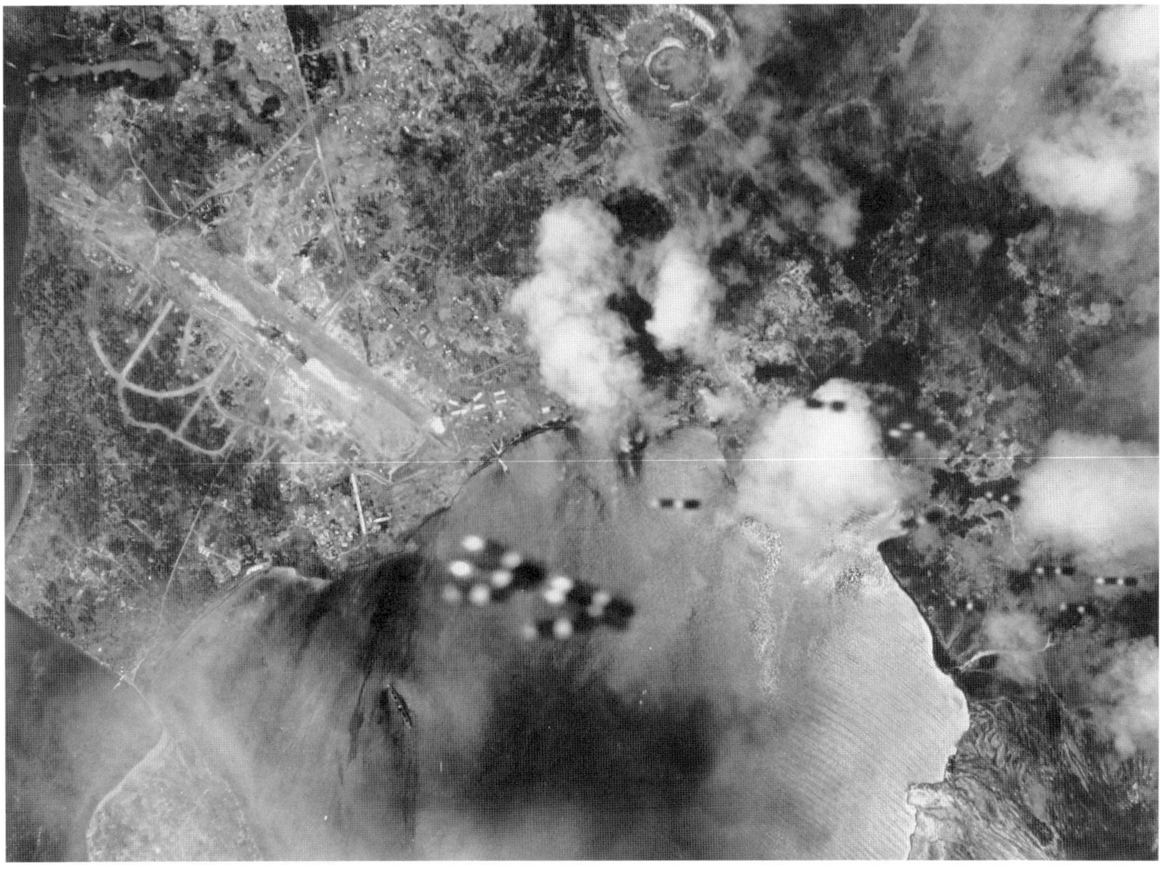

(**Above**) Ground-level photograph taken by a 5th USAAF B-25 strafer aircraft bombing of Tobera Drome, primarily a fighter strip with revetments for seventy-five fighters and two bombers, 20 miles south of Rabaul and deep in the jungle of the Gazelle Peninsula, on 18 October 1943. HE demolition bombs are exploding at one end of the runway while Japanese vehicles and parked planes are situated on either side of the yet untouched runway. Craters are visible from the previous 12 October raid made by RAAF Bristol Beaufighters (foreground). (NARA)

(**Opposite, above**) Marine Douglas SBD Dauntless dive-bombers, with an external bomb load of 2,250lb, fly from their carrier on 5 November 1943 for a raid against a large IJN heavy cruiser force; seven sent from Truk along with the Myōkō and Haguro (both having survived the 1/2 November Battle of Empress Augusta Bay and the 2 November 5th USAAF Rabaul raid), assembling in Simpson Harbour for a repeat heavy cruiser attack to overwhelm Halsey's USN Cleveland-class light cruiser and destroyer screen protecting the American transports and cargo ships off Empress Augusta Bay. Utilizing the great American Civil War general Robert E. Lee's maxim of eighty years earlier, 'I was too weak to defend, so I attacked.' Halsey chose to eliminate Koga's threatening cruiser force refuelling and moored in Simpson Harbour. Halsey's staff quickly devised a plan to attack with Task Force 38 built around USS Saratoga and the light carrier USS Princeton, two Atlanta-class anti-aircraft cruisers and nine destroyers commanded by Rear Admiral Frederick Sherman, which was refuelling off Guadalcanal. (NARA)

(**Opposite, below**) IJN ships attempt rapid exit from Simpson Harbour (right) during a 5 November 1943 USN carrier plane attack. The IJN heavy cruiser Maya (left centre) billows smoke as several other ships steam for Blanche Bay (right) and eventually St George's Channel. Rabaul town and waterfront (top centre) and Lakunai Airfield (top right), adjacent to Matupi Harbour, are visible in this image taken by Photographer's Mate First Class Paul Barnett from one of Saratoga's (CV 3) TBF aircraft, with its wingtip seen (right foreground). B-25 medium bombers, which attacked Rabaul on 2 November, were ineffective against IJN heavy cruisers, such as the Myōkō and Haguro; but over Simpson Harbour, USN torpedo bombers flying parallel to the Japanese ship's length and then turning towards the ship to fire their torpedoes, along with the dive-bombers' descent along warships' lengths, proved effective. The American planes attacked Simpson Harbour from the north, allowing their escape to the harbour's south. After the two USN carriers recovered their aircraft, Sherman's Task Force 38 sped south at 27 knots back to the Guadalcanal area. (NARA)

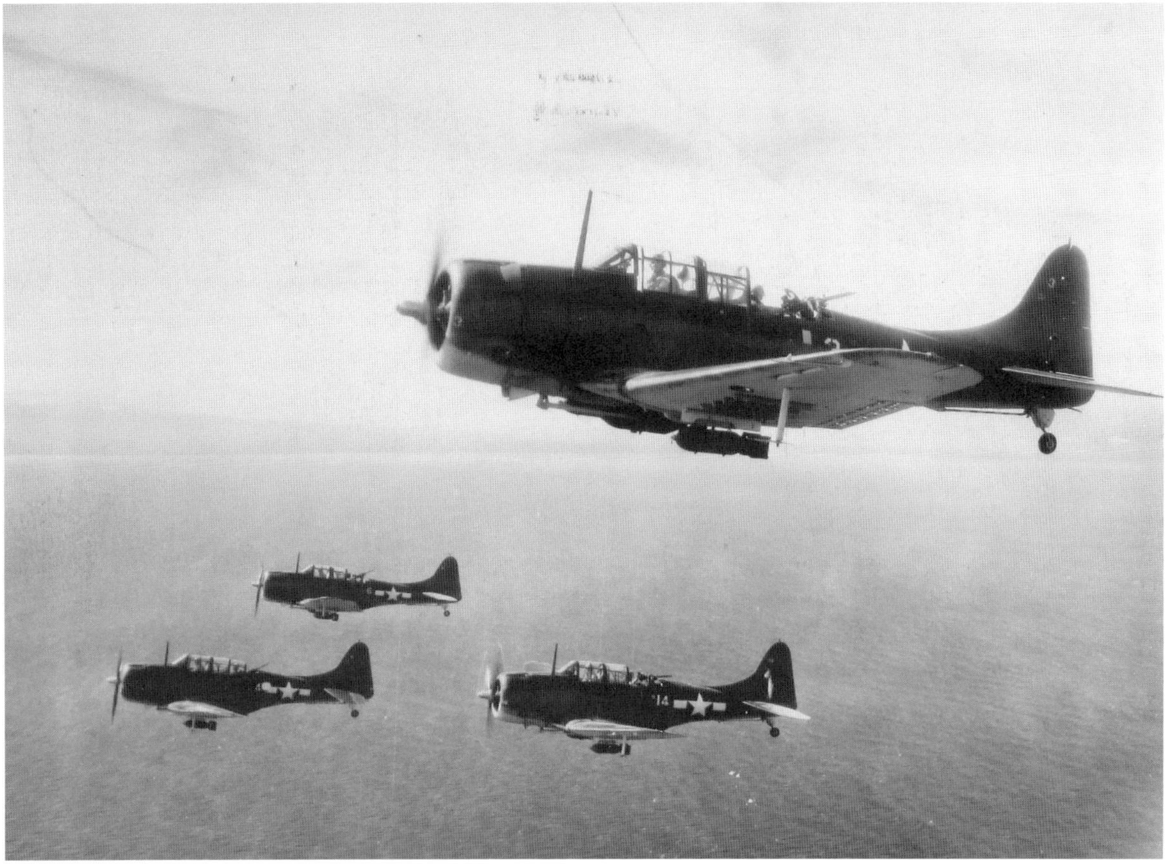
14

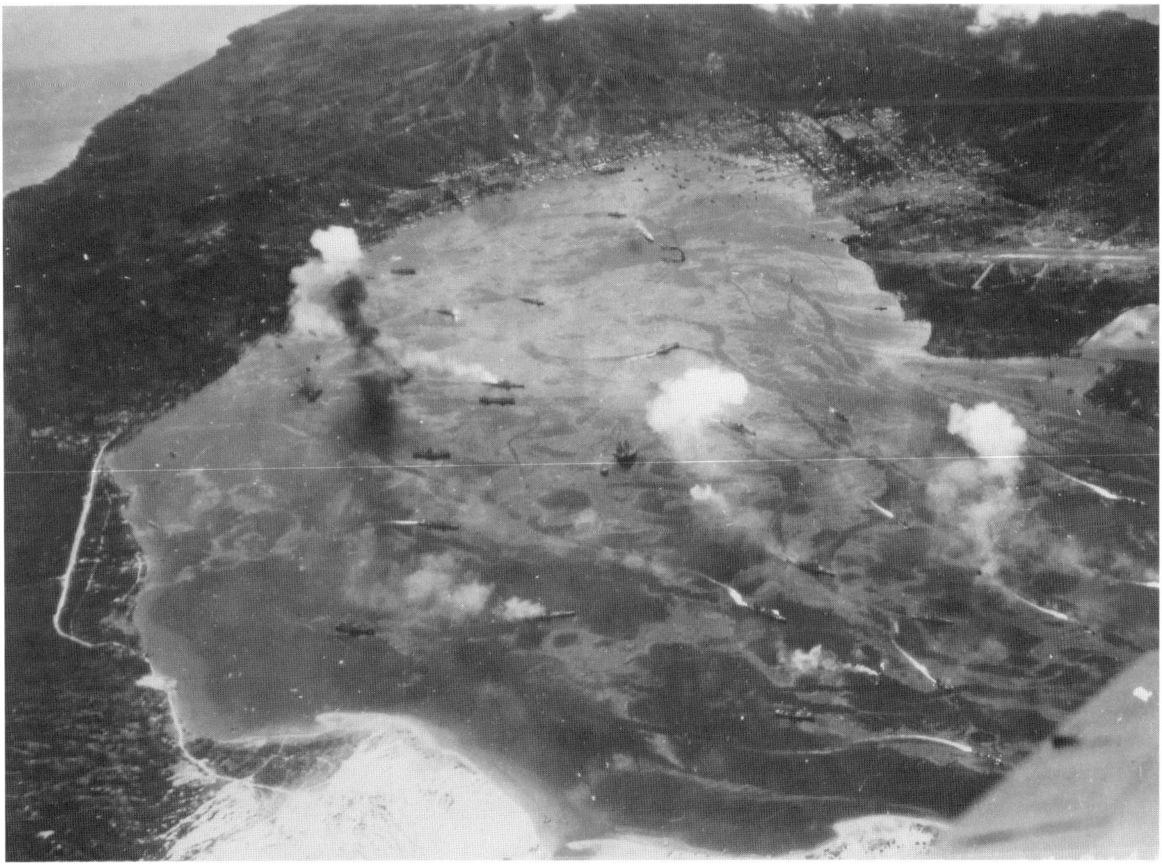

(**Above**) The IJN heavy cruiser *Chikuma*, damaged from a near miss by a bomb landing amidships, was photographed by a USS *Saratoga* (CV-3) SBD Dauntless bomber's gun camera during the 5 November 1943 raid at Simpson Harbour. *Chikuma* was one of five heavy cruisers damaged but none was sunk. Only the *Suzuya* was undamaged. Two IJN light cruisers were hit, as were two destroyers. The USN carrier planes arrived after the Japanese cruisers from Truk arrived and anchored to refuel in preparation for Koga's attack on Halsey's fleet at Empress Augusta Bay that night. Two IJN cruisers finished fuelling. As a result of the 5 November Rabaul raid, the IJN could no longer threaten the Empress Augusta Bay landings, as Halsey feared prior to launching the attack. Under the threat of additional airstrikes, most of the Japanese warships departed for Truk on 6 November, practically ending IJN warship presence in the harbour. (*NARA*)

(**Opposite, above**) An SBD Dauntless dive-bomber's fuselage exhibits an IJN A6M3 Reisen Zero's 20mm cannon damage, which killed the USN sailor manning the twin 0.50-inch calibre trainable machine guns in the rear of the cockpit. American aircraft losses were deemed light, with the USN losing nine aircraft, while one 5th USAAF P-38 Lightning escorting the B-24s was shot down. USN Hellcat fighters shot down two Zeroes, one Yokosuka D4Y1 Suisei reconnaissance plane and one twin-engine bomber taking off from Tobera airfield. (*NARA*)

(**Opposite, below**) Aboard the USS *Saratoga* (CV-3), USN corpsmen and flight deck crewmen remove the casualties from the TBF Avenger air group's leader, Commander Henry Caldwell, exiting from his cockpit (top). The gunner, Kenneth Bratton, was wounded, but the Photographer's Mate First Class, Paul Barnett, who photographed some of the scenes over Simpson Harbour, was killed during a Japanese fighter attack. Caldwell made a one-wheel landing with no wing flaps or radio after being hit over Rabaul by enemy fighters. The one dorsal turret 0.5-inch calibre trainable machine gun is behind Caldwell. (*NARA*)

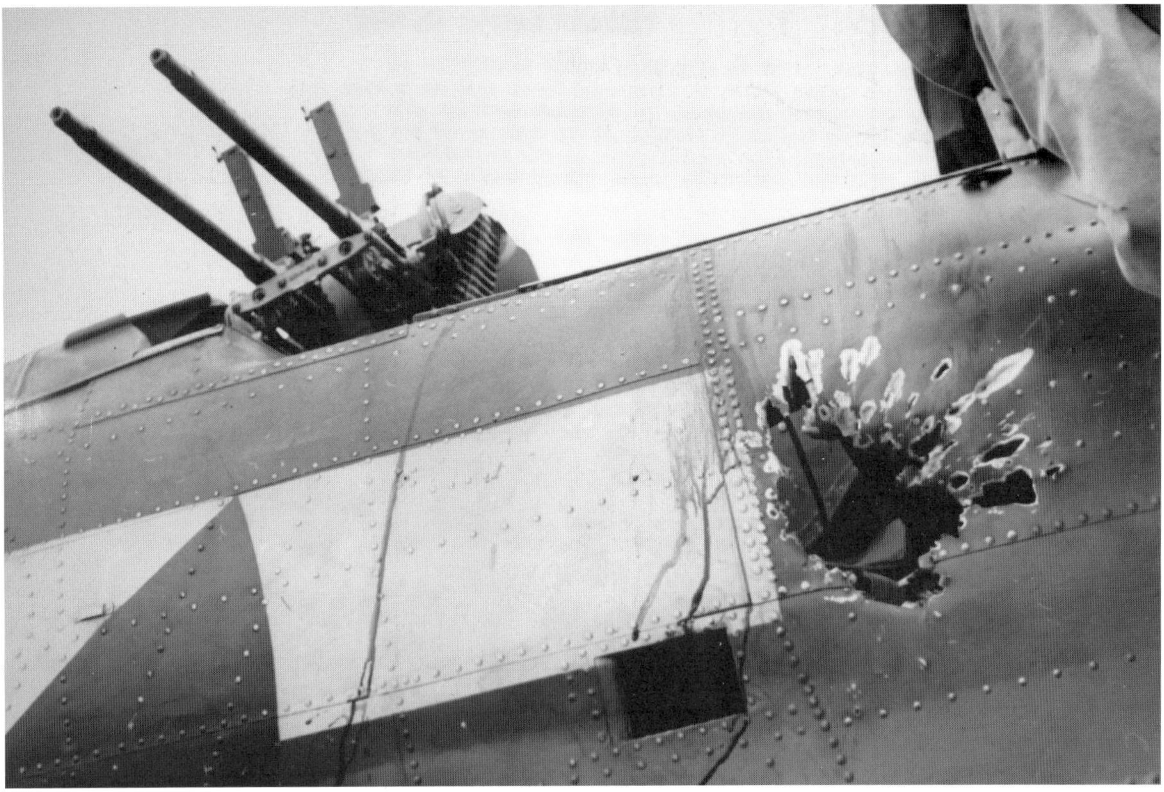

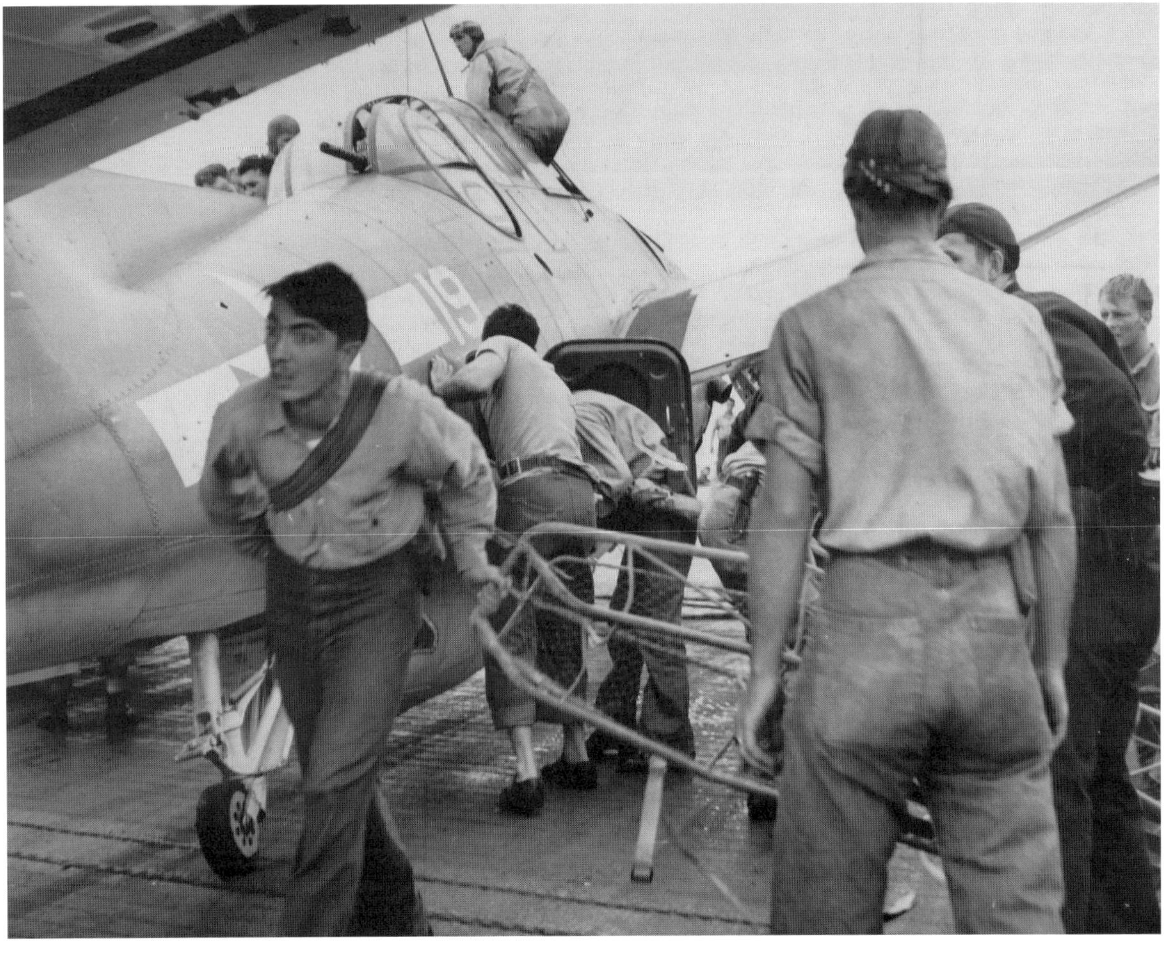
19

(**Above**) After the 11 November USN carrier strike on Rabaul, the Japanese retaliated with an air attack on the USN Task Group 50.3 (of Vice Admiral Spruance's Fifth Fleet), under the command of Rear Admiral Alfred Montgomery, which conducted the raid and included the carriers USS *Essex* (CV-9) (shown mounting AA gunfire against Japanese planes sent from Rabaul), the USS *Bunker Hill* (CV-17), the light carrier USS *Independence* (CVL-22) and nine destroyers, all reaching Halsey on 7 November. Halsey used Montgomery's carriers as well as Sherman's Task Force 38 in a combined strike of over 300 aircraft on Rabaul on 11 November. Most of the IJN heavy cruisers had already left Simpson Harbour although the damaged *Maya* and several light cruisers and numerous destroyers were still there. The weather cleared for Montgomery's air contingent, with hits on the IJN light cruiser *Agano* and destroyer *Naganami*. The IJN destroyer *Suzunami* was hit by a Curtiss SB2C Helldiver, making its dive-bomber combat debut. The USS *Saratoga* and *Princeton* inflicted only minor damage on the IJN warships, principally due to bad weather. The Japanese counterattack consisted of 120 aircraft against the USN carriers during the afternoon, but was intercepted by 24 F4U Corsairs of USN VF-17, a land-based squadron in the Solomons, resulting in 35 Japanese planes shot down by the ships' guns and the CAP, without inflicting damage on the American carriers. The Japanese lost most of their torpedo, dive- and horizontal bombers. (*NARA*)

(**Opposite, above**) AirSols B-25s bomb a Matupi Harbour shoreline supply area, setting it ablaze with Simpson Harbour and the two Beehives (background). Rabaul lay 391 miles from Munda and 349 miles from Barakoma Field on Vella Lavella, the two nearest Allied bases in the SPA, before the Torokina Piva strips were ready for use. When AirSols' first squadrons of fighters arrived at the Torokina's Piva 'One strip' on 10 December 1943, Rabaul was within 210 miles of their striking power. Piva Uncle, a bomber strip 3½ miles inland from Torokina, became operational on 25 December 1943. A second fighter strip at Torokina, Piva Yoke, was completed the following week. Later, a fighter strip on Stirling Island in the Treasury Islands (see Map 2) became operational on 15 January 1944, 279 miles from Rabaul. Munda was still used as a bomber base while most of the four-engine B-24 Liberators stayed at Henderson Field but were staged through Munda for missions. (*NARA*)

(**Opposite, below**) A Marine SBD dive-bombs a Japanese fuel dump, causing it to explode, in Matupi Harbour on 2 August 1944, with a previously sunken Japanese cargo vessel present. To the right is Mount Tavurvur or Matupi volcanic crater, which erupted on 6 June 1937, destroying Rabaul and killing hundreds. During the war, minor eruptions by the Tavurvur volcano sometimes interfered with Japanese air operations from Lakunai Airfield. (*NARA*)

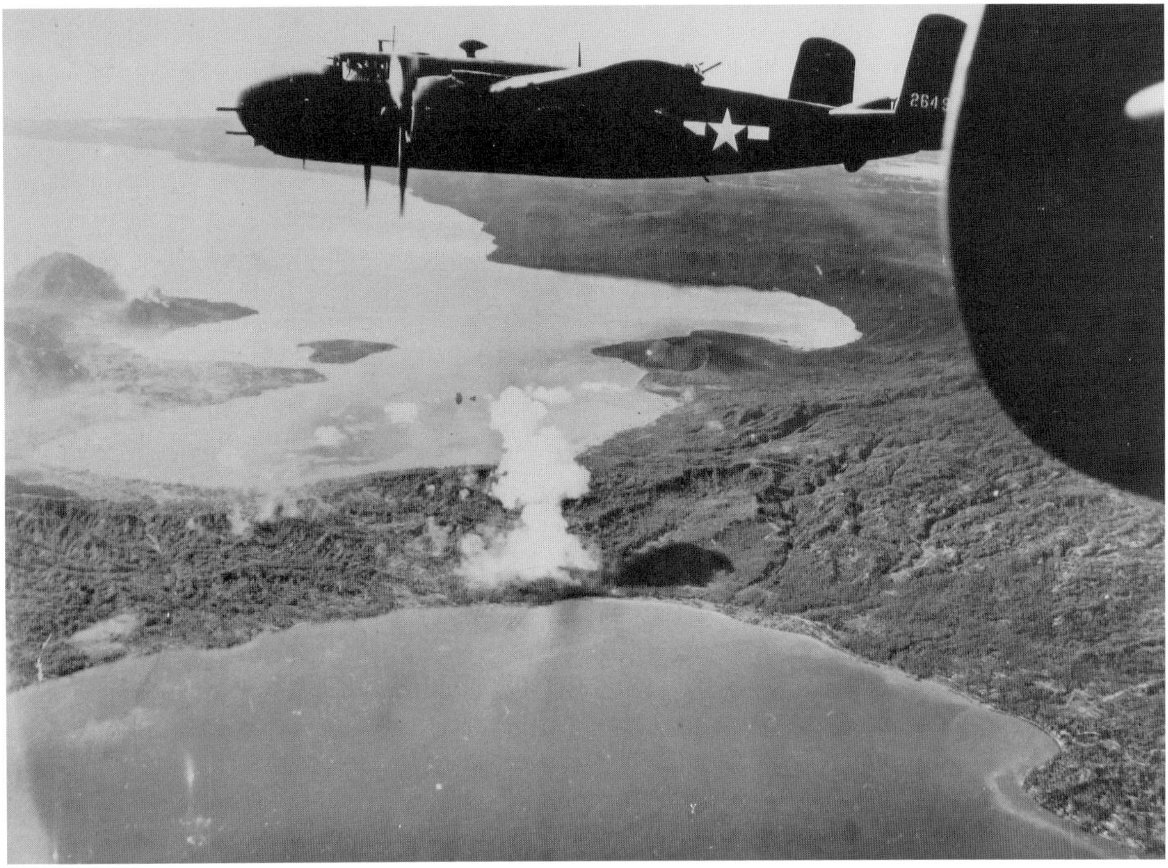

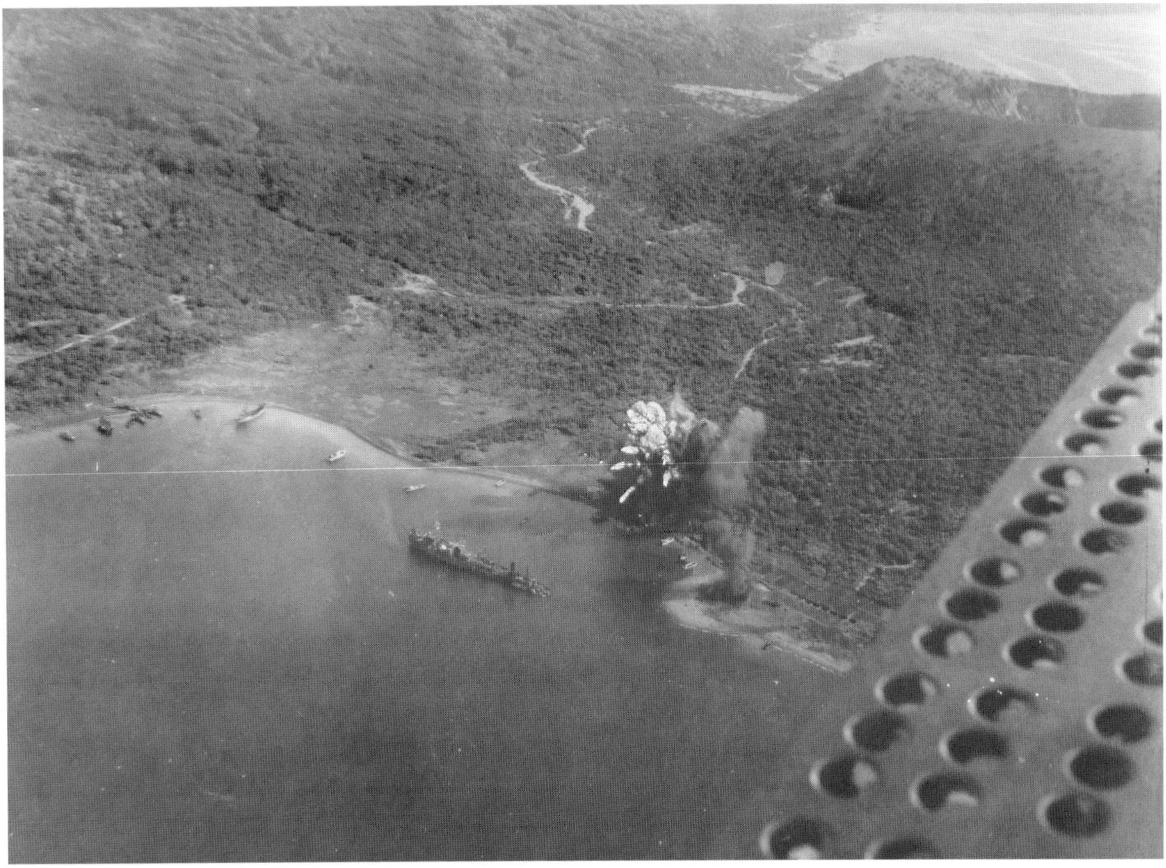

(**Above**) Marine SBD dive-bombers en route to bomb Vunakanau Aerodrome on 22 March 1944. ComAirSols knew from the October 1943 5th USAAF bombing missions that Rabaul could not be neutralized by high-level B-17 and B-24 bombing. Allied photographic reconnaissance on 3 January 1944 showed six destroyers, four submarines, thirty cargo ships, hundreds of barges and nearly 300 Japanese aircraft on four of the Rabaul airfields, including the large Vunakanau aerodrome. Beginning in mid-January 1944, AirSols' SBD dive-bombers and TBF torpedo bombers made frequent attacks on Simpson Harbour and the Rabaul airfields, taking off from Munda at dawn and fuelling at Torokina before and after the raids. By the end of January, Japanese AA defences continued to improve, downing a significant number of American aircraft during the attacks, and enemy ground crews repaired, expanded and improved Rabaul airfields faster than AirSols could damage them. The only deficiency to the Japanese sustaining their airfields was aircraft and pilot replacements. (NARA)

(**Opposite, above**) A low-flying American pilot counted twenty-one wrecked Japanese fighters in revetments at Vunakanau Airfield amid bomb bursts on a runway. AirSols made 3,000 sorties over Rabaul during the first nineteen days of February 1944, almost as many flown since the campaign began with a fighter sweep on 17 December 1943. At Vunakanau, the Japanese kept the concrete runways patched up, so it was possible, even after 1 May, for a few enemy planes to have landed there. (NARA)

(**Opposite, below**) High-level aerial view of Tobera Airfield bombing in April 1944, showing extensive damage and bomb craters to the taxiways near the runway. With the last air battle over Rabaul occurring on 19 February 1944, AirSols dispatched an unescorted bomber strike against Rabaul on 8 March and no Japanese fighter opposition occurred. From 8 to 28 March, AirSols delivered at least one strike on Rabaul every day that weather permitted. An average of 85 tons of bombs was dropped on Rabaul daily from 20 February to 15 May, a total of 7,410 tons delivered by 9,400 sorties. When this final phase of the AirSols assault began, four of the Rabaul airfields were still serviceable and the same was true during the middle of March. The Japanese kept at least part of Vunakanau ready for use even after 1 May. Keravat, the least important airfield of the total of five, was knocked out permanently on 17 April. (NARA)

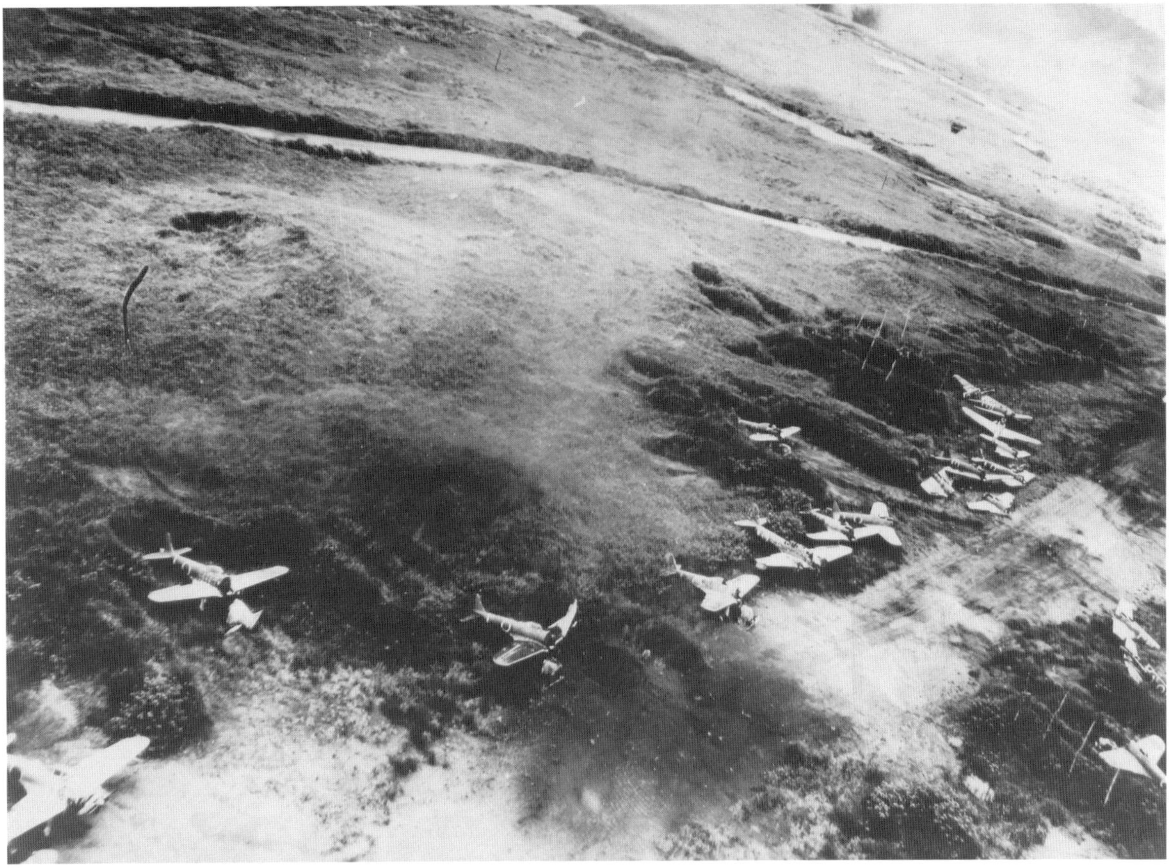

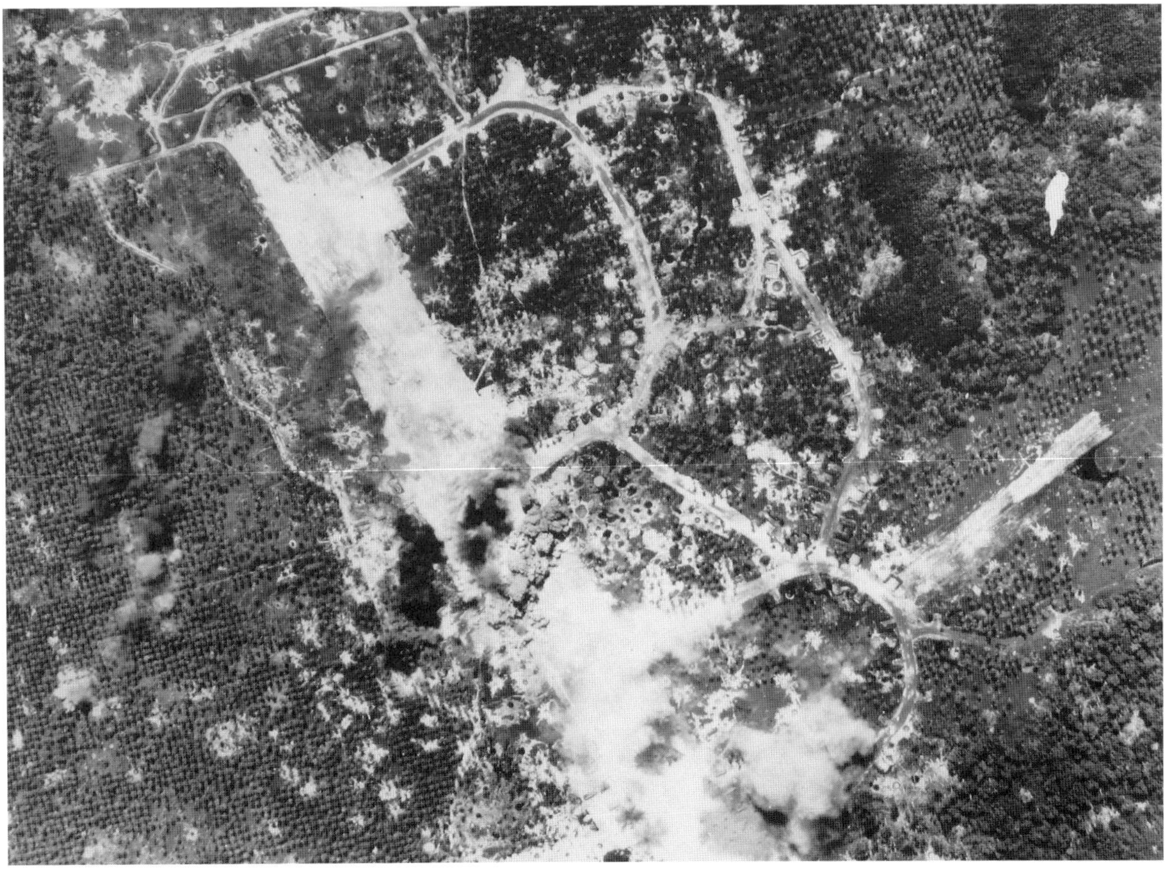

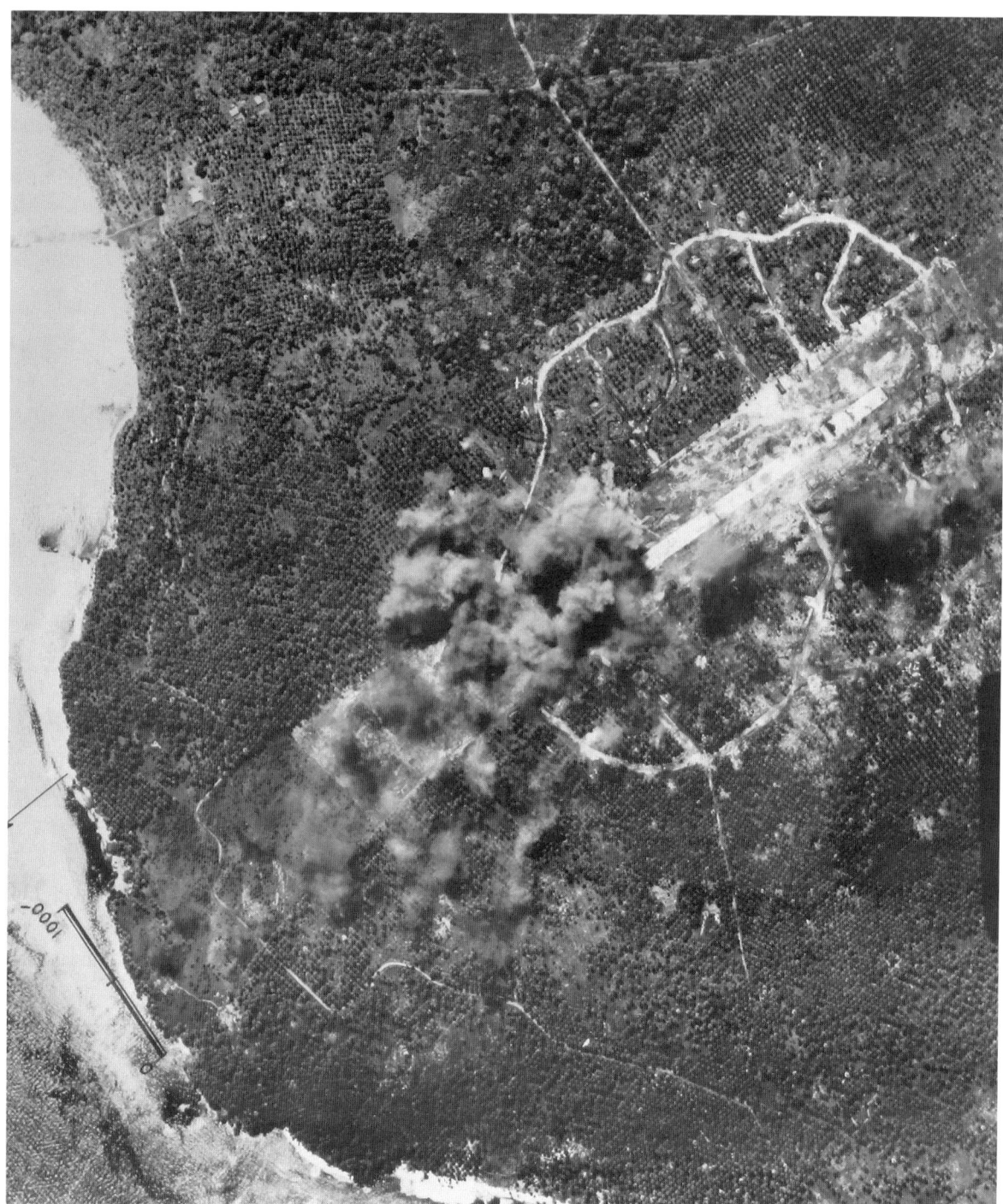

High-altitude aerial view of Allied heavy bombers attacking the Rapopo Drome's concrete runway and surrounding taxiways on 28 February 1944. Rapopo was attacked on 12 October 1943 by 5th USAAF's 3rd Bombardment Group B-25s. Three B-25 squadrons hit Rapopo again on 18 October. On 23 October, 57 B-24s and 100 P-38s were sent to bomb Lakunai and Vunakanau, which were clouded over so the bombers hit Rapopo instead. By the end of February 1944, the runways at Rapopo were so badly damaged that it was virtually abandoned. *(NARA)*

Bombing of Lakunai Airfield by 13th USAAF heavy bombers shows the heavily cratered runway and surrounding installations. On 19 February 1944, AirSols SBD dive-bombers and TBF torpedo bombers arrived over Simpson Harbour in search of enemy vessels. Shipping was so scarce that Lakunai Airfield was attacked with bombs and rockets. Within minutes, B-24s escorted by Allied fighters bombed Lakunai and Tobera airfields from 12,000 feet, with over a hundred 1,000lb bombs. After the 17–18 February 1944 USN carrier plane and surface ship attack on Truk, the Japanese High Command abandoned the air defence of Rabaul and sent the remaining fighters and ground personnel to Truk. (NARA)

Gasmata Airfield, on the southern shore of New Britain, to Rabaul's southeast and north of Arawe, is bombed from high altitude on 24 March 1943. Gasmata Airfield was captured from the Australians on the night of 8/9 February 1942 by the IJN No.2 Maizuru SNLF. The Japanese never permanently stationed planes at Gasmata. From May 1943 onwards, Gasmata was subjected to heavy Allied bombing and not used thereafter by the Japanese for flight operations. Instead, the Japanese built Hoskins Airfield as an alternative strip on the north coast of New Britain to the east of the Talasea Airfield, on the Willaumez Peninsula's east coast. Gasmata was abandoned in March 1944 and soon reoccupied by the Australians, on 28 March 1944. (NARA)

Simpson Harbour was devoid of shipping on a 1 March 1944 aerial reconnaissance photograph. By this date, there were only a few cargo ships, which were promptly bombed and sunk. A photo reconnaissance on 28 February showed over 200 barges in Simpson Harbour itself and nearly 200 in Blanche Bay. It is a testimony to the might of the Allied aircraft and pilots that the splendid Simpson Harbour, which in October 1943 held some 300,000 tons of enemy shipping and had sheltered powerful IJN task forces, was denigrated to a barge depot. Even IJN submarines did not have the temerity to surface in the harbour during daylight. The town of Rabaul, which in 1943 was a small city comprised of 1,400 buildings, was decimated over time. By 20 April 1944, only 120 buildings were left standing and General Imamura's remaining 100,000-strong garrison (about one-third naval personnel), which could not be evacuated or resupplied, remained underground as virtual prisoners. Nonetheless, Imamura and Vice Admiral Kusaka kept the troops strengthening fortifications, digging tunnels, practising tactics, growing fresh vegetables and inventing ingenious weapons in their eager anticipation to use against an Allied land invasion that never occurred. (NARA)

Epilogue

From January 1943 to May 1944, Allied forces under MacArthur and Halsey fought their way from Guadalcanal and Papua through Woodlark, Kiriwina, Nassau Bay, New Georgia, Lae, Salamaua, Nadzab, the Markham and Ramu valleys, Finschhafen, the Treasuries, Empress Augusta Bay on Bougainville, Arawe, Cape Gloucester, Saidor, Hollandia, Aitape, Tanamerah Bay, the Green Islands, the Admiralties and Emirau. They won control of the seas, straits and air in the previously conquered Japanese Southeast Area. Using carrier aircraft and planes based at airfields captured from the Japanese by Allied ground forces, which had been transported and protected by air, and naval surface forces, they neutralized Rabaul to one of irrelevance as Simpson Harbour and the surrounding Japanese airfields were obliterated, with evacuation of any residue of enemy air strength. Hundreds of Japanese planes were destroyed along with a serious dwindling of skilled, trained aircrews. IJN warships were sunk and three Japanese divisions and several brigades were eliminated from the enemy's order of battle. In addition, 100,000 Japanese troops were out of the war as their garrisons were bypassed. After May 1944, SWPA commanders were making plans for an upcoming Philippine Islands campaign in October 1944. Halsey was soon to leave leadership of the SPA, on 16 June 1944, to command the US Third Fleet and was also designated Commander, Western Pacific Task Forces, but his operations at Guadalcanal, the Central Solomons and Bougainville, followed by the early November 1943 carrier raids, were masterful.

In December 1943, there were approximately fifty Japanese merchant ships in Rabaul landing supplies of all kinds, which would keep the 60,000-man garrison alive until the end of the war. The last merchant ship left Rabaul in March 1944. The smashing of Rabaul took longer because of its expansiveness and concentration of AA gunfire. The major airfields were miles apart and neutralizing one allowed another to regain operational status.

Beginning in August 1943, the Allies learned how to destroy Japanese air bases. Major bombing assaults required heavy fighter escorts. From

January to February 1944, hundreds of 13th USAAF sorties were flown against Rabaul by B-24s, B-25s, SBDs and TBFs, with almost 2,000 fighter sorties. Aerodrome installations as well as enemy aircraft were the targets of incessant Allied bombing attacks. Enemy airfields were turned into heavily cratered runways and revetments that would require extensive Japanese manpower to repair. With such frequent air attacks, the enemy would not have the requisite time to make the ground repairs or restore damaged aircraft to an operational status while depriving the Japanese air and ground crews of a needed respite. RAAF steady nighttime bombing of Rabaul's installations with Bristol Beaufort bombers only added to the Japanese physical and mental decline. Japanese commanders at Rabaul identified the B-25 strafers, with their parafrag bombing tactic at low levels, as an excellent weapon against Japanese aircraft on the ground. The low-altitude bombing runs did not allow adequate Japanese fighters the time to get aloft to combat the strafers.

Completely isolated, Japanese forces at Rabaul, Wewak and many other bypassed Japanese garrisons died from disease and starvation waiting for an Allied attack. Only half of the 350,000 Japanese troops bypassed in New Guinea, New Britain and New Ireland lived to return to Japan as the Bismarcks Barrier was nonetheless broken.

Bibliography

Bergerud, Eric, *Touched with Fire: The Land War in the South Pacific* (Penguin Books, New York, 1996).
Bergerud, Eric, *Fire in the Sky: The Air War in the South Pacific* (Westview Press, Boulder, 2000).
Diamond, Jon, *New Guinea: The Allied Jungle Campaign in World War II* (Stackpole Books, Guilford, 2015).
Diamond, Jon, *The War in the South Pacific* (Pen & Sword Books, Barnsley, 2017).
Diamond, Jon, *Guadalcanal: The American Campaign against Japan in WWII* (Stackpole Books, Guilford, 2017).
Diamond, Jon, *MacArthur's Papua New Guinea Offensive 1942–1943* (Pen & Sword Books, Barnsley, 2020).
Duffy, James, *War at the End of the World: Douglas MacArthur and the Forgotten Fight for New Guinea, 1942–1945* (NAL Caliber, New York, 2016).
Eichelberger, Robert, *Our Jungle Road to Tokyo* (Battery Classics, Nashville, 1989).
Gailey, Harry, *MacArthur Strikes Back: Decision at Buna, New Guinea, 1942–1943* (Presidio, New York, 2000).
Gailey, Harry, *MacArthur's Victory: The War in New Guinea 1943–1944* (Presidio, New York, 2004).
Gamble, Bruce, *Fortress Rabaul: The Battle for the Southwest Pacific, January 1942–April 1943* (Zenith Press, Minneapolis, 2010).
Gamble, Bruce, *Target Rabaul: The Allied Siege of Japan's Most Infamous Stronghold, March 1943–1945* (Zenith Press, Minneapolis, 2013).
Gamble, Bruce, *Invasion Rabaul: The Epic Story of Lark Force, The Forgotten Garrison, January–July 1942* (Zenith Press, Minneapolis, 2014).
Hammel, Eric, *Munda Trail* (Avon Books, New York, 1989).
Horton, D., *New Georgia: Pattern for Victory* (Ballantine Books, New York, 1971).
Hough, Frank and Crown, John, *The Campaign on New Britain* (Battery Press Inc., Nashville, 1952).
Hoyt, Edwin, *The Glory of the Solomons* (Stein and Day, New York, 1983).
Lardas, Mark, *Rabaul 1943–44: Reducing Japan's Great Island Fortress* (Osprey Publishing, Oxford, 2018).
Lardas, Mark, *B-25 Mitchell vs. Japanese Destroyer: Battle of the Bismarck Sea 1943* (Osprey Publishing, Oxford, 2021).
Long, Gavin, *MacArthur as Military Commander* (B.T. Batsford Ltd, London, 1969).
Lord, Walter, *Lonely Vigil: Coastwatchers of the Solomons* (Viking Press, New York, 1977).

Mayo, Lida, *Bloody Buna* (Doubleday & Company Inc., Garden City, 1974).

McGee, William, *The Solomons Campaigns 1942–1943: From Guadalcanal to Bougainville, Pacific War Turning Point* (BMC Publications, Santa Barbara, 2010).

McManus, John, *Fire and Fortitude* (Caliber, New York, 2019).

Miller, John, *The War in the Pacific, Cartwheel: The Reduction of Rabaul* (Center of Military History, United States Army, Washington, DC, 1990).

Milner, Samuel, *Victory in Papua* (Center of Military History, United States Army, Washington, DC, 1989).

Morison, Samuel Eliot, *History of the United States Naval Operations in World War II, Vol. VI, Breaking the Bismarcks Barrier 22 July 1942–1 May 1944* (Little, Brown and Company, Boston, 1950).

Shaw, H. and Kane, D., *Isolation of Rabaul: History of the US Marine Corps Operations in World War II* (Historical Branch, G-3 Division, Headquarters, US Marine Corps, Washington, DC, 1963).

Smith, Robert Ross, *The War in the Pacific: The Approach to the Philippines* (Center of Military History, United States Army, Washington, DC, 1984).

Vader, John, *New Guinea: The Tide is Stemmed* (Ballantine Books Inc., New York, 1971).

Wheeler, Richard, *A Special Valor: The US Marines & the Pacific War* (Castle Books, Edison, 1996).

Photographs

Photograph on page 130 (top) is in the public domain and is from John Miller, Jr., *The War in the Pacific, Cartwheel: The Reduction of Rabaul* (Center for Military History, United States Army, 1990), p. 283.

Photograph on page 136 is in the public domain and is from LtCol Frank O. Hough, USMCR and Major John A. Crown, USMCR, *The Campaign on New Britain* (Historical Branch, Headquarters, US Marines Corps, 1952), p. 69.

Photograph on page 162 is in the public domain and is from Naval History and Heritage Command, US Navy, Washington, DC.

Notes

Notes

Notes

Notes